A School at Bearsted

A School at Bearsted

by

Kathryn Kersey

First published in 2003 by Kathryn Kersey

Kathryn Kersey
5 Greensand Road
Bearsted
MAIDSTONE
Kent ME15 8NY

A catalogue record for this book is available from the British Library.

ISBN 0-9545831-0-8

Front Cover:
A photograph of the school and some of the children around 1910. Although undated, it is
possible that this was taken during the celebrations for the Coronation of George V which took
place on 2 June 1911.

The current school badge, as devised by Vernon Finch in 1971, prior to transfer to the new
premises at The Landway, Bearsted.

Digitally set in 10 pt Century Schoolbook and 16 pt URW Antiqua Text Bold
Printed and bound in Great Britain by Parchment (Oxford) Limited

Dedication

To all the children (past and present) at Bearsted and Roseacre Schools.

And in memory of Miss Daphne Clement (1911-1994),
an inspirational teacher at Bearsted and Roseacre
who led my daily way to words.

Acknowledgements

Throughout the process of research, and writing this account, I have been aware that I owe a debt of gratitude to my forerunners in the recording of Bearsted and Thurnham's history. I am conscious of immense debts to Robert Skinner, who wrote the *Centenary Magazine* about the school and the Bearsted and Thurnham History Society Book Committee for *A History of Bearsted and Thurnham*.

I thank most gratefully the staff at the Centre for Kentish Studies in Maidstone in assisting my many document requests, Maidstone Reference Library and the Kent Library Service, the Church of England record centre and Canterbury Cathedral Archives. I have been able to include the photographs that accompany some of the press cuttings, through the courtesy and generosity of the Kent Messenger newspaper group. I thank them.

I would like to acknowledge the kind assistance, together with most generous permission to quote and use as a source of information/illustrations, the following people and organisations:

Alan Sutton Publishing, Paul Ashbee, the late Bernard Banner, Vera Banner (née Croucher), Bearsted and Thurnham Local History Society, Harry Bishop, Rev David Bond, Rev John Corbyn, Boughton Monchelsea Parish Council, Irene Bourne (née Keay), Doris Britcher (née Bentley), Ella Cardwell (née Foster), the Centre for Kentish Studies, Anthony Chadwick, Church House and National Society Publishing, Kay Caliborn (née Graham) Edith Coales, Countryside Books, Brenda Donn, David and Theresa Elliott, Rowland and Janet Fairbrass, Evelyn Fridd (née White), Bruce Graham, Barbara Foster (née Westall), Sheila Foster (née Gould), George Frampton, Froglets Publications, Marjorie Gibson, Norah Giles (née Pettipiere), Barbara Gosden, Pat Grimes (née Robbins), Violet Hales (née Pollard), Winifred Harris (née Guest), Pat Heard, Nell Hodson (née Byam), Joan Harden, Pat Heard, Sally Hook (née Smith), Pamela Horn, Betty Hutchinson (née Pollard), Eileen Jakes (née Young), Jean Jones (née Hodges), Babs Jossi, Kent Archaeological Society, Lawrence and Wishart, Pat Laws, Judith Lovelady, Sheila Murphy, Pam Osbourne (née Town), the late Jessie Page (née Brook), Margaret Peat (née Lang), Rosemary Pearce (née Hardy), Margaret Plowright (née White), Bernice Promtatvethi (née Giles), Roseacre School, Peter Rosevear, Derek Rowe, Thomas Soloman, Jackie Stewart (née Hirst), Miriam Stevens (née Gardner), Roland and Margaret Tomalin (née Baker), Thomas Tate, Taylor & Francis Books, Roger Vidler, Graham Walkling, Trevor Webb, Sue Whittaker (née Baker), Barbara and Jonathan Wraight.

Every reasonable effort has been made to contact the copyright holders of *The History and Topographical Survey of Kent* published by E P Publishing and of images taken by the Photographic Press Agency. I have been wholly unsuccessful in tracing the rights to these. I would be pleased to pursue permission and to insert the appropriate acknowledgement in any subsequent printing of this book.

For access to information from particular records I would like to thank the Kent Archaeological Society, the staff at Roseacre School; especially Dawn Perry, Beth Lloyd, Anne Chalk and Bernard Head. I also thank Vernon Finch for sharing his unique information as a previous headmaster, his enthusiasm for this book, and correcting the shakier parts of my grammar! I thank too, Michael Perring, for some very helpful insights, and for most generously sharing his long-standing memories of Bearsted and Thurnham.

I would like to specially thank Alison Finch for her most generous hospitality over many hours. Immense thanks also to James and Anne Clinch for assistance in the proof-reading and editorial processes prior to publication, and for their contributions in the search for greater clarification. On a personal note, for outstanding technological wizardry, patience endurance of domestic disruption and positive encouragement, I thank my long-suffering husband, Malcolm. I thank too, James and George, for their sharp-eyed observation. During their time at Roseacre they have become an inevitable, but intrinsic, part of Bearsted's history.

I thank and acknowledge an award by the Allen Grove Local History Fund of the Kent Archaeological Society, which was of financial assistance in preparing this book for publication.

Editorial Note

Where I have discovered a particularly helpful description of events or an explanation of circumstances I have incorporated it into the main body of the text for reasons of greater clarity and ease of reading. Any inclusions are subject to a note to indicate that the source used and that the words should not be regarded as mine - by this means I hope to avoid all accusations of that particular horror of all writers: inadvertent plagiarism.

When Bearsted School first opened to admit children, the head of the teaching staff was known as either as Master or Mistress. Latterly, this term has fallen into disuse in favour of the term Headmaster and Headteacher. To achieve a greater clarity in the book, I have used Master or Mistress for the early years of the school. I have then changed to Headmaster and Headteacher as appropriate.

Similarly, it will be seen that the spelling of the School House, Bartie, varies in the text. I have been unable to determine a universally accepted spelling of the name. The rendered spelling therefore reflects the contemporary usage or source.

Abbreviations Used

CCA	Canterbury Cathedral Archives
CCE	Committee of Council on Education
CERC	Church of England Record Centre
CKS	Centre for Kentish Studies
PRO	Public Record Office

Latin

Ibid.	In the same place and refers to the previously named publication.
Op.cit.	In the publication already named.
Passim.	Wording used that is dispersed through the text rather than a direct quote.
Sic.	Thus written in the original text.

Contents

Introduction

Recent years have marked a new millennium and at least 164 years of a school at Bearsted. Whenever I pass the library in Bearsted, I remember that the building once housed the school I attended. History is easily forgotten. Records and documents once made by someone trying to record matters by 'writing it down' largely survive by a mixture of chance and serendipity.

Here then, is my attempt to 'write it down'. I am conscious that it will doubtless contain many errors and I should be very pleased to receive corrections. The more information I receive, the more accurate and detailed will be the inevitable, future revised account. In the meantime, I have prepared this short account with love and gratitude to the school and past and present staff.

Kathryn Kersey

The secretaries reported that they had received an application from the Revd. F St L Baldwin and R Cobb for assistance towards erecting a School at Bearsted for that and the neighbouring parishes of Thurnham Debtling and part of Boxley...

Minutes of the Proceedings of Canterbury Diocese Education Society Board, 12 July 1839

Chapter 1
Why Build a School in Bearsted?

The decision to open a school in Bearsted was taken by the 'National Society of the Education of the Poor According to the Principles of the Church of England'. It was usually known as the 'National Society'. Before the establishment of such organisations as the National Society, elementary education was a largely haphazard affair. Schooling was only available for those able to afford it even though the fees could be modest.

In 1709 there was an attempt to provide schooling in Bearsted and Thurnham through the will of Edward Godfrey. When writing a will, it was quite usual at this time to express humble and pious wishes and to endeavour to leave funds for charitable purposes. When Edward Godfrey,[1] 'a Gentleman of Thornham' drew up his will he decided to leave some money for just such a purpose. His charitable intentions later attracted the attention of Edward Hasted. Hasted was known to be 'a gentleman and a scholar'. He recorded his travels around Kent in several volumes, describing Kent villages and parishes, detailing earlier charities where appropriate. The volume of his work that covers 'Thornham and Bersted' was first published in 1798.

Edward Godfrey's intention was expressed in his will:

> out of all those peeces of land called Crouchfeild in Bersted ....containing seven acres more or less... shall well and truly pay or cause to be paid ...thirty shillings per annum towards the Education (and teaching) at school four poor children of the parish of Bersted and ffour poor children of the parish of Thornham to read and understand the English Tongue....

Hasted recorded that it was deemed that there was no right to devise such a charge upon the estate and thus it did not proceed.[2] Godfrey may have realised that his intentions might not be feasible as the will later directed that the people who undertook the administration of his estate:

> .....for the time being in their discretions shall think fit and approve.[3]

The scheme was probably doomed to fail on a number of points. There is no indication that the charitable provision was a permanent endowment. In addition to the thirty shillings for teaching poor children, other annuities for his family and relatives were also to be generated from the value of those seven acres of land. Further, it is entirely possible that the value of the land dropped significantly in the years between making the will in 1709 and the subsequent grant of probate in 1758, so rendering the scheme impossible. Evidently, as the scheme did not proceed, discretion was indeed exercised.

In the same document Edward Godfrey referred to some land he owned in an area named as 'Russaker Street'. It would be good to think that by one of those curious quirks of history, some of his original holdings included the land now occupied by Roseacre School.

There is an indication that there were some people in Bearsted and Thurnham able to read and write prior to the establishment of the National School. Although the historical sources are fragmentary, there is a record of a library consisting approximately a hundred and twenty eight books. They were recorded as being held in a bookcase at Thurnham church when an inventory was made at Easter in 1751. The contents of this library included leaflets and pamphlets of an instructional or educational nature.

1

Although the origins of the library held at Thurnham are not clear, it has been suggested that it was the result of a clerical bequest. It is possible that the books had belonged to the Rev Henry Dering, who was vicar of Thurnham 1673-1720.[4] The inventory also records thirty books of psalms which were held separately to the library, so there is a hint that the congregation were accustomed to using printed books in their regular services. It is not known what happened to the library.

There are brief details of an establishment for education in the Bearsted area prior to 1839. William Streatfield, who was to become Registrar for births and deaths in the area, is listed in several trade directories as the local Registrar and also a Schoolmaster. The earliest entry for William Streatfield as the proprietor for a 'Boarding and Day School' is dated 1839,[5] but it is likely that the school had been open for some years. Despite this, there are no further details other than brief entries in the 1841 and 1851 Census entries where his occupation is given as 'Private Schoolmaster and Registrar'. He does not seem to have advertised in the local newspapers.

In 1847 William Streatfield was listed in a trade directory under Bearsted as a Registrar in the Loose district and running a Ladies day and boarding school with his wife, Ann.[6] The surname was rendered as 'Straetfield' in the directory. William and his wife are also listed as running schools located in Romney Place and Paradise Row, Maidstone. It is possible that although living in Bearsted, they had further interests in other commercial and residential premises in Maidstone. In the 1861 Census, William is no longer listed as a Schoolmaster although his wife is given as the Mistress of a Private Seminary. William was Registrar for the area for many years. The charges for the schooling offered by establishments such as William and Ann Streatfield's school were beyond the financial means of much of the population of Bearsted and Maidstone.

At the start of the Nineteenth century, England began to industrialise.[7] Some of the living and working conditions in the towns and cities were appalling. Social writers and reformers became concerned that this would lead to serious civil disturbances and rioting. Leaflets and books were published on this matter and discussed the idea that education might prove to combat vice, irreligion and subversive tendencies among the poor. One writer expressed the matter:

> They must be taught to live upright and industrious lives in that station of life which it should please God to call them.[8]

The ideal for education was envisaged as the training of the poor to achieve an honest and industrious poverty. Even among people who were not really interested in politics and economics, there was a growing awareness that the educational provision for poor children needed to be addressed.[9] Eventually, the factory owners came to realise that an educated workforce could be an asset. If the running of a factory could be delegated to a skilled manager, more time could be spent in turning wealth and status into tangible assets such as large country houses.

As the factory system developed, the demand for greater numbers of the population employed in the new factories became evident. In the absence of legislation forbidding it, the employment of children became widespread. For some families, the contribution of the children became an economic necessity. However, factory work left one day free and this made possible the Sunday School movement. The aims of the Sunday Schools were religious and social rather than intellectual, offering a restricted curriculum of religious teaching and reading. Despite this, it was a step towards an education offered to children unlimited by age range and cost.

An education scheme popularised by Andrew Bell and Joseph Lancaster seemed to promote an effective delivery system for schooling. It was known as the 'Monitorial System'. Under this system, the Master was in sole charge of the school, but only taught the Monitors and they in turn relayed the instructions to the pupils. There were many drawbacks to the system - it was mechanical and there was little opportunity for the inquiring mind. Nevertheless, it was a beginning for formal education and emphasised the need for an ordered atmosphere that was conducive for learning. The innovation of dividing the children into groups for formal learning proved to be of permanent value. The Monitorial schools popularised elementary education[10] and part of the system later came to be used at Bearsted School.

There were attempts by the government to consider education in 1816 and 1818. Sir Robert Peel tried to address the matter in his Factory Act of 1818 in what became known as 'The Education of the Lower Orders'. Many of the strong recommendations concerning the education of children had to be reduced in order to secure the Bill's passage through Parliament.[11] The legislation that remained was rendered inadequate and unenforceable.

A further impetus for education emerged from the Great Reform Act of 1832. This Act gave many people the power to vote for the first time. The middle classes who valued education as a means of social progression were able to use their vote to good effect. In 1833 John Roebuck introduced a new plan for education and yet again there was an immense debate on the Bill. The debate was carried by just two votes and resulted in the first annual Government grant in aid of education:

> That a sum, not exceeding twenty thousand pounds, be granted to His Majesty, to be issued in aid of Private Subscriptions for the Erection of School Houses, for the Education of the children of the Poorer classes in Great Britain to the 31st day of March 1834 and that the said sum be issued and paid without any fee or other deduction whatsoever.[12]

Although this sum seemed generous, the National Society only received half the sum with the proviso that an equivalent sum was raised from the National Society's own resources (the other £10,000 went to the British and Foreign Schools Society). In 1839 the government appointed Sir James Kay-Shuttleworth as secretary to the supervisory Committee for the Privy Council on Education. Two inspectors were also appointed as schools were to be compulsory inspected.[13]

By this time, the limits of the Monitorial system had become apparent. It was evident that if any national system of education was to be set up, it required an adequate number of trained teachers. Sir James Kay-Shuttleworth used the experience gained from his appointment as secretary to the Privy Council on Education, to establish a training college for teachers in 1839. This was achieved in association with his colleague E C Tufness. In 1841 the National Society founded St Mark's College in Chelsea for this purpose.[14]

The appointment of government inspectors for schools by the Privy Council Committee was matched by the Church of England who set up diocesan boards of education. As the boards were not keen to have schools scrutinised by the government inspectors, their own inspectors were appointed from among the local clergy. The debate concerning the presence of government inspectors in church schools continued for some time.[15] Many Anglican clergymen continued to view government inspectors as a possible threat to the Church.

In Kent, the Canterbury Diocesan Board of Education had been instituted. On 29 November 1838, it was decided that the board needed to work in association with the Canterbury Diocesan Education Society. The two education bodies aimed to extend and improve education together with the Church of England and the National Society through meetings held four times a year.[16] Almost immediately, the Rural Deans of the Diocese were advised to promote:

> the immediate formation of District Boards within their respective Deaneries and the vicars to encourage and superintend the Establishment of Commercial and Parochial Schools.[17]

Funding for the work of the boards was secured through donations and subscriptions. Sutton Deanery, which included Bearsted, Boxley, Detling, and Thurnham, raised £224 8s towards an overall figure of £1884 10s.[18]

On 12 July 1839, at a meeting of the two education bodies held in Charing, with the Venerable Archdeacon Croft in the chair, it was recorded in the minutes that an application had been received from the Rev F St L Baldwin and the Rev R Cobb for assistance towards a school at Bearsted and the neighbouring parishes of Thurnham, Debtling, and part of Boxley.[19]

The applicants were given notice to apply for a grant of £40 at the next quarterly meeting. Below is reproduced the relevant entry from the minutes:

(Reproduced by permission of Canterbury Cathedral Archives)

From a subsequent minute dated 8 July 1840, it was recorded that at the previous meeting which had been held in October 1839, a grant of £20 had been agreed to establish a school in Bearsted. Grants were also awarded for five other schools in the deanery.[20]

Other funds were still required to secure the amount of money needed to build the school. The National Society awarded grants towards the building of a school only if it could be opened free of debt and it was in union, or affiliated to the Society. The grant covered a proportion of the construction costs as the Society always preferred to assist, rather than wholly replace, local fund-raising efforts.[21]

The National Society awarded a building grant towards the establishment of the school but the document recording the award has not survived. The only record of the award is in later papers in the National Society records. Mr St Leger Baldwin, vicar of Bearsted, then pursued other methods of funding the project.

The land chosen as a site for Bearsted School was owned by the 'Dean and Chapter of the Cathedral Church of Christ and the Blessed Virgin Mary, Rochester'. Over centuries, the Church of England had consolidated finances by a steady series of investments in land and property. It was not unusual for vast areas of land to be owned by the church and leased to tenants. The church maximised income from assets and yet retained the title to the land. The land in Bearsted was rented out to Mr Matthias Prime Lucas (an Alderman of London) by a lease which still had a considerable time to run.

A transcript of the form that was completed in a request to affiliate with either the National Society or the Canterbury Diocesan Board of Education[22] is shown opposite. The next illustration shows the application form that was used for Canterbury Diocesan Board of Education.[23]

TERMS OF UNION

To be subscribed by parties desirous of uniting their Schools with the

National Society,

OR, WITH THE

CANTERBURY DIOCESAN BOARD OF EDUCATION.

Name of the Schools,
description, Street, (if
in a town,) County,
Post-town & Diocese.

The number of School-rooms, { *a Master* } *or Master & Mistress,*
with { *a Mistress* } *Attendance on*

Number of Children.—Boys,   *Girls,*   *Attendance on*
Sunday, or Sunday and Week-days.

Date of Establishment, A.D.

We the undersigned, being desirous that the above-named Schools should be united to the NATIONAL SOCIETY, *or* CANTERBURY DIOCESAN BOARD OF EDUCATION, *declare that*

1. "The Children are to be instructed in the Holy Scriptures, and in the Liturgy and Catechism of the Established Church."

2. "With respect to such instruction the Schools are to be subject to the superintendence of the Parochial Clergymen."

3. "The Children are to be regularly assembled for the purpose of attending Divine Service in the Parish Church, or other place of worship under the Establishment, unless such reason be assigned for their non-attendance as is satisfactory to the Managers of the School."

4. "The Masters and the Mistresses are to be members of the Church of England."

5. "A Report on the state and progress of the Schools is to be made, at Christmas every year, to the Diocesan Board, the District Society, or the National Society; and the Schools are, with the consent of the managers, to be periodically inspected by persons appointed either by the Bishop of the Diocese, the National Society, or the Diocesan Board of Education."

6. "In case any difference should arise between the Parochial Clergy and the Managers of the Schools, with reference to the preceding rules, respecting the religious instruction of Scholars, or any regulation connected therewith, an appeal is to be made to the Bishop of the Diocese, whose decision is to be final."

Signed by the
Parochial Minister
and others the
Managers. }

Dated   18

N.B.—In the absence of the Incumbent of the Parish, it is requested that the Officiating Minister, who signs the above, will state whether the Incumbent approves of the application for Union.

(Reproduced by permission of Canterbury Cathedral Archives)

FORM OF APPLICATION
For aid, prescribed by the Board.

Application for aid towards { building, enlarging, and fitting up } of { one or two, &c. } School Rooms, for

Boys, Girls, or Infants, at near the Post Town of

The Schools are to be, or were UNITED to the NATIONAL SOCIETY, or to the CANTERBURY DIOCESAN BOARD OF EDUCATION (state when) A.D. 184

1.—The Population of the for which the Schools are intended, as taken in the year 1831 .... } was and now is about

2.—Provision exists therein at present for the Education (gratuitously, or at very small charge,) exclusive of the Schools which aid is asked .... } of not more than Boys, and Girls, on .... { Sundays only, or (state which) Sundays and week days.

N.B.—Distinguish Church of England Schools from those of Dissenters.

3.—The New Schools are intended to receive at least boys, and girls, Infants, in Room, to be Sunday and Schools, and to be supported by

4.—The Instruction in the Schools is to be afforded for

5.—The estimated Salary of Master, is about £ The estimated Salary of Mistress is about £ The estimated Annual Charge for Books, &c. &c. is about £
So that there is a reasonable prospect of the Schools being permanently carried on.

6.—The accommodation provided for the Children in the Parish Church .... } is

7.—The Boys' School Room is to be internally, ft. long, ft. wide, and ft. high to the making an area of ft. or sq. ft. to each Boy.

The Girls' School Room is to be internally, ft. long, wide, and ft. high to the making an area of ft. or sq. ft. to each Girl.

The Infants' School Room is to be internally, ft. long, ft. wide, and ft. high to the making an area of ft. or sq. ft. to each Infant.

8.—The Foundation, Floor, Walls, and Roof, are to be of the following materials, viz. and the Property is to be held on the following legal tenure, viz. so that it will be legally secured for ever under Trustees for the purposes of educating the poor, in the principles of the Established Church.

9.—The entire estimated first cost of the undertaking, including the value of any Ground, Labour, or Materials given (as below) is £ viz. of the Ground, £ Building, Labour, and Materials, £ fittings up, £

10.—The exertions that have been made to provide means to meet the estimated cost, actually raised or promised are } viz. { By Grant from National School Society £
By Subscriptions, in Money.......... £
By Collections after Sermons .... £
By Donations of Ground, Materials, Cartage, Labour, &c. valued at .... £

11.—So that the total means already provided, or promised, to meet the first cost are.. £

12.—The only further exertions that can be made, independently of this application, are by and

The utmost that can be expected from them, is about .... £

Gross means to meet the Cost................ £

From details included in the original conveyance: [24]

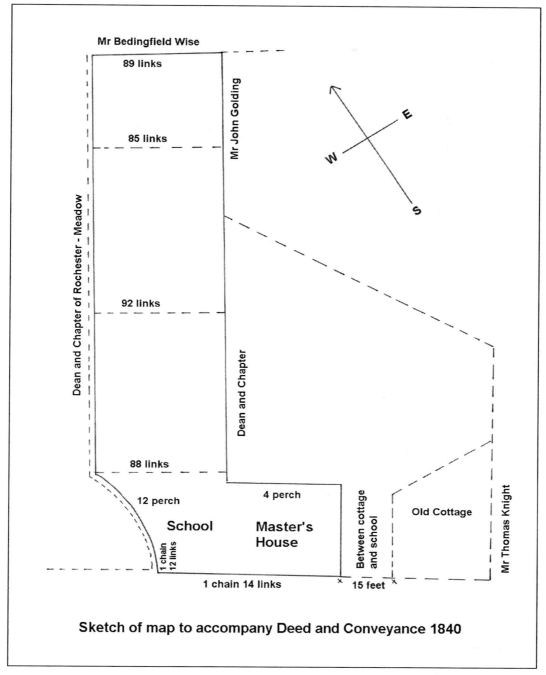

Sketch of map to accompany Deed and Conveyance 1840

(Reproduced by permission of Centre for Kentish Studies, Maidstone)

The site was edged by land owned by Mr Thomas Knight, Mr John Golding and Mr Bidingfield Wise. The 'old cottage' detailed on the accompanying sketch map to the Deed and Conveyance is likely to have been 'The Goose House' shown in *The History of Bearsted and Thurnham*.[25] Hasted certainly showed a property in the area in a map that accompanied his publication of 1798.[26] Part of the map is shown overleaf. The shaded area shows a representation of the plot of land, on part of which the school was later built.

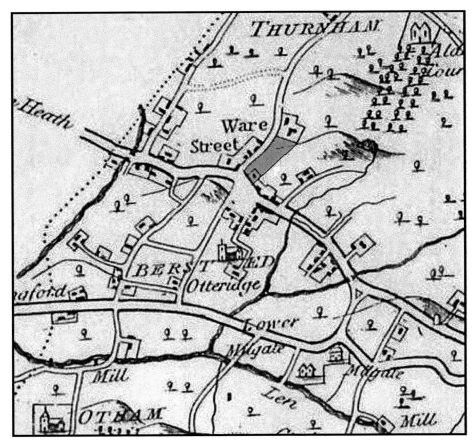

(Illustration courtesy of E P Publishing)

Presumably, the Goose House was demolished so that the school could be built. *Knowle Cottage*, the next house now adjacent to the main school building, was certainly built after this date. Opposite the site would have been the open space of the Green and to one side of the Green still stands the *White Horse* public house. Behind the school building was a large open field measuring approximately 110 yards which the children would use for their games.

It was agreed that Mr Lucas should receive some financial compensation for giving up the lease. The Trustees that were appointed were nominated by the Archbishop of Canterbury. There were four Trustees named in the Deed and Conveyance - the Rev Dr John Griffith, the Rev William Cobb, the Rev John McMahon Wilding and the Rev Charles Cage - respectively, the vicars of Boxley, Detling, Thurnham and Bearsted. The document detailed the agreement to hold:

> *...for ever In Trust and for the purpose of erecting thereon a School Room or School Rooms to be used for the education of such poor children residing or belonging to the several parishes of Detling, Thornham, Boxley and Bearsted in the said County of Kent some or one of them as aforesaid in the Principles of Christian Religion according to the Doctrines and Disciplines of the United Church of England and Ireland....*

The Trustees gave the Dean and Chapter of Rochester and Alderman Lucas five shillings each by way of compensation. The Trustees then became the owners of the site. Alderman Lucas continued to hold an interest in other lands in Bearsted.[27] The contents of the deed documents would give cause for concern to the Managers in later years but at the time they were deemed adequate for the purpose of establishing the school.

Curiously, there are no details of the construction of the building in the school records. However in the Church Vestry accounts for Bearsted there are listed some payments made by the churchwardens for building work: [28]

19 July 1839	To Mr Botten's Bricklayer's bill			14s	4½d
1 April 1840	Mr Samuel Johnson	Carpenter's bill		18s	
8 May 1840	Paid Thos. Botten	Bricklayer's bill		2s	9d
19 June 1840	Paid John Filmer	Bricklayer's bill	£1	15s	9½d
September	Mr Knowles bill			15s	9d
26 February 1841	Mr Johnson a Carpenters bill			17s	
March	Mr John Knowles ditto				
	plumber & Glazier's bill		£2	6s	4½d

There is no indication in the accounts that these bills were the result of a Visitation,[29] but it is clear that there had been substantial building work taking place in the parish at the time when the school was founded. It is therefore possible that these bills recorded in the parish documents comprised part of the cost of construction that was met by the parish.

There is some confusion over the precise date that the school opened to admit children. The earliest surviving document for Bearsted School is held by the National Society. It relates to the terms of affiliation, or union, with the society and confirms the establishment date to be 1839. The document is dated 14 December 1839, but it is not clear if the school had already been opened.[30] There are no documents which would confirm a particular date held in the diocesan records. One of the main reasons for the uncertainty is that the Deed and Conveyance documents bear a date of 6 April 1840. It is possible that the delay in drawing up the official documents was caused by the death of one of the owners of land adjacent to the school site, Mr Bidingfield Wise, and the subsequent administration of his estate by executors.[31] The foundation stone set into the front of the building corroborates the 1839 date as this photograph shows:

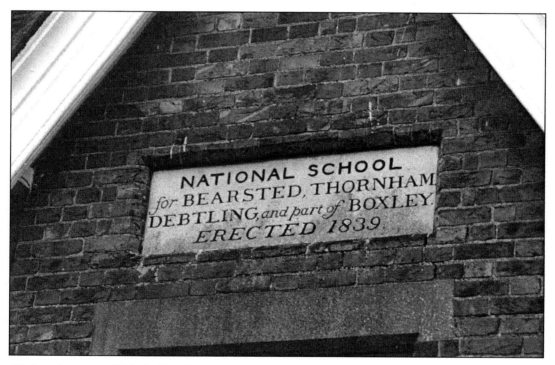

(Photograph courtesy of Malcolm Kersey)

The *History of Bearsted and Thurnham* gives John Peirce as the first Master at the school until 1856 when he departed to be Master at a school in Detling. However, there is no trace of him in the 1841 Census for Bearsted and Thurnham, as would be expected for the Master of the village school. John Peirce's household is listed in the 1851 Census: [32]

Bearsted Street
Bearsted

		Age			
John Peirce	Head	39	Married	National Schoolmaster	born Newenden, Kent
Frances H	Wife	39	Married	National Schoolmistress	Rye, Sussex
Mary A	Daughter	15	Unmarried	Scholar	Rye, Sussex
John	Son	12		Scholar	Rye, Sussex
Elizabeth A	Daughter	10		Scholar	Westwell, Kent
Emily	Daughter	7		Scholar	Bearsted, Kent
Thomas W	Son	6		Scholar	Bearsted, Kent
Fanny J	Daughter	4			Bearsted, Kent
Louisa H	Daughter	3			Bearsted, Kent
Charlotte Homewood		24	Unmarried	House Servant	Westwell, Kent

Using the birthplaces listed in the Census for John Peirce's children as a guide, the first child to be born in Bearsted was Emily. She was born in 1843 and her father's occupation is given as 'Schoolmaster' on the registration.[33] This indicates that the Peirce family arrived in Bearsted village sometime after 1841 but the precise date remains unrecorded. In the 1841 Census there is listed James Simmons, whose occupation is given as Schoolmaster: [34]

James Simmons	Head	55	Schoolmaster
Sarah	Wife	55	
Thomas	Son	15	
Eliza	Daughter	15	

From this information it can be surmised James Simmons was the first Master of Bearsted School until 1843.[35] Short periods of tenure were not unusual for Victorian schoolmasters.

Bearsted School was to be known as a 'National School': a facility for elementary education provided by the 'National Society of the Education of the Poor According to the Principles of the Church of England'. Seemingly unnoticed by the local newspapers, a new opportunity, financed by several organisations that were keen to promote the value of Christianity and education, arrived for the children of Bearsted, Thurnham, Detling and Boxley.

Chapter 2
The Development of the School up to 1914

The Conveyance and Deed for 'Bearsted, Thornham, Debtling and part of Boxley' National School is dated 6 April 1840. The purpose of the Deed is described:

For the purpose of setting a schoolroom thereon for the use of the said school and a house for the residents of the Master and Mistress thereof. [1]

The National Society had previously issued some general advice for the establishment and construction of a school:

A barn furnishes no bad model and a good one may be easily converted into a school...allowance should be made to give each child seven square feet of floor space...but a room narrower than fifteen feet will not admit a convenient space for a class of more than thirty children. [2]

The advice continued that the floor could be made of brick, stone, plaster or wood, and the roof of slate, tile or thatch. Light should be ample and perhaps windows on all four sides would be favourable, but they needed to be placed very high and wider than deep. Evidently, this was considered the best means to prevent distraction of the children's attention by the outside world. Ventilation was regarded as very important and it was recommended that wherever there were horizontal ceilings there were to be apertures to allow foul air to escape. [3] Even hygiene was carefully considered and the following advice given:

If the walls are of brick, they should be worked smooth and lime-washed, not plastered. [4]

The earliest plan located of the school [5] bears the inscription 'United School at Bearsted built 1839'. From the details shown overleaf, the building was basic and followed some of the National Society advice.

It is interesting to see from the plans that it was intended that the children were segregated. The Boys Room measures 7 feet longer than that of the Girls Room, so perhaps it was felt that the boys needed more space! From the outset, an additional area measuring 10 feet long and 20 feet wide was given as a proposed addition to the Boys Room. It appears there was only one point of access for each schoolroom, so if communication was required between staff during the teaching sessions, it was only achieved by walking around to the other room.

There is one obscure point on the plans - the back right-hand side of the Boys Room has a gap in the wall and there is a further small wall approximately three feet in length running in parallel behind it. This is open to a number of interpretations. It is possible that this was a delicate allusion to the sanitary arrangements which otherwise remain omitted from the plan. There is also no indication of a water supply provision or drainage for the school buildings. Drinking water would have been supplied in several buckets every day which were dipped into by the children using the tin mug provided. It may be surmised that the lavatories were that of an earth closet nature and were emptied elsewhere by hand so that any water needed for this purpose could be kept in a rainwater barrel. Such arrangements would have been in common practice in rural areas before the development of mains drainage.

The tithe apportionment details that were drawn up in 1842 but attached to the tithe map for Bearsted in 1844, describe the premises as 'School, House and garden', [6] occupying an area of one rod and thirty-four perches together with another smaller piece of garden which was five perches in area. The landowners were recorded as the National School and there was a tithe charge of two shillings and three pence.

This is a tracing of the 1839 plan of the school:

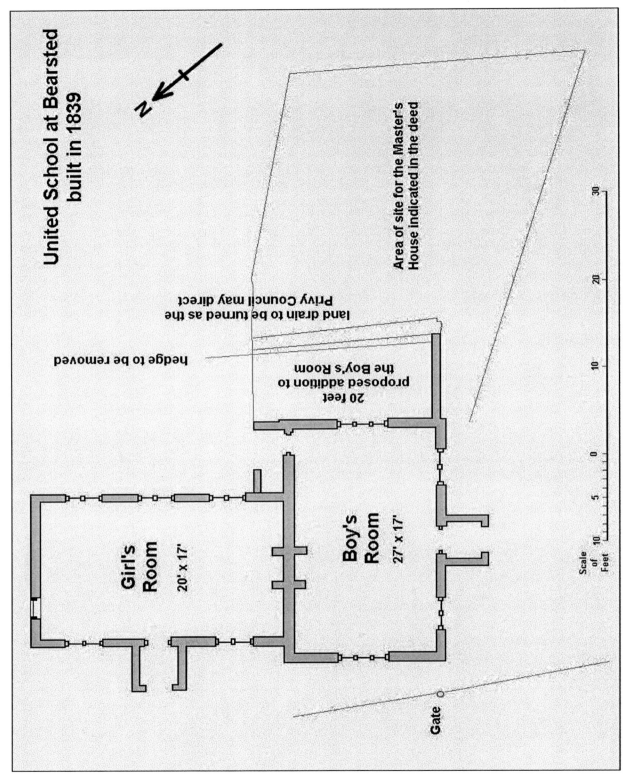

United School at Bearsted built in 1839

N

Area of site for the Master's House indicated in the deed

land drain to be turned as the Privy Council may direct

hedge to be removed

20 feet proposed addition to the Boy's Room

Girl's Room 20' x 17'

Boy's Room 27' x 17'

Gate

Scale of Feet 10 5 0 10 20 30

(Reproduced by permission of Her Majesty's Stationery Office)

This plan contains rather more detail about the land than the conveyance documents. It is specifically noted that there was a land drain that needed to be altered and a hedge was to be removed. Presumably, the hedge marked the boundary of the 'old cottage' premises first noted on the sketch map that accompanied the Deed and Conveyance. An area was also specifically noted as intended for a Master's House.

School House was not added for seven years after the schoolroom was erected. The application for a grant to assist in the enlargement of the school and the construction of a Master's residence, was made to the National Society on 6 August 1847 and is shown overleaf. It was estimated as costing £409 with a further £10 for fittings. However, there had been earlier efforts made to secure other funding as by the time of the application, the Committee of Council on Education had recommended that £125 be put towards this work.[7]

The application for funds from the government had a separate procedure. Applications had to follow the guidelines issued by the Committee in Circular 1, November 1839. It included answers to forty-two specific questions including the nature of the site, and particulars of the building. Fully detailed plans of the building work that were proposed were included,[8] but the contents of this successful application have not survived. In addition to the sum from the government there were funds already raised by local subscription which were listed. Local funds totalled £100 with a further £35 pledged. The Diocesan Board of Education had also granted £50. Curiously, it was particularly noted on the National Society application:

> [*the vicar*] applies for aid towards enlarging his school and adding a teachers residence.
> The schoolroom appears to have been built without aid from the National Society…

This information about the funding for the original schoolroom conflicts with other later papers for the school that list contributions made by the society. It is possible that some of the records were already incomplete and the society did not realise that they had granted some money through the Canterbury Diocesan Board of Education to set up the school. Nevertheless, a sum of £20 was granted on 9 September 1847.

As part of the application to the Committee of Council on Education, the original Deed of Trust had to be submitted to the Privy Council. It was then realised that there was a problem with the document: the formal right of regular admittance of government inspectors to visit the school had not been included. However, there had been regular inspections. In 1834, the National Society had originally accepted the money offered by the government to assist in the establishment of schools. It had also agreed to submit the schools to regular government inspection. When the trust deed had been signed on 6 April 1840, the Church of England had been opposed to the idea of regular inspection of schools by the government. However, as Bearsted School was affiliated to the National Society, the Managers abided by their regulations. This included compliance with the Minutes of the Committee of Council issued in September 1839: [9]

> The right of inspection will be required by the Committee in all cases, an inspector, authorised by Her Majesty in Council, will be appointed from time to time to visit schools to be henceforth aided by public money; the inspectors will not interfere with the religious instruction, or discipline, or management of the school, it being their object to collect facts and information, and to report the result of their inspections to the Committee of Council.

In addition, three months after the deed for the school had been signed in July 1840, agreement had been reached between the Archbishops of Canterbury and York, and the government.[10] Although a clause about regular inspection of the school now needed to be included, the Deed itself was not re-drafted. Instead, a memorandum was attached which covered this requirement:

> Whereas since the execution of the within deed pecuniary and has been sought from the Committee of Council appointed to our permit and the application of any sums voted by Parliament for the purpose of promoting Public Education and the said Committee have agreed to recommend that the sum of one hundred and twenty five pounds be appropriated towards the enlargement of the schools and the erection of a Master's House for the said school upon condition of the same being open to inspection as hereinafter mentioned NOW then it is declared and agreed by and between the parties to the within deed that the school buildings erected or to be erected on the land conveyed thereby shall so soon as the said sum of one hundred and twenty five pounds shall have been paid by the Lords of Her Majesty's Treasury be open at all reasonable times to the inspection of the Inspector or Inspectors for the time being appointed in conformity with the committee in Council bearing date the 10th day of August, one thousand eight hundred and forty eight.

This is the grant application for assistance in the enlargement of the school and towards the construction of a Master's residence, submitted to the National Society 6 August 1847. The original document is in fragments.

(Reproduced by permission of The Church of England Record Centre)

There is another set of plans for Bearsted School dated 1848 [11] which include the designs for the Master's House and proposed alterations to the school. Drawn up on linen, they comprise seven plans. There are exhaustive details of the house basement, ground and upper floors, sections through both of the buildings, the front elevation, the end elevation and an elevation of one of the windows of the house. They were produced by Martin Bulmer of Maidstone, and are a wonderful example of the painstaking art of Victorian draughtsmanship. Tracings of the ground plan and the front elevation are shown overleaf. The impression gained from the plans is of a building in great harmony with the surroundings, and yet still retaining a distinctive character. A great deal of the original 1848 design was built and survives today.

It was proposed to enlarge the Boys' Room (note, called 'Boys' School' here) to measure 36 feet long and 15 feet wide. One large window was to be heightened to measure 7 feet 6 inches and 6 feet wide. The school wall facing The Street would be altered by the removal of the central porch and a window inserted instead. The wall would therefore be punctuated by three windows each measuring 3 feet 10 inches high and 5 feet 3 inches wide. There would be a formal porch sited at the forward front right hand side of the Boys' Room. By this means access would be gained to both the Boys' Room and School House through two separate doors. It is interesting to note that part of the plan is marked 'an old window used to be here', so perhaps there had been earlier alterations to the building, although no record of these has survived.

From the plans, School House had a fairly generous basement although the exact dimensions are not given. The ground floor plans show a living-room and a sitting-room. Both rooms have fireplaces. The upper floor shows two bedrooms at the front of the house and a smaller bedroom at the back. It is likely that only the largest bedroom had a fireplace. There is a brick-paved wash-house and a small outhouse which contained the lavatory discreetly situated some way behind the main body of the house. This outhouse could be directly accessed through a door from the wash-house. Like many village schools there was still no running water on the premises. The water supply seems to have been obtained from a stop-cock in the wash house that was supplied from a well and an iron pump is indicated on the map.

The designs were comprehensive. It was even specified that the windows for School House were to have cement lintels and splays, the sills made of oak and iron sashes for each window. Hay bars would open and shut the sashes with small brass bolts on the inside to fasten the sash. The windows were of an attractive latticed design. Other details such as the chimney pots are included. These measured 5 feet 6 inches high!

School House was sufficiently spacious to accommodate John Peirce's seven children and a house servant during his tenure as Master up to 1856. Twenty years later, in 1871, the house amply accommodated Samuel Johnson's family; comprising husband, wife, step-daughter and three other daughters. In 1891 John Day was also able to accommodate a boarder in the house - Miss Ellen Wallis, one of the assistant teachers for the school.

On 14 December 1848, the Managers were able to give written confirmation to the National Society that the building work was now complete.

A tracing of the front elevation from the 1848 proposals is reproduced below:

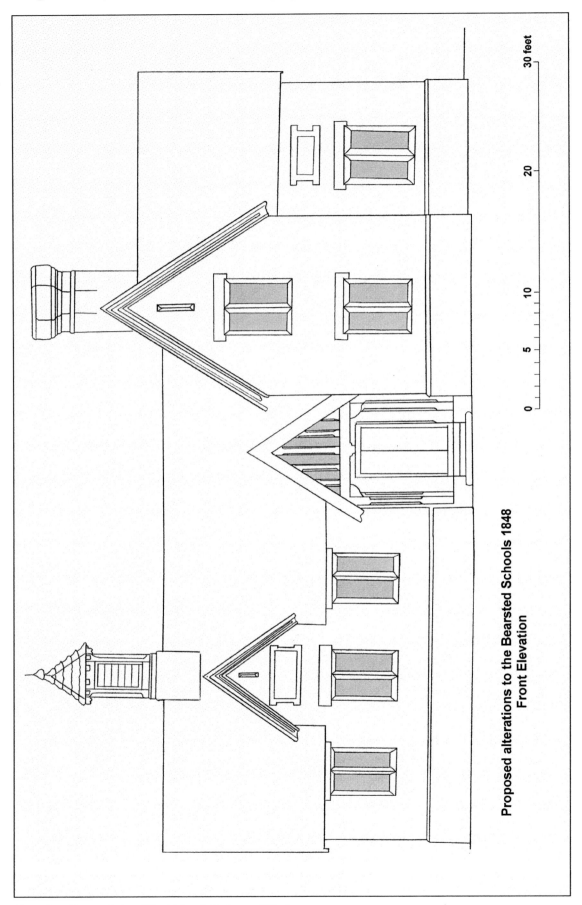

Proposed alterations to the Bearsted Schools 1848
Front Elevation

(Reproduced by permission of Her Majesty's Stationery Office)

A tracing of the ground plan which shows the revisions proposed in 1848 for part of the school and School House is reproduced below:

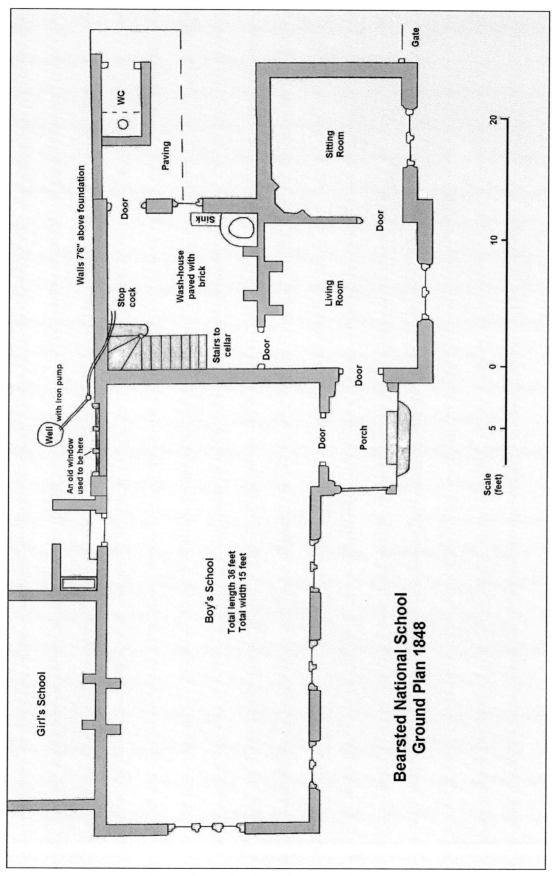

Both the school rooms and School House were subject to the needs of maintenance and upkeep. Until the turn of the century, and changes under a new administration, this was largely carried out on an irregular basis. If deemed necessary, repairs and alterations to the fabric were undertaken as required, but there is no evidence of a continuous programme of regular maintenance. As an example of this, when a school window was broken, the Master advised a Manager, an Order was given and the matter was attended to by a local tradesman from the village. For many years such matters were dealt with by either Mr Wilkinson (who ran a building and undertaking business from Mote Hall Villas in Bearsted) or Mr Knowles (a local builder). Mr Wilkinson had attended the school in the 1860s and later became a Manager. On one occasion in 1885, he also attempted to mend the school clock but to no avail, as it was subsequently sent away for repair. Mr J Wood, a blacksmith in the village, also effected repairs and largely attended to the school stoves.

This sketch, gives an idea of the Bearsted National School site around 1866. The shaded areas show the extent of the premises:

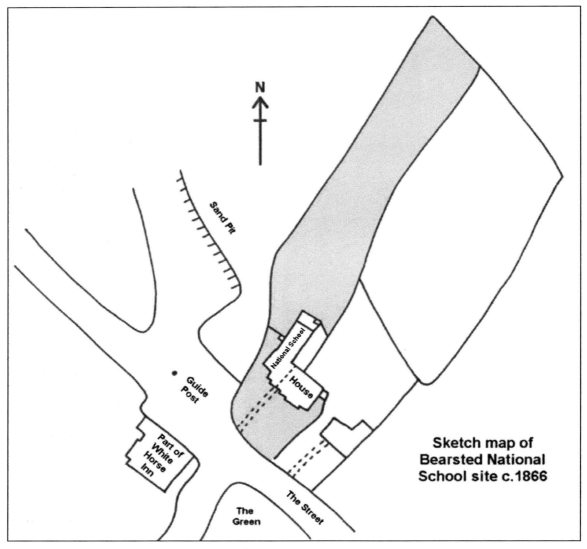

Sketch map of Bearsted National School site c.1866

(Illustration by Kathryn Kersey based on Ordnance Survey)

The school was cleaned by ladies from the village but there is only one person particularly named as cleaning the building and two brief details of incidents involving her in the records. From the log book:

6 January 1893
Mrs Lamkin had to be sent for on Wednesday morning to sweep the school (which was in a filthy state ....[from] the preceding evening)... instead of doing it in the usual course of her duty.

During Miss Love Jones' tenure as Mistress some of the children were ordered to sweep the schoolroom floor at the end of the day. This arrangement was largely unsuccessful and led to a number of minor rebellions. From the log book:

12 November 1872
Two boys unwilling to take their turn in sweeping the schoolrooms.
School left in very dirty state.

As the school became established, it is clear that the size of the building was a constraint on the number of children in attendance. Nonetheless, plans were made to expand. Following advice from a government inspector, the Managers applied to the National Society for a grant to assist in the enlargement of a classroom. It is evident, from the correspondence held by the National Society,[12] that another plan was drawn up by Martin Bulmer. Regrettably this plan has not survived. However, the details given on the application for aid made on 7 May 1855 provide some information. It was proposed to enlarge at least one classroom to the length of 16 feet 2 inches. It was to be 12 feet wide and to have a height of 13 feet and would cost £110. This sum would be achieved through £23 raised locally, with a further £17 promised. The Diocesan Board of Education granted £10, and the Committee of Council on Education promised £50. It was proposed that the £10 shortfall would be met from the National Society. Despite this, the National Society could only offer £5 towards the costs. Unfortunately, no other documentation about this proposed enlargement has survived. It must be assumed that as the cost could not be met in full, it did not proceed. A copy of the application is shown overleaf.

The Infant section opened on 11 October 1869 with Miss Aves as Infant Mistress. The log book records that twenty children were drafted into the new Infant department. It is likely that the room shown as the 'Girls Room' on the 1839 and 1848 plans now became the Infant Room. Despite the division into Infants and Seniors, all the children were still accommodated in the same buildings.

The provision of adequate accommodation for the children of Bearsted and Thurnham was a constant problem. On 30 September 1870 a special meeting took place which culminated in the establishment of a school specifically for the children in Thurnham. The Minute Book records that the population of Bearsted and Thurnham now totalled 1,180 people. The Managers needed to achieve sufficient accommodation for around 196 children to be educated and as each child was estimated to require 8 square feet of floor space, Bearsted only had room for 91 children. A separate school for Thurnham was an attractive proposal, but there would be difficulties in selecting an appropriate site and to secure the necessary funds.[13] Nevertheless, two years later, these difficulties overcome, a school for Thurnham had been built and was opened on 21 October 1872 with Louisa Partridge as Mistress.

From the start, Bearsted and Thurnham Schools were considered as two separate entities but there was a considerable amount of interaction. All the parties governing the schools co-operated over the transfer of children as the local population fluctuated and economic circumstances changed. In later years, on some occasions, there were joint lessons as Thurnham children were invited to participate in some classes at Bearsted.

This is the grant application for assistance towards a proposed enlargement of the school submitted to the National Society, 7 May 1855. The work did not proceed.

(Reproduced by permission of The Church of England Record Centre)

The provision of sufficient desks was another acute problem at times. The first noted shortage of these was in 1865 when a Diocesan Inspection report commented that there were not enough desks for the children. In addition to the lack of desks, it is evident from the records that the staff usually found that the desk provision conflicted with the class sizes and the teaching as the curriculum developed.

The records do not always make it clear what types of desk were in use at the school. However, one desk design favoured by the National Society had a slope of approximately ten inches and a horizontal ledge which was two to three inches wide to accommodate a china ink well.[14] The design meant that it was not easily adaptable for other uses. In 1888, three new desks had to be purchased to enable the introduction of some new Kindergarten activities. In 1906 and 1909 it was recorded in the log book that the cast iron supports for some new 'dual desks' had been received. This design was adaptable for lessons other than reading and writing. These desks were usually constructed from cast iron and wood as the illustration below indicates. The shaded upright parts indicate the metal components. Note that parts of the desk lifted up and a slot was provided to hold writing slates when they were not being used.

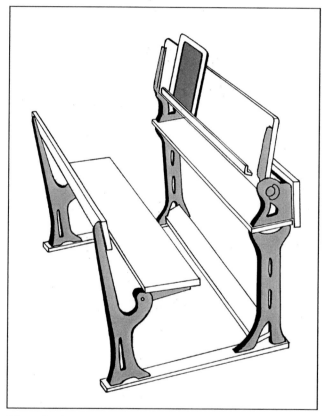

(Illustration by Malcolm Kersey)

In 1891 the curriculum had expanded to accommodate more subjects: Drawing for the older boys and Needlework for the girls. Once again, the seating for the pupils was acknowledged to be inadequate. It is likely that John Day had intimated this to the government inspector before the annual examination. He later commented in the log book:

> Great difficulty however is experienced in the seating of the elder children now in the new Standard II who have come in from the Infant Room. Increased desk accommodation is absolutely necessary if the school is to be worked successfully...

It was a further three months before the situation was resolved with a further supply of desks. From the log book:

> Every child in the Upper Division will now be able to do the school work creditably, especially the pen and pencil lessons...

The number of children that could be safely accommodated in school was a matter for continual discussion. The log books show that there was intermittent overcrowding. For several years in the late 1880s, there was uncertainty over the continually discussed proposal to amalgamate Standard I with the rest of the school. In July 1892 the inspectors advised that Standard I should be kept in the Infant Room but still apart from the other standards. In 1893 the Bearsted Managers met the Thurnham Managers to discuss attendance. As a result it was decided to ask children from Thurnham currently attending Bearsted to move to Thurnham School in an attempt to bring the numbers attending Bearsted to within the guidelines set by the government. This arrangement achieved a limited success due to an immediate influx of new families into the village filling the recently vacated spaces. Overcrowding continued to be a perennial problem.

Just as maintenance was governed by requests from the Master to the Managers to procure the necessary Orders, so too were the supplies for the school. There are many instances recorded in the log book of orders placed and received, together with information when the supplies were low. In 1896, Miss Burnett, a temporary assistant for the Infants was appointed. Being unaware of the system for procuring supplies for the school, she took matters into her own hands. It was some time before she was reimbursed her expenses of 10s 1½d!

On 26 January 1894 the Master had to draw the attention of the vicar and a Manager, to part of the ceiling in the Infant Room which needed urgent repair. Although this was immediately undertaken, two years later in November 1896, part of another ceiling collapsed. John Day estimated that about twenty pounds of plaster had descended into the main room just before the cleaner arrived at 7am. Presumably, he had heard the noise from School House and investigated. Mr Wilkinson was ordered to make immediate repairs but it is not recorded whether this precipitation had any effect upon the timetable for the day.

In addition to maintaining the fabric of the building, Mr Wilkinson also had the unenviable task of looking after the sanitary arrangements or 'offices' as they were known. These duties involved white-washing the walls at intervals and emptying the contents of the lavatories. From the log books, it seems that the emptying procedure was carried out during the holidays or at the weekend. As it was many years before the advent of mains drainage, emptying the offices was an essential activity. In 1898 the Managers decided that there were not enough lavatories or coat pegs for the number of children in the school. Although it is not known how many new lavatories were built in the playing area behind the school, the roll stood at 152 children. The editor of the parish magazine expressed satisfaction with the completed work, but noted that the work would probably have had to have been done before many more years had passed.[15]

Following outbreaks of various diseases in the village, and particularly diphtheria in 1895, all the drains and offices connected with the school buildings became subject to special scrutiny by the Sanitary Officer and Inspector from the Medical and Sanitary Authority for the District. The powers of the government inspectors were similarly extended around this time to inspect the offices, yards, ventilators, walls and the surroundings of each schoolroom. In 1893 the government inspector's report suggested some alterations and additions. From the log book:

> Offices – to have a partition between each seat.
> Windows - to have blinds.
> Doors - to have curtains to keep out draughts and the porch repaired.
> Ventilators - to be made thoroughly effective.

After the inspection, the building of new lavatory arrangements, referred to in the log books for the first time, as 'cloakrooms', immediately began in June. However, John Day noted that the construction and noise made by the workmen had led to some disruption. The following week the children were able to start using the new facilities, but not before it was checked that the efficiency of the school was not impeded. It was carefully noted that the time taken up in crossing the premises was the same as that under the old arrangements!

The advent of the railway in the village had a decided effect upon the school as the construction of the railway line effectively divided the school land in two. Despite the lack of a playground, there was a field used by the children for games directly behind the school which extended approximately 110 yards. During the passing of the Act in 1880 which enabled the railway line to be built, the Maidstone and Ashford Railway Company deposited funds into the Court of Chancery as payment for the land they intended to use. Although the money was ultimately the property of the Dean and Chapter of Rochester Cathedral, the situation had become complicated due, once more, to the contents of the original Deed and Conveyance documents for the school.

In October 1879 it was realised that there were several problems which needed to be remedied. The site had originally been conveyed as a personal interest to the Vicars of Bearsted, Thurnham, Detling and Boxley, rather than to their offices. Only one out of the four original Trustees was surviving, and he had no vested power for the sale or disposal of school property.[16] The National Society was consulted by the Managers who, in turn, sought legal opinion about the matter. As a result, a fresh Deed of Appointment of Trustees was signed on 9 July 1883. The proceeds of the land sale to the railway company were then invested in £78 17s 6d, 2½ per cent Annuities to supplement the income for the school.[17] It is curious to note that once the legal problems had been resolved and the parcel of land was purchased, the railway company only used it to build the railway through Bearsted. A hedged boundary structure which outlines the extent of the original school field is still visible from the footpath that cuts across the fields at Thurnham Lane. The boundary is still marked on Ordnance Survey maps.

The construction of the line through the village must have provided quite a spectacle for the children. In addition to the usual gang of 'navvies' that worked on building the railway line, it provided another source of employment in the village which was well paid. Norah Giles (née Pettipiere) recalled that her great-uncle, Stephen Bridgland, once showed her a bag of gold sovereigns that he had earned 'putting the railway through the village'. There is only one reference to it in the log book, and concerns the attendance at the school:

15 February 1884
Several families who came to the village on account of working on the line have now left, others will be leaving shortly, as the line gets near to its completion, so children gradually drop off.

The subsequent opening of the line on 1 July 1884 did not merit a comment.

On 25 April 1890 the railway was to prove troublesome when the schoolroom was flooded by water that had gathered in the fields and had run along the railway line following torrential rain. The School House cellar was also flooded to a depth of three feet. Unsurprisingly, the school was closed for the day in order to sort out the problems but opened as usual on the following Monday. Sixteen years later, in 1906, heavy rain caused the main room to be flooded on 30 October and so the school did not re-assemble for that afternoon.

Other landscaping around the school was achieved by Mrs Knight, who was a most generous friend to the school. She suggested in August 1889 that the trees in front of the building needed to be cut down, the sides of the path to the school would then need to be turfed and the path itself to be asphalted. She offered to pay for all of these works and the improvements were soon achieved.

The grounds were further landscaped in July 1890 when the wind blew over one of the lilac trees near the school. Fatally weakened, the tree finally fell down during the same week. Yet more inadvertent landscaping was achieved in 1897, as John Day wrote in the log book:

19 February 1897
Mr Marley's goat has been in the garden in front of the school, eating the bark off the trees. He comes in nearly every time the gate is open to admit the children. The Master, school cleaner and pupils have driven him out again and again but unless the gate is kept closed altogether, all efforts to keep him out are fruitless!

The heating was largely supplied by two stoves, one for each room. These needed regular attention as they were disposed to be troublesome. When the stove malfunctioned or failed to draw properly, the resulting smoke filled the rooms and thick black smuts landed on the desks spoiling paper and needlework alike. This happened many times and on at least one occasion the smoke irritated the eyes and throats of both teachers and pupils. Due to the temperamental nature of the stove in the Infant Room, in 1889 there was no fire in the room for a week. In winter the limits of the heating arrangements were particularly apparent. In 1884 John Day recorded that the stove merely heated the room to the extent of a three foot radius with the result that the children were crying with cold. Despite constant maintenance of the stove, the situation was acutely similar in January 1895.

On 25 October 1895, the Managers finally decided to purchase a new stove for the large room as twice during the previous week, the room temperature barely rose above 44°F. It was also decided to attend to the chimney of School House as the front room had been uninhabitable owing to the smoke filling the room every time a fire was lit. A week later, the new stove was installed but almost immediately cracked at the back! It was still awaiting repair fourteen days later. It was not until 22 November before some sort of order was restored but the new stove continued to give intermittent trouble. There was further trouble with the stove in 1897 when the Infant Room was filled with smoke. This later incident culminated in Mr Wilkinson removing the errant piece of stove pipe altogether whilst Mrs Knight kindly supplied a paraffin stove for use in the Infant Room until the proper stove had been repaired by Mr Wood.

If the winters were marked by cold, frozen ink and fingers due to the ineffectual heating, the children suffered the opposite problem in summer. The schoolroom windows were quite small until 1900 when they were eventually widened. However, the main problem in the summer, commented upon by many of the staff, was the sun beating down upon the children's heads. Due to the lack of blinds at the three south-west facing windows in 1893, the children had to be moved to various other parts of the building to achieve some respite and rest from the sun.

In 1892 there was an alteration to part of the boundaries as John Perrin, a grocer and businessman, who was trading from premises which included a shop with some accommodation at Chestnut Place. This was adjacent to the school. It was agreed to exchange several strips of land with the Trustees. John Perrin agreed to build and maintain a 6-foot high wall on the school side. A 4-foot high gate was to be built in addition to making provision for an opening in the wall.[18] Mr Perrin was now able to develop the range of shops at Chestnut Place. The shops had two storeys and he expanded a commercial operation for a jam factory premises behind the shops. This was to cause a nuisance in 1894 as John Day complained that the air of the Infant Room was filled with unsavoury odours and smoke from the chimney of the factory.

There are two documents held in the Centre for Kentish Studies that illustrate the finances of the school. The first is dated 29 July 1892 and acknowledges the receipt of £1 9s 10d, this being a collection taken at Bearsted church and was forwarded from the churchwardens.[19] The Managers always welcomed such donations and had a formal printed receipt book. The second document is a printed account of the income and expenditure for the year ending 28 February 1895.[20] In 1894-95 the voluntary contributions received were by means of a subscription list. The list included prominent members of the community and one or two local tradesmen who had sent their children to the school: William Tomsett, the baker, donated 10 shillings. The most generous subscription was that of the Earl of Romney who had given £5, but the majority of the donations were in the range of £1 to £2.

The annual running expenses in 1894-1895 amounted to £224 16s and 10d. Of this, the staff salaries accounted for £185 and 7d. The income was largely based upon a grant from the Committee of Council on Education, the Annuities purchased from the proceeds of the sale of land to the railway, some voluntary contributions, and a legacy from Major Wayth, a former Manager. Three shillings had also been earned by the hire of a room for the parish council election. The accounts were produced by Henry Tasker, treasurer and audited by Major General Talbot. A printed account[21] is shown opposite.

The school account sheet for 1894-1895:

ACCOUNT OF THE INCOME AND EXPENDITURE

OF

THE BEARSTED NATIONAL SCHOOL,

For the Year ending February 28th, 1895.

Income.

Dr.	£	s.	d.
To Balance on 1st March, 1894	0	16	8
Grant from Committee of Council on Education	111	13	0
Ditto, Fee Grant	58	7	6
Voluntary Contributions	45	12	0
Major Wayth's Legacy	1	5	4
New 2½°/₀ Dividend	1	19	4
Sale of Needlework	2	10	0
From Department of Science and Art ..	2	10	0
Hire of Room for Parish Council Election	0	3	0
	£224	**16**	**10**

Expenditure.

Cr.	£	s.	d.
Salaries :—Master	130	0	0
Assistants	45	8	7
Monitors	9	12	0
Books, Apparatus, and Stationery	19	16	11
Fuel, Light, and cleaning	7	14	0
Replacement of Furniture, and Repairs to Buildings, &c.	1	18	6
Rates, Taxes, and Insurance	6	1	8
Other Expenses......................	3	5	7
Balance in hands of Treasurer	0	19	7
	£224	**16**	**10**

Examined and approved
March 11th, 1894.

R. TALBOT, Major-General,
AUDITOR.

HENRY TASKER,
TREASURER.

Subscription List for the Year ending February 28th, 1895.

	£	s.	d.		£	s.	d.		£	s.	d.
Adams, M. A., Esq	1	1	0	Lushington, Rev. T. G. L. (donation)	5	0	0	Tasker, H., Esq.	5	5	0
Bensted, H., Esq.	0	10	6					Tasker, H., Esq. (donation) ..	2	0	0
Blunt, Mrs...................	2	0	0	Perrin, Mr. J.	1	1	0	Tasker, Mrs.	1	1	0
Darby, Mr. E...............	0	10	0	Procktor, Mr. E. C.	0	10	0	Tomsett, Mr. Wm.	0	10	0
Harnett & Co...............	2	2	0	Romney, The Earl of	5	0	0	Whatman, James, Exors. of ..	2	2	0
Isherwood, Foster, and Stacey, Messrs.	2	0	0	Scarth, Rev. Canon J.	1	1	0	Wilkinson, Mr. C.	0	10	0
Jewell, Mr. J.	1	1	0	Scarth, Mrs.	1	1	0				
Laurence, William, Esq.	2	2	0	Shaw, Mr. H.	0	5	0				
Lushington, Miss	4	0	0	Style, A. F. & Co., Messrs....	1	0	0				
Lushington, F., Esq.	1	0	0	Talbot, General.............	2	0	0	**£45**	**12**	**0**
				Tapply, Mrs.	1	0	0				

₊ Mr. H. J. Knowles' Subscription of 10/0 received after account was closed.

(Reproduced by permission of Centre for Kentish Studies, Maidstone)

Although the finances were of a largely sound nature, there was very little money to carry over until the next year and some greater investment would be needed for future development. The question of finance for the school was to remain open to discussion by the Managers for many years.

The sketch map below shows the school premises around 1897. Note the effects of the railway line running through the playing field and the expansion of Chestnut Place.

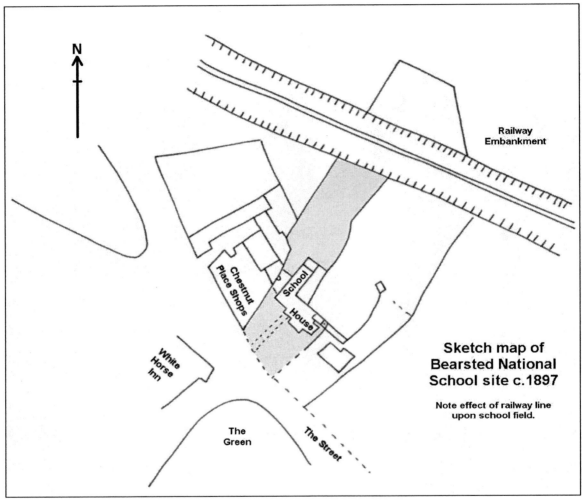

(Illustration by Kathryn Kersey based on Ordnance Survey)

From the log book entries of 1899 it is evident that the continual questions about the condition of the school and the problems posed by the overcrowding had still not been adequately addressed. As the annual government inspector's report commented:

> The condition of the school shows very little improvement....The school itself is old, inconvenient and often overcrowded, some of the windows want mending. The offices which under present conditions are unavoidably too close to the school are dirty and no urinal is provided for the boys taught in the Infants class room. The desks are old and need replacing.
>
> I am to call your attention to Her Majesty's Inspectors remarks as to the condition of the premises and the want of suitable desks and of sufficient office accommodation...

Clearly, the renovations were needed but how was this to be achieved? Any development and improvement required adequate finance.

Several months after the government report, plans for improvements were abruptly influenced by outside events. A fire at Mr Perrin's premises at Chestnut Place caused damage to the school on 14 January 1900 when the parade of shops burnt down. The local newspaper covered the event in minute detail. A transcript of the report in *Kent Messenger and Gravesend Telegraph and Dartford News* dated 20 January 1900 is shown below:

DISASTROUS FIRE AT BEARSTED

JAM FACTORY AND SHOPS DESTROYED

Early on Saturday morning a fire occurred at the extensive premises of Mr J Perrin at Bearsted. The establishment, which was well known in the district, consisted of three large shops, with post office, jam factory and store-room, and the whole premises have been burnt to the ground.

It appears that about half-past four a.m. one of the domestic servants in the upper rooms was awakened by a strong smell of smoke, and Mr Perrin and the household being aroused, it was found that the ceiling of the store-room over the drapery department was on fire, and the rafters were extensively burnt. The shop assistants and other helpers used their utmost endeavours to prevent the fire spreading to other parts of the premises, but their efforts proved futile. The flames spread with alarming rapidity, in consequence of the inflammable nature of the stock-in-trade and the large quantity of woodwork used in the construction of the buildings. The boot and provision departments were quickly enveloped in flames, and after the roofs fell with a tremendous crash the central and outer wall gave way. Amid the fierce roar and crackling of the fire, numerous tins of meat etc., in the grocery shop went off with sharp reports resembling small explosions. The cellars contained a large quantity of bacon, lard, etc., and this as well as a big stock of calico, was destroyed. The old jam factory was soon attacked and tons of jam and marmalade in bottles and nearly all of the appliances were utterly

destroyed. The residents in the neighbourhood rendered every assistance possible, and a portion of the household furniture, a valuable piano, and the books were saved, although those who rescued the latter did so with hands muffled in towels. Two horses in the stables got out early, without sustaining any injury. As soon as possible too, a messenger was dispatched for the Kent Office Fire Brigade but by the time of their arrival, under Capt. Oates, the fire had obtained such a hold on the main premises that their efforts were largely directed to the saving of adjoining property. In this they were to a large degree successful, the National School escaping with comparatively little damage, while a new building recently erected by Mr Perrin for the requirements of his growing business was also saved, together with boilers, coppers and other machinery. A plentiful supply of water was obtained from the pond on the Green.

So great was the heat from the fire, that the paint on the White Horse Inn, which is on the opposite side of the road, was much blistered. The origin of the fire is unknown. The damage which is estimated at about £5,000 is covered by insurance in the Kent Fire Office. A temporary shop and postal office has been opened in the Village Hall, where Mr Perrin is carrying on his business for the present. It is gratifying to know that the new and commodious buildings at the west end of the scene of the conflagration escaped destruction, as here Mr Perrin will be able to continue the manufacture of Kentish fruit jam, which has secured such a good reputation.

Rarely has the village had such a concourse of visitors as on Sunday. It was a fine day, and all roads leading to Bearsted were crowded, especially during the afternoon with people all going to the scene of the disaster.

The log book entry for the following day gives a straightforward account of the matter as Agnes Barclay recorded:

<u>15 January 1900</u>
A fire broke out early yesterday at Mr Perrin's adjoining the school. The flames spread rapidly and soon caught the school. By strenuous efforts they were extinguished before much damage was down. The western window, the roof belfry and two front windows are however burned.

It does not take a great leap of the imagination to envisage that day's working conditions; the sodden, blackened school, the wrecked burnt-out building immediately next door, and air heavy with smoke, smuts and dampness from the Fire Brigade's attentions. Despite this, Agnes Barclay stoically finished the record for the day:

> School opened as usual.

In the face of all the discomfort and the children's natural curiosity, the teaching given that day was probably not the most effective.

The school was subsequently closed for a week while the building was swiftly repaired and re-opened on 13 February. To her great satisfaction, Agnes Barclay recorded that the school now had a new large window, two front windows, the roof was repaired and the stoves in both rooms were removed further from the woodwork. The shops were subsequently rebuilt but the parade became a single storey. This photographic postcard shows the view from Chestnut Place towards the Green around 1910. The front of the school is just visible, behind the lamp post on the left hand side.

(Postcard courtesy of Roger Vidler)

Despite the renovations, the buildings were criticised by the government inspector's report for 1900, issued three months later. There were clearly grounds for concern as the buildings were now over sixty years old and there was still no water supply on the premises other than that supplied through the pump at School House. Although the log book does not give the Managers' reaction to this criticism, they were able to use an enforced closure due to a mumps outbreak, 25 April to 14 May, to good effect to attend to the toilet provision. Unfortunately, this work caused a further three-day delay in re-opening until 17 May.

Further small improvements followed in 1901 as drainage repairs were carried out. The architect's certificate for this work survives.[22] Later on in the year, persistent concern about overcrowding led the Managers to request twenty children who were not resident in the parish to attend other schools.

The financial provision was boosted in 1901 for the next two years by grants awarded to the school by the government.[23] The money was designated for improvements to the existing premises and provided a new Gallery in the Infant Room, a wooden block floor, redecoration and further attention to the stoves. A Gallery was a small platform which was installed to accommodate further desks. It was reached by a series of steps. Such a facility made it possible for oral lessons to be delivered to a large number of children at the same time. Despite this, the government inspector's comments in the annual report remained:

> The room is an old and inconvenient one…

Clearly, change was now needed to achieve improvements in the funding, maintenance and administration. That change was achieved, but on a gradual basis and as part of a larger reform of local government which partially focused upon education provision. Under the 1902 Education Act, the County Council became responsible for elementary education in Kent. It was not until July the following year that the Kent Education Committee took over responsibility for elementary schools.

Once more the contents of the deed documents continued to give cause for concern. A few months earlier, in January 1903, the school Correspondent wrote to the National Society. He sought advice as to whether a new Trust deed was required as there were now only two surviving Trustees from the 1883 document. There was also no provision for the appointment of Managers. Evidently, the Correspondent was concerned to determine whether under the provisions of the new Education Act, the role of the Trustees would be assumed by the Kent Education Committee.

The school was still affiliated to the National Society but there was confusion whether the Managers role would now change. An assurance was sought that Managers who were in post at the time of transfer to the Kent Education Committee would continue. It was confirmed that this was the case but any future appointments should be by free vote elections. Further, if any Manager needed to be replaced during the three year tenure of office, the vacancy could be filled by the nomination of the remaining Managers.[24] The rest of the correspondence about this matter does not survive but a new deed was not drawn up, so perhaps the legalities of the situation were already adequately covered. However the letter is a good illustration of problems encountered during the transition period.

Although the Kent Education Committee continued to assume overall responsibility, most routine maintenance such as re-decoration continued to be carried out spasmodically and on a local basis. The parish magazine advised:

> During the holidays the School has been thoroughly done up. The walls have been washed a delicate primrose colour and with permission of the Managers, the Vicar is painting on the east wall, a large outline map of the world…[25]

On 3 July 1903, there was an entry made in the log book:

> F C Bennett Esq, [*Correspondent of the School*] visited on Monday, bringing papers to be filled in for the Kent Education Committee.

The entry looks routine, but it marks the start of the school's association with the emergence of the local education authority. Over the next few years, although the strong links to the Church of England would be maintained, the Kent Education Committee gradually took over the administration and maintenance. Amongst the early indications of the Kent Education Committee's increasing influence are the entries in the log book noting that a card giving the monthly attendance figures had been completed and returned. For renovation work, whilst the Education Committee would sometimes employ their own contractors, and for minor repairs and maintenance, a Local Order Book could be used if deemed appropriate. The overall administration by the Kent Education Committee proceeded, but the links to the local business community in Bearsted would continue as before.

Whilst the beliefs of the Church of England continued to play a pivotal role, it was undeniably true that further funding was urgently required. Accordingly, as the Education Committee established its working relationship with the school, the Committee's assistance was largely to provide new desks and other appropriate equipment. It would be a mistake, though, to presume that the Kent Education Committee was providing resources in a similar manner to the county-wide remit of today. Resources were largely provided through the local districts, and Bearsted was included in the local district of Maidstone. The increase in provision did not immediately impact upon the school as the annual government inspection report for 1904 still noted that parts of the building seemed cold and dark.

After the correspondence with the National Society in January 1903 concerning the Trustees and Managers, as a move towards the greater scope and establishment of the Kent Education Committee, the Trustees of the school were discharged from their duties. This was achieved by an Order of the Board of Education dated 23 June 1905. As an interim measure, the vicar and churchwardens of the parish were appointed Trustees for the administration of another Foundation. Income from the school which was estimated to be £1 19s 4d, was then transferred into the Official Trustees of Charitable Funds. This move was then consolidated by an Order of the Charity Commissioners, dated 12 December in which the site and buildings were vested in the Official Trustee of Charity Lands.[26] Robert Skinner, in the *Centenary Magazine* described the school property as comprising in 1905:

> The freehold of Land.
> Two Consols £78 17s 6d and £36 12d 4d from which a small annual income was derived.
> There were also funds from several subscribers which generated £40-50.[27]

A demonstration of the new administration's efficiency was provided in 1906 when the need for more desks became apparent after an inspection on 8 January. Barely a week later, a Kent Education Committee inspector had visited concerning this, and the new desks were received in March. This provision of equipment doubtless answered the repeated critical comments about the furniture in the annual government inspector's report. There were further alterations to the school resulting in the gallery being removed from the Infants Room in favour of more desks.

1907 brought yet more change as during this year the school ceased to be known as the 'National School for Bearsted, Thornham, Debtling and part of Boxley'. Henceforth, the school was to now to be known as:

Bearsted Church of England School [28]

The new name was written in the annual government inspection report for the following year:

Kent Local Education Authority
Bearsted Church of England School [29]

As there is no copy of the annual government report in the log book for 1907, it is probable that an annual inspection did not take place as the administration was in transition to the Kent Education Committee authority. There were a number of persistent problems to exercise the attention of the Education Committee. Once again, the question of overcrowding arose following a three week closure due to a chickenpox epidemic in 1907. During a routine visit by a government inspector, concern was raised over the number of children in attendance. A further number of the desks used by the children were also condemned as unfit for use. Replacements were swiftly provided.

Barely a month later, there were a series of meetings with representatives from the Education Committee for the Master and several Managers. These representatives included the government inspector, Mr Hitchins, an inspector of stores from the Education Committee, and a Manager, Mr Wilkinson. Perhaps these meetings were an attempt to define the problems of the school. When the school re-opened in October, it was with an evident degree of satisfaction that

Frank Goodman, who had been appointed Master in 1905, was able to record that the children had returned to a re-decorated building with twelve new desks and a new cupboard. Despite these welcome additions, the wall map of the world started by Canon Scarth that had been announced by the parish magazine, was painted over during the re-decoration and lost to posterity.[30]

Whilst the school was being re-decorated, the Education Committee tried to deal with the matter of overcrowding. In November there was a joint meeting between the Managers, the Thurnham Managers and Mr Harrison, the Assistant Secretary to the Education Committee. As a temporary measure, it was decided that no child under five years of age would be admitted due to lack of accommodation. Frank Goodman was asked to implement this decision in January of the following year 1908. The authorities were not in any great hurry to alleviate the matter of overcrowding as the letters which advised parents of children living in Thurnham parish that they would need to apply for immediate admission to Thurnham School, were not despatched until the end of February. Twenty children were transferred. In May, the number of children that could be officially accommodated was now 126; comprising 96 junior children and 30 infants.

In 1908 there was a further material change in the buildings. The Managers agreed to move back an old wooden partition which, for some time had separated the two rooms, and inserted another partially glazed partition. Although it is unclear when the partition had been built, it is possible that it had been in use since the Infants Section first opened in 1869. It was hoped that the result would be an Infant Division clearly separated into two parts. It was noted as a great improvement, as was the new floor laid in the main room later on in the year. However, this did not stop the inspector suggesting that further structural alterations were desirable for improved working. The commencement of a library the following year, 1909, was a further welcome addition to the facilities.

This photograph bears the date of 1906 on the reverse and shows some children at Bearsted School together with some of the teaching staff.

(Photograph courtesy of Roseacre School)

This second photograph is not dated but was also taken around this time. A note on the reverse indicates that it includes both Miss Hearnden and the father of Violet Hale (née Pollard). Miss Hearnden taught at the school from 1906 to 1920.

(Photograph courtesy of Roseacre School)

This sketch map shows the school premises around 1908. It indicates the slight change in the outline of the buildings after the alterations:

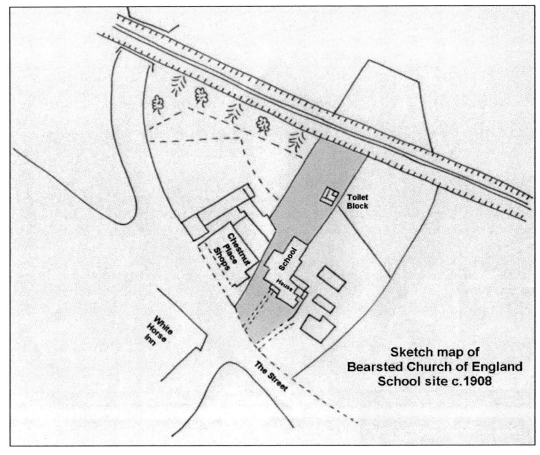

(Illustration by Kathryn Kersey based on Ordnance Survey)

In the *Centenary Magazine,* Robert Skinner recounts that around 1907, the Managers began to concentrate upon the improvement and updating of the buildings. To this end an architect's report was commissioned. Apart from a brief note that a proposal concerning the building was to be put before the Managers, there are no further details in the log book. However, in the National Society records for Bearsted, there is a discussion paper on the architect's proposals.[31] There are difficulties in reading the document, written on tissue-like paper in ink which has begun to decay with age. Nevertheless, it is evident that the report gave the Managers some alarm, as the proposals did not seem to meet the demands of the Board of Education or the recommendations of the government inspectors!

The architect had certainly given an assessment of the buildings and their potential for modernisation much consideration. The proposals included converting part of the south east corner of the Mixed Room into an Infants Room and adding another partition. The former Infants Room would then be converted into a Master's Room, there would also be a new Main Store Room and, most intriguingly, a 'Marching Room' for the Infants with a flat roof and a floor area measuring 19 feet in length, 11 feet 6 inches wide, at the back of the school. Presumably this room was intended as accommodation for the drill exercises popular at the time.[32] There was considerable debate over whether all the desks should be renewed and the replacement of all the casement windows with sash windows.

The conclusion of the report was that a minimum expenditure of £600 was required to put the buildings into a satisfactory condition. To secure the money looked a daunting task. Nevertheless, the Managers began to address the problem. There was a somewhat over-wrought appeal in the parish magazine (all italics are in the original): [33]

> We regret to say that a very serious crisis has arisen in the history of our Schools. Built as they were by Churchwardens, long *before the State showed much earnestness about the education of the poor* they have given many generations of scholars the beginning of a sound education. But we now suffer from having been, as it were, pioneers in this noble work, and in their present structural state, our schools no longer meet the modern *requirements* of the Board of Education. The Parish will therefore have to choose before long between two alternatives. EITHER we must close our present school and build a new Council School at *enormous* cost (we say 'enormous cost', for as far as we can judge such a school would cost about £3,000 to repay which (with interest) would apparently entail *an additional shilling rate for about 30 years* OR we must raise sufficient funds *voluntarily* to adapt our present schools to modern requirements. We have good reason for believing that this could be done for a *comparatively* modest sum, i.e. for about a sixth of the other scheme. This is the grave question that we must shortly face. Of course, even £500 is a large sum to raise BUT surely if ratepayers have to choose between the expenditure of £500 or £3,000 it ought not to take them long to choose which is the cheaper and wiser plan. We put this side of the question first because this is a side which affects *all* ratepayers alike, whether they be Churchmen or not. But to Churchmen we make this further appeal. Churchmen and Churchwomen in the past have handed down to us these Schools, in which those parents who desire it can have their children taught the Church's faith (while other parents can withdraw their children from such teaching if they wish). Are Churchmen and Churchwomen of the present day going to abandon this precious privilege? God forbid.

The Canterbury Diocesan Education Board awarded £40 and an application to the National Society for assistance resulted in a further £40.[34] The majority of the funding was achieved through some very large donations from several generous local residents.

The Diocesan Inspector commented in his report for 1909:

> I congratulate the Managers upon their decision to enlarge the accommodation.
> I am sure it will materially benefit the children and the teachers.[35]

Once funding had been secured, the alterations were begun in July 1910. In order to have a safe environment for the children, the Green became a temporary playground whilst these alterations were carried out. Despite the absence of the children from the school during the hop-picking holidays for the entire month of September, the start of term had to be delayed for a further week to enable the builders to fully complete the alterations.

After the school opened on 3 October, the children were able to take immediate advantage of the changes. Frank Goodman recorded in the log book that the improvements included the replacement of the old latticed windows throughout the school, a welcome increase in accommodation due to the addition of a new classroom at the back of the building and a further twenty five desks. A new cloakroom was also added. To reflect these alterations, a new arrangement of the classes was now adopted: Standards I-IV were now accommodated in the main room, the Upper Standards were in the middle room and the infants were in the new classroom.[36] A further project to provide a new playground and the proposed Marching Room did not proceed.

The improvements were heartily endorsed by the government inspector, Mr C J Phillips, who visited a little over three weeks after the start of term. Nevertheless, his comments were tempered by a note of caution:

> The additions and alterations in the school premises have been carried out successfully and much benefit to discipline and the general efficiency of the school will probably result from what has been done. It is to be hoped that no damp will be found in the Infants Room from the sloping ground on the north side.[37]

The doubts about the drainage were resolved in 1911 by Mr Robinson, the architect and surveyor to the Kent Education Committee, who inspected and satisfactorily reported, although his report does not survive. The accommodation and maintenance of the buildings were now on a sound footing. The Managers were then able to sign a certificate for the National Society to confirm that the works were now complete at a total of cost of £560.[38]

The next three years were characterised by a process of steady consolidation. The staffing, financial support and resources were now administered by the Kent Education Committee. The school medical service, introduced several years previously, was also now beginning to make a valuable contribution to the general standard health of the children. Both of these wide-ranging developments meant that for virtually the first time, the school could deliver an education which was adequately supported by an appropriate administration.

Although a better horizon glimmered for the children attending the school, 1914 marked the beginning of cataclysmic world events that would lead to parts of small and relatively ordered communities such as Bearsted changing. Some of the change would happen slowly, some of the changed world order would be for the better, but most of the change would be irrevocable.

Chapter 3
Staff, Training & Teaching at Bearsted School

When Bearsted School opened the staff comprised a Master and a series of assistants. Local clergy undertook some of the religious teaching. There were many different categories of staff employed at the school. The change in staff categories and the nature of the teaching supplied reflects the evolution of the teaching profession. The title of the person appointed to be in charge of the school also changed from Master to Headmaster and then to Headteacher.

The National Society was founded in 1811 but it was some years before it was realised that formal training of teaching staff was required to achieve a consistent standard of teaching. The National Society provided some basic training but it was very brief. In 1834 the clerical superintendent of the central school of the Society admitted that five months was the average period of training for probationary teachers. Applicants were expected to possess a moral and Anglican religious character. Applicants also had to display a minimum level of education: the ability to read, write legibly, have knowledge of the first four rules of arithmetic and be generally intelligent and energetic.[1]

Robert Skinner wrote in the *Centenary Magazine,* that a daily log book was kept from the first day the school opened. However, if such existed, the earlier volumes have not survived. The log books deposited at the Centre for Kentish Studies commence July 1863. It is not clear from the entries whether the log book was a new enterprise or the continuation of a regular administrative duty. The keeping of such a record did not become mandatory until the Revised Education Code of 1862.

One of the earliest hints as to the form of teaching delivered at Bearsted during the first two decades of school is in the 1841 Census. As previously discussed, this entry contains the details of the household of the Master for Bearsted school.[2]

Bearsted Green

James Simmons	Head of household	aged 55	Schoolmaster
Sarah	Wife	aged 55	
Thomas	Son	aged 15	
Eliza	Daughter	aged 15	

There are no further returns on this census which would indicate other staff for the school living in Bearsted.

The number of children in attendance would not have been considered large by the Managers. In 1863 the school roll was recorded as 148 children. The teaching was initially delivered by James Simmons, his wife, Sarah, and a number of Monitors. Under legislation introduced by the government in 1846, the number of assistants permitted was regulated by the size of the school. One teaching assistant was allowed for every 25 scholars in attendance. In 1848 this was amended. In schools where apprentice staff were already employed, there was to be one member of staff to every 50 children in attendance. It was not until 1890 before an average of 30 pupils to one apprentice member of staff was achieved.[3] These regulations were to give concern to the Managers on a number of occasions as staff left and were not easily replaced.

The Monitorial system of teaching was one of the first attempts to impose an organised structure to the task of teaching a large class of children in one room. This system popularised by Joseph Lancaster and Andrew Bell, worked as a 'pyramid' with the Master solely teaching the Monitors. The Monitors in turn taught the pupils whilst the Master kept order and supervised the school. There was therefore a teaching 'cascade' of information. Naturally, the system was full of drawbacks as it was dependent upon the information being accurately conveyed and understood between the Master and Monitors prior to being passed on to the pupils. Through the work of the

Monitorial system, it was realised that dividing the children into smaller groups for formal learning was an effective method of teaching.

Under the National School system of teaching there were desks or benches for writing and reading lessons which occupied the outer space and faced the wall. Some schools had benches facing the wall so that the children could look at wall charts. Sometimes these benches had a chalk circle drawn upon the floor to indicate where the pupils had to stand to receive instruction. They were known as 'teaching points'. The central floor area was used by classes of children standing or seated at desks arranged in open ended squares for instructions by their Monitors who were called 'teachers' or 'assistants'.

This diagram shows a typical National School layout:

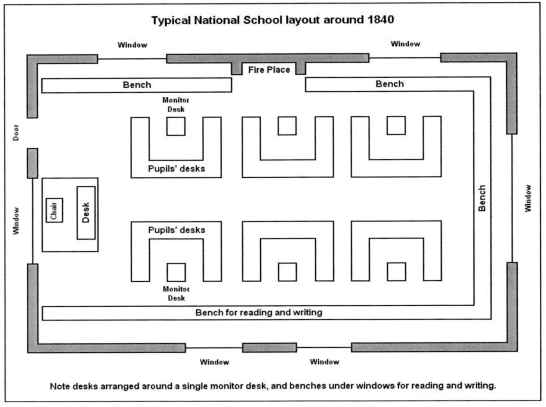

(Illustration by Malcolm Kersey)

The Monitorial system was used for many years at Bearsted School. The earliest mention of Monitors in the log book is 18 January 1864. It was noted that the Managers had decided to apply to the Diocesan Board for permission to appoint another Monitor. The first Monitors directly named in the log book were Eliza Cocker and Sarah Foster who worked at the school in 1865. The Monitors role in school was to teach the units of work, to recommend promotion of pupils and to keep order.[4] Some Monitors were more effective at teaching in the school than others. There were also occasional problems caused by the Monitors' lack of difference in age as some were barely only two years older than their charges. From the log book:

<u>18 June 1875</u>
The Monitors are neither of them very much use at present and their classes require much more supervision than I can at all times give them.

<u>8 June 1881</u>
The two Monitors are very idle. The Master has been obliged to send them to their places several times. One Monitor plays with the boys in his class and been cautioned some dozens of times. He is not in anyway more attentive than formerly. The other Monitor, though better, on the whole gets with him and talks. Master has to frequently speak to them about it.

Not every Monitor that was appointed at Bearsted received a stipend. On 7 February 1890 it was recorded in the log book that the Senior Monitor, Emily Hickmott, had received notification she was due to receive a salary increase of a shilling a week!

The 1851 Census records John Peirce and his wife, Frances, as National Schoolmaster and Schoolmistress respectively. In 1854, the staff at the school listed in a local trade directory were John Pierce as Master for the boys and Mrs Pierce as Mistress for the girls,[5] although the surname has a different spelling. These entries would support the implication from the plans that the school was initially segregated. It is clear from the log book that commences in 1863 that the school had been taught in mixed groups for some time. When the Infant Section opened in October 1869 it was recorded that Miss Aves was now in charge of that part of the school. This was a mixed group from the start.

The log book chronicles Emma Potter's teaching career. In 1867 she was appointed Diocesan Monitor. Two years later, following the opening of the Infant department of the school, she became an Assistant in the Upper School. There was further promotion for Emma in 1872. From the log book:

> 19 April 1872
> Emma Potter approved Pupil Teacher.

Although the post of Pupil Teacher was introduced in 1846, Emma was the first person to hold the position at Bearsted. Pupil Teachers were introduced by the government in 1846 as a means of improving the quality of teaching supplied and to provide a supply of qualified students for the teacher training colleges. Like many Victorian innovations, this development within the teaching profession was subject to a rigorous prescription and administration.

In a National School the aspiring Pupil Teacher had to satisfy many requirements before apprenticeship. Only candidates approved by one of Her Majesty's Inspectors could be apprenticed as a Pupil Teacher to a school that had received a favourable report. The Managers had to testify before the government inspectors that the candidate was of good moral character, had an understanding of the catechism and attended to religious duties. A candidate also had to present a certificate from the Managers and Master of the school testifying to good conduct, punctuality, diligence, obedience and attention to their duties.[6] The Inspectors then tested each candidate according to a formal schedule. Each candidate was required to:

1   Read with fluency and expression.
2   Point out the parts of speech in a simple sentence.
3   Write in a neat hand with correct spelling and punctuation a simple prose narrative slowly read to him.
4   Write from dictation sums in the first four Rules of Arithmetic, Simple and Compound, and work them correctly and know the Tables of Weights and Measures.
5   Show an elementary knowledge of Geography.[7]

Once the initial hurdle of appointment was passed, there followed a five year apprenticeship from the age of 13. As it was an apprenticeship, indentures were drawn up between the parents of the Pupil Teacher, the Master and the National Society. The indentures prescribed that the Pupil Teacher should:

> Faithfully and diligently serve the said (*Master's name here*) in his business as schoolmaster in the school...and shall not except from illness absent himself from the said school during school hours and shall conduct himself with honesty, sobriety and temperance and not be guilty of any profane or lewd conversation or conduct or of gambling or any other immorality but shall diligently and obediently assist in the instruction of the scholars...and shall regularly attend Divine Service on Sunday.[8]

At the same time parents were bound to provide:

> All proper lodging, food, apparel, washing, medicine and medical attendance.[9]

The Master agreed that the Pupil Teacher was to receive opportunities to observe and practice teaching, and to provide an agreed amount of time every day, usually one and a half hours, to the instruction of the Pupil Teacher. It was long working day as the instruction was taken before or after school and did not include the homework that accompanied these lessons. Girls, especially found it taxing as they were expected to continue their domestic chores as before; in fact it was regarded as important that girls should be competent to pass on these skills to their pupils as future wives or servants.[10] Mr Day particularly went to great lengths to record in the log book that he was fulfilling his extra duties in instruction:

18 October 1893
The Pupil Teacher is allowed forty minutes each morning for private study.

20 March 1896
The Pupil Teacher, with permission from the Master, has had about five hours allowed her for extra study in addition to the usual time each day.

The stipend was £10 per annum and rose by increments of £2 10s to £20 per annum. For instructing a Pupil Teacher the Master received an addition to his salary of £5. The Pupil-Teacher's salary was drawn through the Post Office using a money order that was made to them personally. Later, this arrangement was changed so that all salaries were paid to the Managers, who then allocated them to the staff.[11]

After the completion of the apprenticeship there was an examination for a Queen's Scholarship in the hope of gaining a place at a training college. However, many successful candidates were prevented from taking up scholarships as they did not always include living expenses whilst attending a training college. As a direct result of this financial shortfall, it was estimated in 1901 that little more than a quarter of successful candidates went on to teacher training colleges.

Some successful candidates for the scholarships became provisionally Certificated teachers in charge of small schools instead. However, this lapsed at the age of 25, so the ex-Pupil Teacher then reverted to an Assistantship, unless they were able to pass the certificate examination. From 1852, unsuccessful candidates for the Queen's Scholarship were allowed to continue as uncertificated assistants. This provided the economically sensible option of retaining some experienced staff.[12] In addition to Samuel Taylor, several other Masters at Bearsted: Edward Barnacle and John Day, were Certificated teachers.

Some of the new appointments to the school were announced in the parish magazine. Occasionally there are brief previous career details too. From the parish magazine of June 1874:

On 23rd July the charge of our school will be assumed by Miss Vincent, Certificated and trained Mistress from Whitelands Training College. It is now ten years since Miss Vincent took charge of the girls' school at Strood and during that period the school has flourished to a remarkable degree and we feel confident that our school here will do well under her care.[13]

There is no record in the log book of Emma Potter taking the Queen's Scholarship examination. However, on 2 April 1875 having completed her apprenticeship as a Pupil Teacher, Emma left the school to take up a post as an Assistant Teacher at a school in Sittingbourne. The same year, and possibly inspired by her sister's example, Maria Potter also began a five year apprenticeship as a Pupil Teacher at Bearsted. From the log book:

27 March 1880
Maria Potter (fifth year) completes her apprenticeship. Her diligence and perseverance has been very satisfactory to the Master.

After the First World War, the Pupil Teacher system of training slowly fell into disuse as there were now many other routes to teacher training.

There are very few photographs of the staff and children from Queen Victoria's reign that survive in the school records. It is possible that the earliest photographs were taken over successive years and are those shown below. They have been dated from the commercial advertisement for a portrait saloon for D A Stickells printed on the reverse, a photographer listed in trade directories during the decade of the 1870s. At this time Miss Vincent was Mistress (1874-1879) and a Miss Rosa Edwards was in charge of some of the children. Rosa Edwards was originally appointed Monitor in 1874 and later became a Pupil Teacher at the school.

(Both photographs courtesy of Roseacre School)

In 1854 the category of 'Registered Teacher' was created by the Committee of Council on Education. The government hoped that this would address a growing problem in securing a sufficient supply of staff for schools. There were many thoroughly experienced teachers who were over 35 years old but who had been unable to benefit from a Pupil Teacher apprenticeship. These teachers held no formal qualifications. However, becoming a Registered Teacher was not an easy option as applicants still had to sit a rigorous examination commensurate with that of a Pupil Teacher.[14] Many of the Masters and Mistresses that ran Bearsted School held this qualification.

As part of the legislation to create this category of staff, the government offered a grant. However there were still drawbacks as the financial award was based on the number of children that attended the school and all applicants were subject to annual inspection. It was not until the Revised Education Code of 1862 that the criteria for the grant changed to that of examination results achieved by the pupils. Nevertheless, the inspection always led to immense pressure upon the staff to achieve an acceptable attendance or annual examination results.

Another early photograph in the school records:

(Photograph courtesy of Roseacre School)

There is nothing recorded about the date of this photograph, apart from a note on the reverse saying 'Mr and Mrs Smith' and that it was taken on the school steps. If this is correct, the photograph was taken by the front door of the school. William Smith was Master of the school from 1881 to 1884 and taught with his wife. The two boys flanking them are likely to have been Frederick Smith and John Wood, who were noted as Monitors in 1881.

In addition to some other categories of staff – Monitors, Pupil Teachers, Certificated and Registered Teachers that were employed at Bearsted, there was a further category of teacher introduced in the Education Code of 1875: the 'Supplementary' or 'Additional' teacher. As a result of the legislation, these teachers were known as 'Article 84s' and later, 'Article 50s'. Ellen Wallis and Emily Day, wife of John Day, are listed under these categories in the annual government reports for the school.

Later, under the Education Code of 1890, such staff became known as 'Article 68s'. The only requirements for 'Article 68' assistants were that they were over 18 years old and vaccinated against smallpox. They were accepted by the government inspectors as suitable to assist in the general instruction of the scholars and in teaching needlework.[15]

There are other early photographs of the staff pictured with the children at Bearsted School which survive. The reverse of this photograph bears a date of 1890 together with a note that indicates Edith Mary Watcham, aged 12, and A J Watcham, aged 7, are included in the picture. There is no information, however, whether the adult female included is Mrs Day or Miss Wallis.

(Photograph courtesy of Roseacre School)

It is interesting to trace the early teaching career of Miss Ellen Wallis through these changes of category. She is listed as an 'Article 50' assistant at the school from 1889 to 1890. She was then employed as an 'Article 68' assistant from 1891 to 30 June 1893, after which she left to take up a post at St Paul's Infant School in Chatham.

It is evident that there was an extremely good relationship between Mr and Mrs Day and Miss Wallis. On at least one occasion when Mrs Day was unwell, Miss Wallis was noted in the log book as looking after her. In the 1891 Census, Miss Wallis was boarding with the Day family at School House. Later on, Miss Wallis married and became Mrs Ovenden. In 1898 she returned to the school to provide temporary help as an Assistant Mistress but retained the Article 68 category in her description. There were many occasions over the next few years when Mrs Ovenden was regularly employed as a temporary assistant for short periods.

There is a further set of photographs from 1895 kept in the school records. They depict Mr and Mrs Day with some of the children and teaching staff.

This photograph shows Mr Day with Bearsted School Group 4, and includes Edith and Elizabeth Watcham:

The next photograph in the group shows Group 3 with Mr and Mrs Day, Miss Wallis and may include Carrie Smith, who was a Monitor:

(Both photographs courtesy of Roseacre School)

The last two photographs in the set are strikingly similar. This is Bearsted School Group 1 pictured with Mr and Mrs Day:

The photograph below shows Bearsted School Group 2:

(Both photographs courtesy of Roseacre School)

In 1898 Agnes Barclay copied three letters into the log book which advised that the school was to receive a £25 grant for 'strengthening the staff by engaging a male Head Teacher'. Evidently, this was not possible as the purpose for this grant was immediately amended to increase the Mistress's salary. The final letter in the group noted that the Education Department also approved a £15 grant to provide an additional teacher and an ex-Pupil Teacher. Funded by these grants, Miss Flora Fox was appointed as an assistant in the Infants. Miss Fox then passed her Certificate examinations and in the following year she is listed in the annual government inspection in 1901 as a Certificated Mistress. Miss Fox left the school in 1903.

In the Education Code for 1900, there was further financial change as the previous grants for special subjects such as Drawing, Geography and Needlework, were now abolished. Despite this, additional payments could still be made for teaching cooking and 'manual instruction', although what the latter category included remains unclear - possibly such subjects as woodwork. The funding for schools changed again as capitation grants of seventeen shillings for each infant child and twenty two shillings for an older child were introduced. The power of the inspectors was slightly reduced in scope as they were now only able to reduce grants by a shilling for defects in the running of the school. At Bearsted, in addition to grants of £15 to maintain staff salaries in 1900 and in 1901, there was also a £10 provision for an Organising Visitor. There was a further £15 grant to maintain the staff salaries in 1902.

As part of the 1902 Education Act, organising bodies called Local Education Authorities were devised. These Authorities delegated their work through Local Education Committees. The Local Education Committee was advised by a member of staff called the Director of Education or Chief Education Officer, who had his own staff. An important feature of this new relationship was that the policies formulated by government were handed to the local education authorities for administration.[16] The Kent Education Committee began to oversee the appointment of new members of staff but the exact date at which the church authorities were relieved of the financial burden of funding and meeting staff salaries is not recorded. The first indication of the Education Committee's involvement in the appointment of the staff is given in the log book on 22 April 1904. Miss Apps is recorded as appointed as a temporary help by the Kent Education Committee, rather than by the Managers.

The majority of the early entries in the log book concerning staff and the Kent Education Committee are recorded by the permanent successor to Agnes Barclay, Mr Frank Goodman. This is an undated photograph of Mr and Mrs Goodman from *The Kentish Express* as they celebrated their silver wedding anniversary:

(Photograph courtesy of Derek Rowe and the Kent Messenger group)

Frank Goodman's tenure of office marks the formal introduction of staff now known as 'supply teachers' to the school. They provided temporary assistance to the usual teaching staff when they were absent. On one occasion, in 1906 when the Monitor was absent for three months at the Pupil Teacher centre in Maidstone, Mrs Goodman was appointed as a temporary 'supply' assistant. During Frank Goodman's tenure as Master of the school, Mrs Goodman became the regular supply teacher, often standing in at very short notice.

With the advent of the Kent Education Committee, although the daily routines of the school changed little, there were greater administrative demands upon the Master or Mistress. The log books indicate a growing amount of paperwork and forms to be completed about matters that had previously been considered routine. An example of this is shown below. Previously, if a teacher requested a formal absence this was verbally agreed between the Master and managers. The Education Committee would expect this form to be completed and returned for their records.

One of the forms used to notify staff absence: [17]

	Form S.M. 315
Kent Education Committee	

....School

No. ....   Elem   ....Department

NOTIFICATION OF ABSENCE OF TEACHER.

Name of Teacher.	Grade.	Commencement of Absence.	Returned to Duty.	Cause of Absence.

..........................190........   ....
                                                                    Head Teacher.

(Reproduced by permission Centre for Kentish Studies, Maidstone)

Other modern-day professional management procedures were introduced and regular conferences were held by the Education Committee. Further training was also offered, and it was expected that staff would take advantage of the opportunities offered. The Board of Education assisted by writing and distributing publications such as *Suggestions for Teachers* which was published in 1905.[18]

In 1920 the senior members of staff, Mr Goodman, Mrs Dibble and Miss Hearnden, were all noted in the log book as separately attending Teachers Conferences held in Tonbridge, Chatham and Canterbury, respectively. The only teacher from the school who did not attend was Miss Clayton, who at that time, was in charge of the Infants department. Later, Miss Hearnden attended the Teachers' Conference in Canterbury and it is also recorded that she had been awarded a month's sabbatical to attend a 'Refreshers Course' at Goldsmith's College. Two years later, Miss Clayton again updated her training by attending a conference with the school inspectors and by visiting St Luke's Infant School. Clearly, the benefits of further training for qualified staff were beginning to become apparent as the Education Committee recovered from the contingencies of the First World War and began to address some of the problems of a changed world.

Some of the changes in educational theory and thinking were slow but continuous. A further breeze of change was felt when *Suggestions for the Considerations of Teachers,* which had been regularly updated since it first appeared in 1905 was withdrawn. It was re-issued in 1925 under a new title: *Handbook of Suggestions for Teachers.*[19] The need for evaluating different educational ideas began to be addressed and the Education Committee began regularly to offer courses of training and issue some policy documents in addition to their directives. In 1923 the Committee decided to distribute copies of the *Times Educational Supplement* to schools for use by the teachers.

After the First World War many organisations that were controlled by local government were reconsidered and reviewed. The Kent Education Committee's role within the county was to ensure that an effective teaching service could be supplied. Part of this was achieved through the far-sighted vision of Maidstone's Director of Education, Mr E W Abbott. By the time he retired in 1932, the need for an education service that had reasonable terms of employment for the staff, together with an appreciated need for budgetary control and an open-minded attitude to new ideas, was apparent.[20]

As Mr Abbott retired, wider world events began to occupy more time in public life as Hitler continued his rise to power in Germany. Educational thinking and staff development would have to take a less prominent role in county council offices whilst the Second World War was fought and won. Widespread public awareness of the required changes in education would only be achieved after the 1944 Education Act began to be implemented, and the local education office became part of the divisional offices of the Kent County Council.[21]

Chapter 4
The Effects of Social Problems on the School

Attendance at school became compulsory under the 1876 Elementary Education Act. In order to stop the exploitation of child labour, the Act decreed that no child under the age of ten was to be employed. In times of recurring agricultural depression it was particularly hard for some very poor parents to pay the school fees.

Fees for school had been introduced in 1862 at the tariff of 1d per child per week and were known as 'School Pence'. By 1875 the fees had risen to 3d per child a week: an almost impossible amount for poor families to find from the weekly wages of an agricultural labourer. The Act gave the Poor Law Guardians the power to pay school fees where parents were unable to do so.[1] This legal provision was used in Bearsted to good effect as the Relieving Officer for the Poor Law Guardians was also the Attendance Officer for the school. On 28 October 1882, the amount of School Pence received was first noted down in the log book as £1 3s 1½d. It was to become a regular feature in the school records.

If a child was persistently absent without good reason there was a threat of legal action and a fine to pay. Often the parents of an absentee child were summoned to appear at either a Police Court in Maidstone or at the Petty Sessions. The latter were meetings of local justices to deal with minor offences. At Bearsted, the Petty Sessions were held at either the *White Horse* or the *Royal Oak* public house. Often the proceedings were reported in the local newspapers. This is a transcript of a typical report from the *Kent Messenger and Maidstone Telegraph*, 21 July 1888:

> ### SCHOOL BOARD PROSECUTIONS
> Several Bearsted parents were each fined 1s 6d and 4s 6d costs, for neglecting to send their children regularly to school.

Sometimes poverty-stricken parents who were desperate to supplement the meagre family income, encouraged their children to leave school before they were of an age to be legally employed. In a small community like Bearsted, this move was usually unsuccessful as the deception was discovered fairly quickly. Parents could be ordered to send the child back to school immediately or suffer the penalty of a heavy fine.

When a child was absent from school with good reason, i.e. ill through an infectious disease such as diphtheria, the Attendance Officer had to be given a medical certificate. This certificate cost the preposterous charge of two shillings and sixpence. There were many cases, even when schooling became free, where financially hard-pressed families could not afford this extra demand and were summoned. These proceedings also made a good source of information for the local newspapers. The first record of the Attendance Officer trying to enforce attendance was entered in the log book in March 1878. In 1880 an Education Act was passed which made school attendance compulsory until a child had reached thirteen years of age. Under the Act's regulations, some children over ten years of age could leave providing that parents applied for exemption.

In 1886 the Master ignored the regulations governing the entries made in the log book which stated that nothing of a personal or political opinion should be entered. He commented that the death of a local landowner, General Knight, had thrown many out of work and that there was widespread poverty. It did not take long for some children to exhibit the effects of poor nutrition and diet. Although the children came to school, they were too ill to work at their lessons. For some families, poor economic circumstances were not helped by a decision on 21 May 1886 by the Managers to turn away any child who arrived without the fee.

Mindful of the distress in the village, the vicar of Bearsted, Canon John Scarth, and his wife, decided upon practical examples of Christian compassion. John Day noted in the log book:

11 December 1885
The vicar called on Wednesday morning at 11.15am and brought a little shawl to be given away to some deserving child.

A few weeks later, early in 1886 Mrs Scarth had opened a soup kitchen, located at Milgate, for the poor families in the village. This proved a great boon to many of the children of the district and the soup days were greatly anticipated. The log book gives details of the success of this idea:

24 February 1886
For several weeks past Mrs Scarth has arranged a soup kitchen which has proved a great boon to many of the poorly-clad and ill-fed children of the district. The soup days are looked forward to with eagerness.

29 February 1886
About 52 children availed themselves of the privilege of having soup on Tuesday.

It was briefly re-opened through necessity in 1888 and in 1893-94. During the latter period it was in a slightly different form. From the log book:

20 January 1893
On Tuesday Mrs Scarth and the Vicar brought some soup for the dinner children (about 25) and on Thursday some cocoa - the children supplying their own basins. This attempt to give to the children something nice and warm with their usual cold dinners is greatly appreciated on the part of the recipients.

During a government inspection on 23 March 1887, the Managers were informed that no child above seven years of age should be kept in the Infants. If the child was judged too backward then their name had to be entered in the Exception Schedule for the Inspector's assessment. It is evident that many of the children deemed 'backwards', 'indelicate' or intellectually deficient would have benefited from decent nutrition, housing and medication. The examinations for intellectual weakness and deficiency feature regularly in the log books.

On 25 April 1890 John Day was advised by the Attendance Officer, that the Master now had no right to turn away any child from school for any reason other than a skin complaint, and only then upon the production of a medical certificate. The officer features regularly in the first two surviving log books, earning his £50 yearly renumeration by taking lists of absentees, issuing cautions and sending summons to various families. It was also part of his duties to give the Master any money for school fees that had been paid to him.

In 1891, there was at last some relief from financial pressures for poor families as schooling became free under Lord Salisbury's 1890 Education Act. The Act included an amount of flexibility for school hours which it was hoped would enable two hours compulsory attendance to be accommodated around children's working hours. Instead of school fees there would now be a payment made by the government for each child. On 17 August 1891 there was a Managers meeting at which it was decided to accept the government grant of ten shillings for each child in lieu of fees. A great deal of time was spent at the meeting discussing how best to protect and secure the financial footing of the school. Mr Day recorded in the log book on 9 October:

Re-commenced school this week after an interval of five weeks, the school being entirely free.

The vicar visited the school at the start of term. He gave a short talk to the children on the subject of 'Thrift'. He also talked about a proposed school bank and the idea of a subscription scheme for parents. It remains a matter of conjecture how well this homily was received by some of the children. There is no record that the bank scheme was ever implemented.

The move to free schooling was not greeted with universal approval. John Day recorded in November 1891, that considering there were no fees to pay, the attendance had been fair. However it was not as good as might have been expected as no less than nineteen children were still absent for the whole of the week. He then added:

> The old Irregulars seem to be irregular still.

Was it hoped that the intellectual needs of the children might have been more important than family economics and financial income?

One of the major economic factors to affect school attendance also constantly governed the poorer families of the village - that of achieving continuity of paid employment. Much of the industry in the Bearsted area comprised agricultural work or other seasonal employment. Labourers and their families therefore had to remain relatively mobile in order to be continually employed. The properties occupied by many labouring families in the village were either rented weekly or were tied accommodation. Occasionally, properties were sold with tenants in occupation, as this transcript of an advertisement shows from *Kent Messenger,* 4 June 1892:

FIVE FREEHOLD COTTAGES
ROUNDWELL, BEARSTED near MAID-STONE
MR. STEPHEN P. WALTER

Is favoured with instructions to SELL by AUCTION, at the Star Hotel, Maidstone on THURSDAY, JUNE 9th, 1892 at 3.15.

Lot 1-A FREEHOLD COTTAGE, situate above, let to Mrs Earl, at a rental amounting to £8 9s. per annum.

Lot 2-A Terrace of FOUR FREEHOLD COTTAGES, situate near the above, in the occupation of Messrs. Swift, Earl, Fairwell and Mrs Tompsett, at rentals amounting to £23 16s 6d per annum.

Particulars and conditions of sale may be had in due course at the place of sale, of the Auctioneer, or of C H White, Esq., Solicitor, West Borough Offices, Maidstone.

Roundwell was an area of Bearsted that had a constantly fluctuating population as many people worked in the brickfield leased by Mr Knowles.[2] Brick manufacture was seasonal work and particularly avoided winter and early spring. However, despite the seasonal work, the attendance figures at the school remain relatively stable in the latter half of the Nineteenth century, particularly in the period when fees had to be paid. The log books are full of entries nearly every week detailing the arrival, re-admittance and departures of children. A typical set of entries for 1879:

5 November	Two new infants admitted.
10 November	Admitted one infant.
13 November	One boy re-admitted.
17 November	One infant re-admitted.
5 December	Two girls have left the school.

One practice that now seems strange was the admittance of children to the school if a family was spending a few days locally visiting relatives. Again, a typical entry from 1882:

> 9 June
> Taken one boy's name off the register - he was only a visitor.

Although a full demographic study of Bearsted is outside the scope of this book, the probable explanation for this relative stability can be ascribed to the available seasonal work being widespread in the area. Despite the constant movement of people, the totals largely remained the same. In the decades between 1851 and 1891, the population of Bearsted as recorded in the Census entries, average 630 with a maximum variation of 35.

Many of the entries in the log book seem to involve minor offences of behaviour and the pursuit of social order in the school. Any offences were dealt with rather firmly by modern standards although the Punishment Book which would give specific details no longer exists. Sometimes the Master or Mistress had great difficulty in keeping order as these log book entries from Miss Love Jones in 1872 show:

> 15 July
> Order and work greatly interrupted in the afternoon by Upper section boys who brought matches to school and caused them to explode with a loud report.

> 16 July
> Wrote a statement of elder boys bad conduct on the blackboard and showed the same to Rev Cullum[3] who visited in the afternoon. Order improved.

> 17 July
> Order not so good as I could wish.

> 19 July
> Order unsatisfactory throughout the week owing possibly to several bad boys who attend and the number of children attending being too large for a mistress and a pupil teacher to instruct properly.

It was the use of bad language that particularly exercised John Day, who usually cancelled the attendance of any offender. In January 1886 he used the occasion of the twice weekly visit to the school by the vicar to pass on the names of boys who had used bad language. All offences of this kind were always punished severely. As the log book records, the vicar used the occasion for a display of authority by laying out the enormity of the offence before the whole school. He also observed his disappointment that the problem was continuing to occur after a year of making encouraging remarks to the children to stick to the right path. He then concluded by suggesting that further offences might well result in the expulsion of offenders. It is evident from the log book that this address met with a limited amount of success.

There are very few incidences of theft recorded in the log book. The details are sparse and usually record that the matter had been referred to higher authority for a decision about expulsion. There is one theft mentioned, however, that is curious:

> 4 October 1889
> Several hoops belonging to the boys having been stolen, one boy was caught in the act and was sent home pending the vicar's decision upon the same.

A number of queries present themselves about this entry, including *how* were the hoops stolen and having obtained them, what did the thief do with them? They could not have been easy to conceal! As there are no further details about this incident, it is possible that a prank had gone badly wrong.

A prank that did go wrong certainly landed three boys in trouble. The log book indicates that John Day and the vicar had previously remonstrated with the culprits but as this transcript from the *Kent Messenger and Maidstone Telegraph* reported, 26 March 1892:

BEARSTED BOYS IN TROUBLE

Three Bearsted boys pleaded guilty to damaging an out-house, to the extent of 5s, the property of Henry Smart, at Bearsted on 28th February. Albert Trendall, builder etc., of Maidstone, said he had been carrying out repairs to the prosecutor's cottages, and on inspecting the outhouse in question on the day named he found that a number of the newly fixed tiles on the roof had been broken, evidently by stones thrown by someone. P C Ellis said he questioned the defendant Smith, who admitted having thrown at the outhouse twice, while the other two defendants, whom he subsequently interviewed, made a similar admission. P C Ellis said, in answer to the Bench, that he had previously received a complaint respecting of the defendants throwing stones. The Bench bound the mothers of the defendants over in £5 to answer for their children's good behaviour for six months. They were also ordered to pay the costs of 6s 2d. each.

John Day's duties as Master included trying to enforce an acceptable standard of rudimentary cleanliness for the children. This was a major problem for many families as clean water was not easy to obtain. It was not until 1897 that social conditions began to be improved in many areas of Bearsted, as Mr Fremlin, concerned at the ease of water contamination in the village, improved many water wells and pumps. Until the installation of a pump at Roundwell many of the residents still used an open dip well as the most convenient supply of water.[4] For the majority of the village though, a piped water supply and mains drainage was to be an unimaginable luxury for the future.

A postcard showing a photograph of the Roundwell area taken in the early years of the Twentieth century:

(Original photograph courtesy E A Sweetman and Son)

Whilst the Master oversaw the standard of sanitary arrangements at the school, he could not always admit the children if they arrived obviously dirty or unclean. There were many occasions that some members of the poorer families in Bearsted were sent home for this reason and the log books repeatedly record this too:

25 May 1890
Master had to send the same girl home twice this week for coming in a dirty state.

10 July 1894
Master had to send a girl home this week as she came to school in such a filthy state that the children could not sit near her. Nearly all complained of the offensive odour proceeding from her clothes and person.

17 August 1894
The Master had to send a boy home to get his head free from vermin as the children objected to sit anywhere near him.

Use of the words 'dirty' or 'untidy' were sometimes employed as contemporary euphemisms to describe infestations of lice - an unpleasant and contagious condition, but a common occurrence in some Victorian families.

After these entries, the Managers decided to try to sort out the problem. John Day, acting under their direct instructions, sent a written notice to parents that any child that was not entirely clean and tidy in appearance would not be admitted to the school. This probably resulted in an improvement in appearance for some children.

Despite this new authority that had been given to him by the Managers, there was at least one occasion when Mr Day felt that he needed the reassurance of a Manager to approve the admittance of the children from one of the poorer families. The events were recorded in the log book:

13 June 1900
The children were brought to school again on Monday.

They were certainly cleaner than before and in general appearance were presentable.
The Master sent a note to Mr Darby (the nearest Manager to the school)) to ask him to come down and look at them and give his opinion whether they were fit to stay. The answer was to use your own discretion.

The Master kept them for the vicar to see at the close of the morning.

From these entries it is all too easy to imagine the problem being passed all round the parish! All the parties concerned must have found this sequence of events quite embarrassing. Whether any effective teaching was either delivered or lessons learned during the day remains unrecorded.

There were occasions when a family in the village, through poverty caused through illness or bereavement, had no other economic option left but to enter the workhouse. There are examples of this recorded in the log book, if only to account for the attendance figures. John Day noted on 7 November 1890, the Attendance Officer had reported to him that a village family had gone into the workhouse at Linton. Maidstone Poor Law Union included Bearsted. The workhouse was situated in Linton parish. Eleven days later, on 16 November, the father died and was interred in the workhouse burial ground.[5] The records that would have advised the duration for the rest of the family's stay in the workhouse have not survived. However, on 28 November 1890, there was a note in the log book that two of the family had been re-admitted as the fees were now being paid by the Guardian.

Was it decided that it was economically cheaper for the Union to keep the family living in Bearsted and the children attending the local school rather than living in the workhouse? There was a school at the workhouse but the records have not survived. The records for the workhouse which detail outdoor relief commence 1897, and are therefore too late to be of assistance in this particular matter. Nevertheless, the deciding factors that were considered in the administration of outdoor relief for the workhouse Trustees, included whether there was at least one child of a sufficient age to be earning a living to help support the family.

In the early 1890s, there were occasions when the Maidstone Trustees of the Poor did pay some outdoor relief (mainly a small sum of money and a quantity of bread and flour) in a number of categories, which included women with families to support.[6] It would be good to think that there was some sort of compassion in operation.

The Attendance Officer, in his capacity as the Relieving Officer for the Poor Law Union in the area, would have been familiar with the circumstances of the poorer families in the village. Upon occasion he would have been able to advise the Guardians about the most convenient solution. The introduction of free schooling in 1891 would have undoubtedly assisted the poorer families to stay in the village.

In the last years of the Nineteenth century, there was a slight easing of the social conditions that had caused such problems. Agriculture was beginning to experience rather more favourable economic conditions. The industry slowly began to expand as the demand for food increased. More opportunities for regular, decently paid employment resulted in a slightly more stable economic environment for the poorer families in the village.

The departure of John Day in 1897 and the arrival of his successor, Miss Agnes Barclay, marked a change in the entries in the log book. There is far less detail so many indications of the manner in which village families coped with some very tough economic and social problems disappear from the records. Despite experiencing the difficulties of poor social and economic conditions, the children of the village managed to receive some sort of education. It is a tribute to the professional determination of the staff at Bearsted School.

Chapter 5
Illness and Disease in the Village and School

In the Nineteenth century, people readily died from diseases that are easily treatable today. This is largely because modern medicines were only just beginning to be discovered. Housing and hygiene were major contributory factors in the high death rate and contagious diseases were dispersed in the village through close contact. Everyone was susceptible but an essential difference was that the richer inhabitants enjoyed a better standard of living and had stronger constitutions. In the event of debilitating illness wealthy people had a better chance of surviving poor health.

Inevitably, contagious diseases and illness were contracted by the staff and their families from contact with the children. On one occasion in 1898 the Pupil Teacher contracted mumps - presumably from the class. There are a number of entries in the log books that indicate the staff were suffering from relatively minor complaints and struggled to meet their duties. Most illnesses that afflicted the staff were usually treated with an absence of duties which facilitated rest. In 1868 the Master, Samuel Taylor recorded in the log book that he was unable to speak due to a severe cold. A subsequent entry indicates that he had gone away for a change of air and to recover. Most poor people did not have this luxury - they had to work to earn the money that put bread on the table. The alternative was the workhouse and its accompanying indignities in a pre-Welfare State age. It was not until 1911 and the provisions of the National Insurance Act that some treatments became free to those in employment.

Despite the lack of effective medicine and the professional hazards of contracting illnesses from the children, the majority of the staff were healthy. In the log books there is only one death of a teacher chronicled. Emily Trewren, appointed as an Infant teacher in August 1916 was absent from her post due to 'congestion of the lungs' on 31 May 1917. Barely four days later, the Master, had the melancholy duty of recording her death due to pneumonia. She was forty three years old. Despite teaching at the school only a short time, her loss was keenly felt and there was a tribute paid to her in the log book from Frank Goodman:

> In her death, I have lost a loyal colleague and the children a true friend…

There was a small memorial service led by the vicar at the school. The school was closed on the day of the funeral in order for the pupils to attend the service. It is also interesting to note that that her gravestone was supplied by the firm of one of the school managers, Mr Wilkinson. It is an indication of the respect which the village held for Miss Trewren.

Bearsted, like many rural communities suffered from epidemics of infectious fevers. These have been largely eradicated through the introduction of widespread vaccination in childhood. In 1875 there was an epidemic of 'Hooping cough' which greatly reduced attendance. The attendance figures determined the amount of money that the school received and largely generated the remuneration of the staff. The Managers were concerned about this but there was an element of compassion. The vicar subsequently decided to close a week earlier than usual in August. The school was re-opened on 8 October with a very small attendance. The following week the Infant classes were still small as the log book recorded:

> The Hooping cough was still in many families.

The attendance took some time to return to the usual size. There were outbreaks of whooping cough in the village for some years.

Outbreaks of measles were troublesome to the school. In 1905 an epidemic culminated in the resignation of a Master. Barely seven weeks after he was first appointed to succeed Agnes Barclay, James Cripps recorded that eighteen children were absent due to measles. On 10 July it was noted with some alarm that nearly fifty children were now absent, and the Chairman of the Managers gave authorisation for closure. When the school eventually re-opened on 7 October, James Cripps tendered his resignation. It is not clear whether he was paid during this period of closure but a lack of income combined with concern at the infection prevalent in the area would have contributed to his decision to resign.

In the Nineteenth century, smallpox was one of the most feared diseases, as it cast a long post-recovery shadow of physical disfigurement for survivors. From 1854 every infant was supposed to be compulsorily vaccinated against smallpox, but it was not until 1871 that the legislation for this began to be effectively implemented.[1] In Boughton Monchelsea in February 1866 a surgeon vaccinated the school population[2] but there is no record of such a procedure being carried out at Bearsted. Despite the introduction of growing immunity for some of the population, there was considerable resistance to the vaccination. After years of lobbying by the Anti-compulsory Vaccination League, in 1898 the government finally conceded that conscientious objectors were allowed to apply to the local magistrate for exemption. But by this time the vaccination campaign had done its work and smallpox as a major killer had been eliminated.[3]

Widespread vaccination notwithstanding, in 1885 part of Bearsted suffered an outbreak of smallpox. In January, the Master noted that six cases of smallpox had been diagnosed and that all sixteen children from the Roundwell district would be remaining at home by order from the Vicar until further notice. The district was eventually clear of smallpox by March, but not before John Day had to write several Certificates under Statutory Authority to cover the continued absence of children from Roundwell for the School Attendance Committee. It is not apparent if there were any deaths.

A major disease of the Victorian period was tuberculosis. It was generally known as 'consumption'. During the 1880s the disease was endemic in the Maidstone area and was responsible for thirty-seven per cent of all deaths in the age group 15-35. There was provision for tuberculosis cases at the Maidstone Union Infirmary at Coxheath but many people preferred to use the Outpatients department at the West Kent General Hospital.[4] In any case, treatment of the disease was generally palliative despite the advertised claims of such medicines as *Owbridge's Lung Tonic*! It is surprising that there are only a few occasions in which the disease is clearly mentioned in the log book, although there are myriad recordings of children suffering from chest complaints.

It is not until the first decade of the Twentieth century that tuberculosis begins to mentioned in the log books in any detail. Following the introduction of the school medical service, the children were subject to regular inspection. The first direct hint of the disease was recorded in the log book on 17 February 1911, stating that a child had been excluded 'with lung trouble' and was a patient at Maidstone Hospital. Another child was initially excluded the following year for three months for 'lung trouble' and was sufficiently unwell to merit a further exclusion up until 1913. Such was the infectious nature of the disease that in January 1913 the doctor asked for the rest of the family to be examined too when the case was under review. However, school attendance was resumed as the children from the family were awarded several Medals and Certificates for regular attendance in later years.

Bronchitis, coughs, colds and other chest complaints seem ubiquitous throughout the years covered by the log books. Despite this there is only one death of a child noted as specifically due to bronchitis. For many children, chest problems were considered a normal part of village life. It is likely that many underlying chest complaints were aggravated by damp housing and poor heating. Heating was usually supplied through coal fires - the irritating smoke of which did little to help inflamed chests and lung tissue, especially when there were damp clothes to be dried by the fire.

In 1886 the log book chronicled a different sort of health problem. On 19 February, the Master had to deal with a stabbing, as a child had attacked his older brother during the mid-day break over a dispute about their respective dinners. The profuse bleeding was staunched and the doctor called. The child was revived from fainting with some brandy and rested in School House until Dr Rivers and the child's mother arrived. It was decided to send him to the West Kent Hospital. He arrived there on a mattress supplied by the vicar and swaddled in some of Mrs Day's blankets, but his mother was advised to take him home and report again the next day. John Day was happy to conclude that the child was doing well and recovering from the incident. Whether the attacker suffered any punishment for this onslaught is unknown - perhaps he had to make a contribution to the doctor's fee.

Diphtheria was present in the village in 1895 and the children witnessed a tragedy when a small girl was taken ill in school and subsequently died of the disease. The following weeks were marked by the absence of many children whose parents were too afraid of contagion to let them attend. At this time, another twenty two children were also absent suffering from other ailments. The uneasiness of the parents was not helped by the decision of a local farmer to operate a policy of isolating his tenants. He ordered the children from the area to stay away from school. Following consultation with the vicar and the Attendance Officer, it was resolved to mention the matter at the next meeting of the Attendance Committee. The outcome of the meeting is not known as the Committee minutes do not mention the matter but the attendance gradually returned to a normal figure.

In 1907 there was a three week closure between 23 March and 15 April due to an epidemic of chickenpox. One local name for chickenpox was 'grass-pox', but this rather confusingly, was also used for cases of hayfever! Despite the closure, it is evident from the subsequent entries in the log book that the attendance took many weeks to be restored to usual figures.

The School Medical Service was founded around 1908. Although medical inspection by the service was compulsory in elementary schools, it is disconcerting to find that actual *treatment* did not become compulsory until 1921. Amongst the reasons for the delay in enforcing treatment was a hesitation by the authorities to involve parents in further expense.

This type of postcard was completed and sent to the school when an inspection was arranged: [5]

FORM 2. M.I.

KENT EDUCATION COMMITTEE.

MEDICAL INSPECTION OF SCHOOL CHILDREN

Date...............................

I purpose visiting your School on ....

at .... o'clock, for the purpose of medically inspecting certain of the children.

Kindly make arrangements in accordance with instructions which have already been forwarded, *i.e.*, for children born in 1   , and entrants since the last inspection,

....
Medical Inspector

To the Head Teacher

(Reproduced by permission Centre for Kentish Studies, Maidstone)

The log book contains few details about the introduction of the regular visits of the Medical Officer. At first, little more could be done about Reported Cases other than making the managers aware of the children's general state of health. Regular inspections of the children were made by the District Nurse or nurses from the School Medical Service of the Kent Education Committee. The first formal medical exclusions were recorded in 1910 for cases of ringworm and chickenpox.

A typical exclusion certificate is shown below: [6]

```
┌─────────────────────────────────────────────────────────────┐
│                                                             │
│  No.  4149    C.                          Form              │
│                                           S.A. 237          │
│            KENT EDUCATION COMMITTEE                          │
│                                                             │
│      I certify that I have examined_____ │
│                                                             │
│   residing at_____ │
│                                                             │
│   that he or she is suffering from _____ │
│                                                             │
│   and should be excluded from School for _____ days from this date. │
│                                                             │
│      The child should return to School on _____ 190  , unless a │
│                                                             │
│   further certificate is obtained                           │
│                                                             │
│                  Signed _____ │
│                                           Medical Officer   │
│                                                             │
│   Date ........................................ 190  .      │
│                                                             │
└─────────────────────────────────────────────────────────────┘
```

(Reproduced by permission Centre for Kentish Studies, Maidstone)

In addition to the epidemics of infectious disease, there were other problems concerning the health of the children. In 1914 a road traffic accident was recorded in the log book as a child was knocked down by a motor-cycle outside the school. There were several other traffic accidents of a similar nature that were recorded around this date as they involved children making made their daily journey to school.

Another, slightly bizarre, incident concerning the health of a child was recorded on 11 May 1916 when a boy arrived complaining that he had been shot in the leg on his journey to school.[7] When Mr Goodman examined his leg and found a wound, he wisely sent for the District Nurse who sent the child home.

In addition to all the hazards of everyday life in the village, there were risks in the curriculum too: at least two girls sustained accidents whilst in Needlework lessons. In 1917 a pupil broke a needle in her hand during the lesson. First aid was unsuccessfully ministered by the District Nurse and she was then transported to the West Kent Hospital for fuller attention. In 1920 another pupil managed to entangle her thumb in a sewing machine which resulted in completely removing the nail. Once again, West Kent Hospital received a Bearsted child for attention and Mr Goodman recorded his relief in the log book that her thumb was healing.

On the whole, the village of Bearsted, like many small communities enjoyed a reasonable standard of health. However, infections did occur in the village and these caused problems for communal institutions. The basic policies of isolation and closure were exercised where appropriate, as they were the only effective means of controlling disease. Few people living in Bearsted during the Nineteenth century would have realised that it would take many decades before the communal benefits of the National Health Service and truly preventative medicine became apparent. Today, children are generally healthy, enjoy infancies that are comparatively disease and illness-free, and parents are confident of effective medicines. These are some of the greatest benefits of modern life.

Chapter 6
The Curriculum Before the First World War

The majority of historical sources for the first twenty years of the school have not survived, so this is not a detailed account of the general curriculum followed by the children. In some communities there is evidence found in parish registers which can indicate the number of agricultural labourers being able to sign their names prior to a school being opened, but this remains outside the scope of this history.

There may have been a set of rules for the school but there is no evidence for them. The school day lasted from 8.50am to 4pm. There was a reasonable amount of time allowed for lunch as most children had to go home for a meal at noon. The afternoon session started around 1.15pm with an Assembly that lasted fifteen minutes. The day finished with prayers around 4pm. Upon occasion, the times of sessions could be slightly adjusted to achieve longer days in the summer. The day could also be shortened if the weather conditions were adverse. Lessons lasted around thirty minutes but it was not until the Education Code of 1891 that the length of some infant lessons was actually specified.

The curriculum concentrated upon prayers, scripture, mental arithmetic, writing, spelling, dictation and reading. Reading was taught with wall charts and started with single syllable words before progressing to words with two or more syllables.

From a typical elementary reading wall chart:

```
                    -at
        c-at              m-at
        f-at              r-at
        m-at              s-at

   1.   A fat cat.
   2.   The fat cat sat on a mat.
   3.   The fat cat ate a rat.
```

(Illustration by Kathryn Kersey)

Early lessons in writing were undertaken in the infant classes by the use of sand trays and slates with slate pencils. It was not until a child moved into the main school that lessons were given that involved using ink and paper exercise books that were known as 'Copy Books'. It was a major offence to make errors or ink blots in a Copy Book. Many writing lessons included copying out proverbs, homilies and maxims, together with parts of the Bible, from a blackboard that was either hung on the wall or set on an easel.

Most elementary schools used the Bible as a universal teaching resource. It was the main reading book for many schools. Schools that were affiliated to the National Society normally only used books that were obtained from the catalogue produced by the Society for the Promotion of Christian Knowledge. These included such titles as:

The Catechism Broken into Short Questions
An Abridgement of the Bible, by the Reverend Ostervald
The Chief Truths of the Christian Religion[1]

The latter was a child's book of Church doctrine. To a modern reader, all of these titles seem to possess little attraction to a child developing reading skills. However, at this time there was not very much literature that had been written especially for children that was readily available and approved for use by the National Society.

In 1855 a depository for school books and equipment was opened in Maidstone. Sales to local schools were encouraged by offering incentives such as specimen books at half-price.[2] After the introduction of the Education Codes by the government, schools such as those run by the National Society, were permitted to introduce other printed material into their classrooms. Book publishers were quick to respond and produced books that were specifically advertised as including reading material that was approved by the government. However, these books were expensive and their quality was variable. It is astonishing that despite the government guidelines, there was still no assumption that an entire book needed to be read or enjoyed. There were many schools which made little real effort to introduce children to major authors and literature, but there is no evidence that this happened at Bearsted.

The school year was punctuated by two events for which intense preparation was undertaken by the staff and pupils. Both the annual government inspections and the annual diocesan inspections were of paramount importance to the staff. The school was subject to regular inspections from the day it opened as part of the affiliation to the National Society.

From a Letter of Instruction to the Society's Inspectors, 1840: [3]

> You will ascertain whether the School House is substantially built, commodiously fitted up and kept in good repair, whether it is of adequate dimensions, and situated in a central and accessible position, well lighted and warmed and thoroughly ventilated, whether there is annexed to it a yard or playground, well-drained and fenced, whether the children are taught habits of cleanliness and have time allowed them at proper intervals for exercise and recreation.
>
> You will enquire whether school materials in sufficient quantity and of a proper kind are provided and what are the books employed; and how much time is devoted to study. With respect to the method of instruction, you will, when it is Monitorial, enquire how far the Master or Mistress is acquainted with the principles of that system....the age and proficiency of the Monitors, whether they are allowed to teach all subjects indiscriminately or are confined to the more mechanical and elementary departments of instruction, whether they are paid or apprenticed, whether they receive tuition at extra hours apart from other pupils, whether this is an assistant Master or Mistress and how paid, and whether the Master confines his attention to a single class or extends his instruction to the whole school.
>
> ...you will consider how far the Master or Mistress possesses the necessary art of communicating ideas in clear and popular language....the Master is of far more importance than the system, the spirit than the mechanism... you will endeavour to satisfy yourself whether the replies or answers are given intelligibly or mechanically and by rote....

The diocesan inspection was held once a year and a copy of the report was written into the log book. As would be expected in a school run by a Church of England voluntary society, the diocesan inspectors were ordained clergy. The reverend gentlemen (there were usually two) conducted their examination by asking the children questions about the Bible and the Catechism. (which was a formal series of questions and answers about the principles of the Christian faith). Children were expected to display a good knowledge of the Church of England doctrine of faith, bible history and events in the life of our Lord that were celebrated within the church year. The children that displayed the best knowledge and gave good, accurate answers were rewarded with prizes of books - usually a copy of the Book of Common Prayer and a Holy Bible. Perhaps some of these prizes, with the details inscribed upon the fly-leaf, still survive in some families resident in Bearsted.

It was rare for the diocesan inspectors to be less than satisfied with the religious instruction and teaching of the school. Most reports were polite and bordered upon the self-congratulatory. An example of a Diocesan Inspection report, entered into the log book, is shown below:

<u>1 March 1872</u>

Copy of Diocesan Inspection
Deanery of Sutton
Report of Bearsted School
Inspected Feb 16th 1872

<u>Mixed School</u>
The Upper Division have a good knowledge and understanding of Christian doctrine. A few of them have a good, and the remainder, fair, acquaintance with the portions of scripture text they have studied. The younger children are taught with great ability by the Monitor, and their knowledge both of scripture and Catechism are satisfactory.

<u>Infant School</u>
The Scripture Instruct appears to have been painstaking and comprehensive and to have interested the children. They answered in fair numbers and with intelligence. They repeat nicely suitable portions of Hymns and Catechism and are nicely behaved.

In later years there was a separate Diocesan Prayer Book examination. Occasionally, the parish magazine bears reports of this (it was usually a good opportunity for some excellent publicity for the school). This is an early example from the parish magazine for July 1875: [4]

Diocesan Prayer Book Examination

It may not be generally known to our readers that an Examination in Knowledge of the Prayer Book is annually held for the children of our National Schools throughout the Diocese of Canterbury (by direction of the Archbishop) under the management of the Diocesan Education Society. The examination is held in different centres throughout the Diocese by means of printed papers of questions, and the children who pass creditably are arranged in three classes according to their performance and their names are published in the Report of Examiners which is sent to each member of the Society.

Of course, the children presented for examination are but few in number compared with the number at school in the Diocese which is 52,890 for the year 1874. The total number examined in March last was but 162, of which 13 came from this neighbourhood viz.: 6 from St Paul's; 2 from St John's, Maidstone; 1 from Harrietsham; 1 from Boxley; 3 from Bearsted

First Class	16
Second Class	78
Third Class	38
Failed for satisfactory examination	30
	Total 162

As regards our 3 Bearsted candidates we are happy to state that Mercy Silk obtained a place among the 16 of the First Class, Ellen Mercer a Second Class and Rosa Edwards in the Third Class. The portions of the Prayer Book chosen for examination on this occasion were: The Order for Morning and Evening Prayer, The Confirmation Service.

The annual government inspection was of immense importance for the Master. Under what became known as 'The Revised 1862 Education Code', payment of government grants towards education became dependent upon results. There was a basic grant to the school of twelve shillings per child for all pupils over 6 years of age. From this sum, four shillings related to regular attendance and the remaining eight shillings depended upon a successful annual examination in reading, writing and arithmetic. If the child did not pass the examination, there was a forfeit of two shillings and eight pence for each subject failed.

Infants were not examined every year, but each infant child earned the school money through an attendance grant of six shillings and sixpence. This award depended upon the government inspectors' satisfaction with the standard of teaching. As the amount of money granted to the school was dependent upon the number of successful pupils, teachers became accountable on many different levels. The salaries of the staff were also dependent upon the same assessment.

The government grant could also be withheld if the inspector was not satisfied with the condition of the school. It had to be ascertained that the building was properly lit, drained, ventilated and supplied with offices. The inspector's report was sent to the Managers by the Education Department and had to be entered in the log book by the secretary to the Managers.[5]

The 1870 Education Act led to further pressure on schools run by voluntary religious organisations such as the National Society. The Boards of state schools had the power to levy a rate for their properties, so some voluntary organisations felt that these schools were in a better financial position. At this time, new ideas for economical government and education began to be introduced into Britain.[6] The term 'efficiency' began to be used as both a government bench mark and whipping post for many staff in voluntary schools.

An example of a government inspectors report from the log book, 9 May 1873:

Substance of the Government Inspectors Report					
			Grants		
			£	s	d
Average attendance		73	21	18	--
Infants presented		12	4	16	--
Qualified for examination		29			
Presented		25			
Passes	Reading	21			
	Writing	22			
	Arithmetic	13	11	4	0
	Total	56			
			£37	18	0

The children read and write very fairly but the Arithmetic is moderate and must be improved [under Education Code] Article (32.b).

The School accounts should in future be made up to the end of the School Examination.

Names and standing of teachers continued on staff

Miss Love Jones	3rd Class treated as 2 by Clause 64
Emma Potter	Pupil Teacher

signed   W Edwards
                    Correspondent

Extra salary payments to the staff were made on the basis of the number of children who passed the examination. These extra payments could add up to twenty-five per cent of a basic salary. This system meant that where a reduction in grant was deemed necessary through a lack of successful pupils, the staff salaries could also be reduced. It could also mean summary dismissal as Managers were reluctant to retain a teacher who could not secure the maximum cash return for the school.[7]

The best results were therefore achieved by hard work and a good relationship with the inspectors. In 1888 only one child failed the annual government examination. The Managers and vicar were delighted with this achievement and Mrs Scarth decided upon a reward. From the log book:

> 23 March 1888
> By kindness of Mrs Scarth, every child who has passed will be presented with a nice illuminated certificate.

The government included guidelines in the Education Codes. These guidelines became the models for the lessons which many schools adopted. The shape of the syllabus was to survive, with many adaptations through to the latter half of the Twentieth century. From the 1862 Revised Education Code: [8]

Standard I	
Reading	Narrative in monosyllables
Writing	From on blackboard or slate, from dictation, letters, capital and small manuscript
Arithmetic	From on blackboard or slate from dictation figures up to 20
	Name at sight figures up to 20
	Add and subtract figures up to 10 orally from examples on the blackboard

Standard II	
Reading	One of the Narratives next in order after monosyllables in a elementary reading book used in the school
Writing	Copy in manuscript character a line of print
Arithmetic	A sum in simple addition or subtraction and the multiplication table

Standard III	
Reading	A short paragraph from an elementary reading book used in the school
Writing	A sentence from the same paragraph, slowly read once and then dictated in simple words
Arithmetic	A sum in any simple rule as far as short division (inclusive)

Standard IV	
Reading	A short paragraph from a more advanced reading book used in the school
Writing	A sentence slowly dictated once by a few words at a time from the same book, but not from the paragraph read
Arithmetic	A sum in compound rules (money)

Standard V	
Reading	A few lines of poetry from a reading book used in the first class of the school
Writing	A sentence slowly dictated once by a few words at a time from a reading book used in the first class of the school
Arithmetic	A sum in compound rules (common weights and measures)

Standard VI	
Reading	A short ordinary paragraph in a newspaper or other modern narrative
Writing	Another short ordinary paragraph in a newspaper or other modern narrative slowly dictated once by a few words at a time
Arithmetic	A sum in practice bills of parcels

Despite the Code prohibiting opinions and personal comments in the log book, it is evident that many Masters did not always abide by this injunction. In 1864 Samuel Taylor was not impressed with some of the new teaching arrangements and wrote in the log book:

> 12 May 1864
> By promoting the classes of the whole school under the New Code I find the children more dull than individually promoted.

In later years, additional grants for specific subjects became available, so English grammar, geography, needlework, elementary history and drawing were introduced into the curriculum. However, this also meant the staff were assessed in their teaching of these subjects. Some inspection reports include comments that the pupil teacher needed to show improvement in specific subjects.

Even when a school was deemed efficient by the inspectors (*efficient* was the highest accolade awarded) they usually managed to issue some fairly stern warnings. From the log book 6 April 1882:

<u>Copy of Inspectors Report received</u>:

The results of the Examination in the Elementary subjects are fair or pretty good on the whole. Arithmetic in the Second, Third and Fourth Standards is good but on the other hand some of the writing especially in the higher classes is somewhat inferior. Needlework is very satisfactory throughout but the other class subjects were not successful. The grant for Grammar is earned by the barest majority and almost entirely by the lower standards and Geography is much below the requirements.

The Infants have been fairly taught.
The tone and order are satisfactory.

signed F O Mayne   Correspondent

School Staff

	William Smith	Master Second Class
	S O Smith	Assistant Mistress
	B Edwards	Assistant Mistress

The local clergy greatly assisted the teaching staff at Bearsted. In particular, two vicars of Bearsted, the Rev Frederick Mayne and Canon John Scarth, together with their families, became heavily involved with the life of the school. The incumbent of Bearsted parish usually fulfilled duties as a School Manager and acted as Correspondent to the school for any official paperwork received from the diocese. There are many entries in the log book for the daughters of Canon Scarth assisting with needlework lessons for the girls and accompanying music lessons by playing the piano.

Other local clergy regularly gave lessons on religious instruction to the children in school. Any formal lessons on religious teaching were reinforced by the work of the Sunday School. In Bearsted this acted independently of the village school. Church services were attended throughout the year and became part of the curriculum. The log books show that church services for Ash Wednesday and Ascension Day were attended before formal lessons commenced for the day or a half-day holiday.

In order to encourage good attendance and conduct by the children, Samuel Taylor was blessed with the imagination and foresight to organise some school prizes in August 1864. These were supplemented through the generosity of Mrs Louisa Whatman who was a local benefactor whose family lived in Boxley parish. It was quite an innovation, although only bare details of these prizes are recorded. From the log book:

<u>Names of children who received Reward Books</u>

<u>First Class</u>   Sarah Foster, Mary A Potter, John Cocker, David Taylor
<u>Second Class</u>   Sarah Morris, Fanny Tolhurst, William Booth, Charles Tucker, John Cooper
<u>Third Class</u>   Harriet Winchester, Maria Glover, Ed. Knowles, Charles Foster
<u>Fourth Class</u>   Jessy Stanford, Sophia Rose, Chas. Wood, Stephen Bridgland, William Stickings

<u>Mrs Whatman's prizes</u>
Emma Constable, Emma Winchester, Elizabeth Glover, Jane Harland

Three years later, in 1867, there was a further distribution of school prizes distributed for good conduct. Details of the prize winners can be found in Appendix Two.

It seems curious that the scheme for prizes and awards did not continue. However, when William Smith became Master, the idea was revived in 1883. Mr Smith was inspired to institute a series of marks for each attendance which were then added up and prizes awarded accordingly. As the parish magazine advised: [9]

<u>January 1882</u>
At the suggestion of the hard-working Master of our schools, Mr Smith, rewards have been given at the end of the last two quarters to those children of the various divisions who are most regular in attendance and good in conduct.

<u>Conditions</u>
Each child is credited with two marks at every school meeting: these are forfeited in cases of absence or misconduct. The following all secured prizes at Michaelmas:

First class	Boys	Frederick Silk
	Girls	Gertrude Colgate
Second class	Girls	Kate Woollett
	Girls & Boys	William Washford
Third class	Girls & Boys	Adelaide Kingsnorth
Fourth class	Girls & Boys	William Hunt

<u>At Christmas</u>		
First class	Boys	Ernest Smith
	Girls	Emily Perrin
Second class	Girls	Kate Geer
	Girls & Boys	Mary White
Third class	Girls & Boys	Alice Brown
Fourth class	Girls & Boys	William Hunt

Later on the annual prize-giving was developed by both the school and the Education Committee to include certificates, medals and bars for good attendance. A superb example of a silver medal for achieving perfect attendance was awarded to Harry Hodges and is shown opposite. For every subsequent year of perfect attendance, a further bar was awarded. Harry actually attended Thurnham School but the medals awarded at Bearsted were of an identical design.

As part of the regulations covered by the later Education Codes, brief outlines of the curriculum were included in the log book. John Day was one of the most conscientious of the staff to do this and thus there are regular 'snap-shots' of the sort of education delivered to the children. His second entry in the log book gives an idea of the curriculum:

<u>9 October 1883:</u>
The Infants are in sole charge of Miss A. Turner (from London School Board) who is responsible for the Needlework. I have made several changes to the approved Time Table (to suit New Code) viz. Elementary Drill and Music or Drama and Needlework two whole afternoons per week. Boys take Map Drawing and Geography with Readers.

(Reproduced by permission of Jean Jones)

The inspectors finally awarded Bearsted 'efficient' status under John Day's charismatic and resourceful leadership. An example of a Government Report bearing this status was recorded in the log book on 20 April 1887:

Received Government Report

Bearsted United National School, Kent

<u>Mixed School</u>
The results of the Examination shew that the high level of efficiency attained last year is fully maintained.
Order and tone are very good and the work throughout is characterised to a marked degree by industry, accuracy and intelligence. Needlework is very praiseworthy.

<u>Infants Class</u>
The Infants are very well taught.

	£	s	d
Grant Ed	100	18	0
Reduction under Rule 114(a)	2	0	6
Amount of Grant Received	98	17	6

<u>School Staff:</u>

Master	John Day	Cd II	Class
Sewing Mistress	Emily Day	Assistant	Article 84
Infants	Charlotte Watts	Assistant	Article 50

Signed	John Scarth, Vicar
	Correspondent

In 1895 a new Education Code abolished the annual examination for senior pupils and finally ended the insidious 'payment by results' scheme. At long last, teachers became slightly freer to devise their own approaches to teaching.[10] John Day embraced this change and two years later, in his penultimate year of office, recorded the most detailed example of the curriculum followed by the school. Full details of this can be found in Appendix Three.

There is ample evidence from the log book to suggest that Mr Day did his best to make lessons interesting for his pupils. When elementary science was introduced into the curriculum; he decided to make it interesting for his pupils by using simple everyday substances. He also took the bold step of introducing swimming lessons into the curriculum. By the time of John Day's departure in 1897, kindergarten lessons had been introduced. Many infants spent time in kindergarten lessons making string mats, stencilling, threading beads and building with bricks.

No discussion on the development of the curriculum prior to the First World War would be complete without a brief mention of the regular series of lectures by the Church of England Temperance Society on the perils of alcohol. It is unclear if the children were expected to take a Pledge of Abstinence as there is no record of this. Certificates of Proficiency were awarded in 1914, as shown opposite.[11]

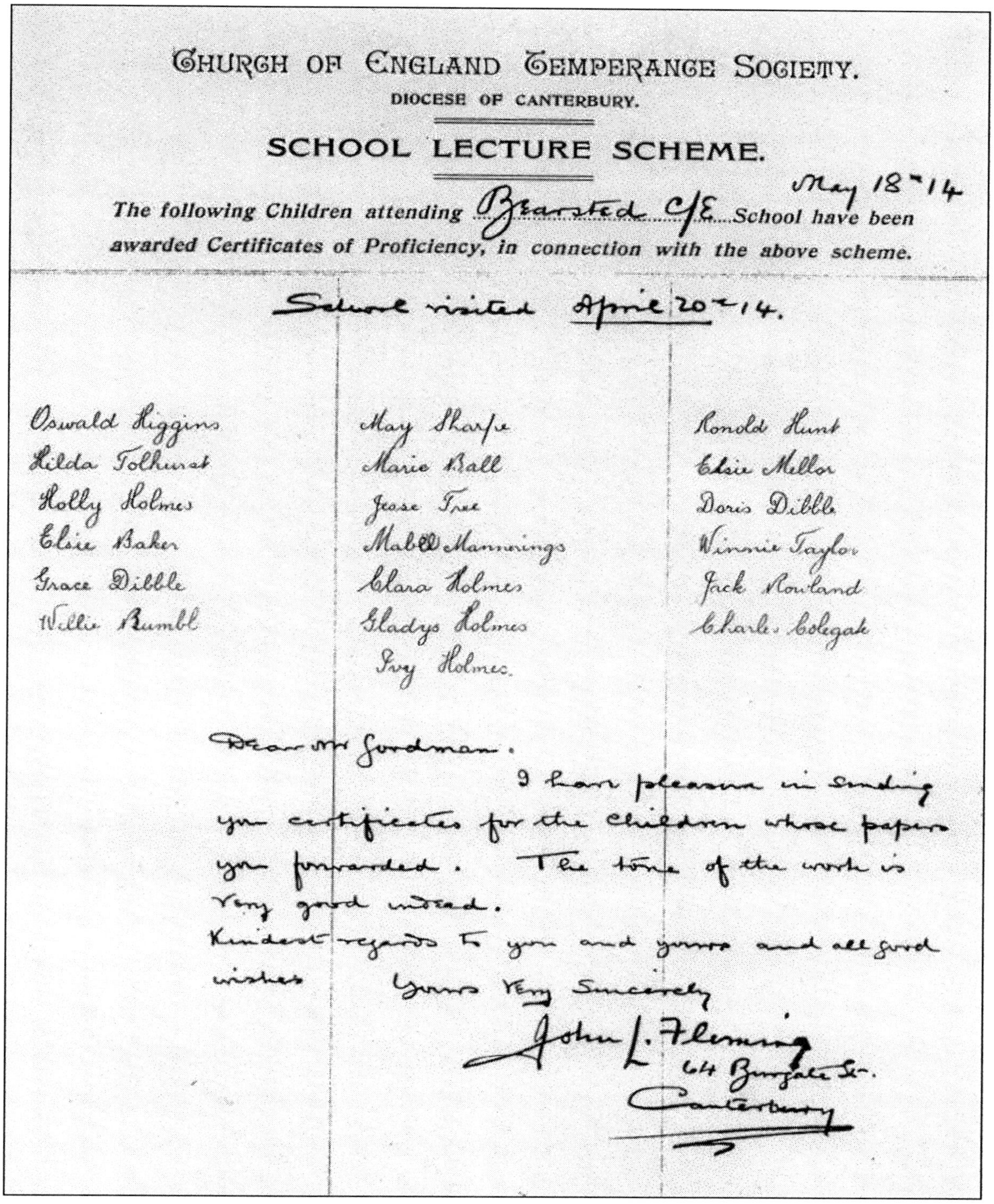

CHURCH OF ENGLAND TEMPERANCE SOCIETY.

DIOCESE OF CANTERBURY.

SCHOOL LECTURE SCHEME.

May 18" 14

The following Children attending *Bearsted C/E* School have been awarded Certificates of Proficiency, in connection with the above scheme.

School visited April 20" 14.

Oswald Higgins
Hilda Tolhurst
Holly Holmes
Elsie Baker
Grace Dibble
Willie Rumble

May Sharpe
Marie Ball
Jesse Tree
Mabel Mannings
Clara Holmes
Gladys Holmes
Ivy Holmes.

Ronald Hunt
Elsie Mellor
Doris Dibble
Winnie Taylor
Jack Rowland
Charles Colegate

Dear Mr Gordman,

I have pleasure in sending you certificates for the children whose papers you forwarded. The tone of the work is very good indeed.

Kindest regards to you and yours and all good wishes

Yours very sincerely

John L. Fleming
64 Burgate St.
Canterbury

(Reproduced by permission Centre for Kentish Studies, Maidstone)

As the Nineteenth century ended, the curriculum slowly began to be developed in an effort to produce lessons that were relevant and of practical use. It was hoped that by this means, children would be equipped with the skills for a life outside school. In 1900 there are entries in the log books that the Mistress, Agnes Barclay, had taken Standards II and III for short walks to gather leaves for a nature lessons. This welcome development was followed by the introduction of an hour of physical exercise for the children once a week.

Agnes Barclay also introduced small concerts that were given by the children. As the parish magazine reported in June 1909:

Successful Children's Concert

In spite of many unavoidable drawbacks and disappointments our School Children presented an excellent programme on the evenings of May 18th and 19th to large and appreciative audiences at the Institute Hall. The chief items in the attractive programme were Musical Sketches: Nursery Rhymes, Washing Day, The Jumble Sale.

Much time and labour must have been expended by the Master and his colleagues in the preparations and practices which produced such excellent results. All went well from the start to the finish without a hitch.

Added to the children's parts, an amusing and instructive sketch was given by some elders who doubtless remember the days when they went to school and are now trying to face the serious side of life. 'Henpecked' was the title of the sketch and it was heartily received as it deserved. We sincerely trust that 'Henpecked' are few and far between. We congratulate all concerned and assure our performers and teachers that on another occasion they will be sure to secure crowded audiences.[12]

Much of the 'revolution' in teaching was magnified by the new ideas in education that were beginning to be published. It had taken a long time for teaching to be regarded as a profession. The associated ideas of regular revision and opportunities for further training now began to be developed. The arrival of the Kent Education Committee had many effects upon the school. One of the most important was that the ideas governing the curriculum were strengthened and developed in the years leading to the First World War and beyond.

Chapter 7
Celebrations, Commemorations and Holidays

There were many opportunities for children to spend time away from school! The early years of Queen Victoria's reign coincided with an expansion of leisure industries because technological advances, such as railways, made cheap and swift travel available. Further opportunities for leisure were opened up by the 1871 Bank Holiday Act which provided six bank holidays throughout the year: Good Friday, Easter Monday, Monday in Whitsun Week, the first Monday in August, Christmas Day, and if it fell on a weekday, 26 December.[1] The passage of the legislation through Parliament was shepherded by Sir John Lubbock, (later Lord Avebury) who was the Member of Parliament for Maidstone.

The local village and religious festivals that marked the year's round in a small community were all celebrated in Bearsted. Easter and Christmas were particularly anticipated by the children but were kept in a fairly quiet manner: a marked contrast to our modern extended celebrations. Between 1909 and 1911 the children had the unexpected pleasure of each receiving an orange for Christmas whilst at school. As the log book recorded:

22 December 1909
School was closed this afternoon.
Before parting, the children received oranges from the staff and amid best wishes for each and all, the school work for 1909 came to an end.

In later years other well-wishers gave a supply of ice-cream, bags of peanuts and bars of chocolate to the school at Christmas for distribution to the children.

In addition to formalised days of absence, there were plenty of other opportunities away from the school room. The log books bear evidence that a surprising number of half-day holidays were called throughout the year. Sometimes these were after the inspections of the school but also festivals of a religious nature: confirmations or Ascension Day occasioned a half-day holiday after the service. It was a tradition that on the latter, older children were allowed up the tower of Holy Cross church. Norah Giles recalled that one Ascension Day, there was an eclipse. All the children were given pieces of smoked glass to look through at the eclipse whilst they were up on the top of the tower.

Days were also set aside for other religious observances as the log book detailed:

9 March 1866
A Fast Day for the Cattle Plague.

A Fast Day was a day set aside for special prayers and abstinence from food as a form of penance or purification. The intention here was that the prayers and penance would be answered by the ending of the illness from which the cattle were suffering. Unfortunately, the Master only recorded the bare facts in this entry. It is not clear whether the day included a special church service or if the children were also expected to abstain from eating.

Occasional half day holidays were given for other civic events and ceremonies. These included the 'Beating-of-the-Bounds'. The following two photographs show some of the details involved in the ceremony for Bearsted parish. Although the photographs are not dated, the Rev Frederick Brown (vicar of Bearsted 1914-1928) can be seen in the first picture which was taken at the start of the ceremony outside the shops in Chestnut Place. Everyone is carrying hazel wands which were used to beat the boundary stones or parish markers. Other people in the photograph include Mr Harry Brook, Mr Whitehead, Mr May and Mr Oswald Jones.

The photograph below shows Mr Spenceley and Mr Brook bouncing 'Panky' Wickens on the boundary stone. This was performed throughout the ceremony at every boundary stone to ensure that the children remembered the location of the parish boundary markers!

(Both photographs courtesy of the late Jessie Page and Photographic Press Agency)

Norah Giles recalled that on one occasion she was able to have some time off school along with Fred Martin as they were chosen to witness the beating-of-the-bounds in Thurnham parish. The Thurnham parish boundary was so large that the ceremony took two days. On the second day Norah walked a great deal of the distance with the vicar of Thurnham, the Rev Arthur Scutt, and Mr Scott, who lived in a house in Thurnham called 'The Friars'. At the end the day, the men decided to celebrate by taking tea at *The Tudor House* tea room and invited Norah along too. She felt very grown-up indeed!

Sometimes holidays that were either whole days or half-days were called in order that the children could attend celebrations, weddings and funerals. The first of these was recorded in the log book in 1878:

11 January 1878
A whole holiday was given on Thursday on honour of the marriage of Miss Helen Mayne, daughter of the Rev Mayne, vicar of Bearsted. 120 children sat down to tea in the schoolroom at her visitation at 4pm on that day.

From the very full account in the *Maidstone Telegraph*, June 21 1890, the children were given a half-day holiday to attend the wedding of Miss Agnes Scarth to the Rev Herbert Maitland. Agnes was one of the daughters of Canon John Scarth, vicar of Bearsted, School Correspondent and Manager. The children scattered flowers before the bridal couple as they left the church through a triumphal floral arch and gave a silver-mounted biscuit box as a wedding present.[2] The Misses Scarth assisted on many occasions in the teaching of the school.

Funerals of people associated with the school were rather more sombre occasions. Some children from the school usually attended funerals and memorial services of people associated with the school. In 1923 when Henry Tasker died, the Master, Mr Goodman, recorded in the log book:

6 March 1923
The funeral of Mr H Tasker, who for over fifty years has been a Manager and Treasurer of the School, took place today, and some of the children under my care, represented the school at the two services at 9am and 2.30pm.

When the vicar of Bearsted, Mr Brown, died after a painful illness in 1928, the school was closed for the day as a mark of respect. Three years later, the boys that were in the church choir, accompanied by Mr Goodman, attended the funeral service of Mr Monckton, who had been a later school Correspondent and Treasurer. In 1936 the school was closed on the day of the funeral of King George V.

Sometimes a child's absence from school was due to purely economic reasons: looking after the baby in the family and younger siblings whilst mother worked was a constant excuse for non-attendance. Illness was another major reason given for absence but there were also the persistent demands of labour for local agriculture. There are countless entries in the log books that detail reduced attendance due to seasonal work in fruit and hop cultivation.

Absence through hop pole-shaving persisted until the later years of the 1890s when the system for growing the hops changed. Originally, hops were trained to grow up against wooden poles but a system of growing the hops against wires and strings was then introduced and became known as "wire gardens" in some parts of Kent. Picking the hops affected school attendance if the picking season was deemed a poor one. The season normally lasted six weeks but in a bad year the picking went on until late into September, beyond the official holiday dates. During the picking season the local towns and villages were almost deserted during the day and there were few children in school. In Maidstone and the surrounding villages, the traders kept their shops open until very late in the evening so that people could purchase food and goods when they had finished the work for the day. The harvest of other crops and gleaning also regularly reduced school attendance.

The weather was a marked participant in the reasons for absence: extremes of cold, wind, rain and snow all resulted in low attendance. Once thoroughly wet, children had to stay in their uncomfortable and heavy clothes with little prospect of being able to dry out. On 4 December 1874 the attraction of a completely frozen pond on the Green proved irresistible for several boys, who then received a caution for arriving late. In the 1920s there was a series of regularly flooded roads around Bearsted which led to an enforced absence for some of the children from outlying areas. It was not the first time that 'Water Lane' lived up to the name.

The yearly round of life at Bearsted involved the Green being used on many occasions. It was an ideal location for various local organisations to hold annual events. These proved irresistible to some of the children. Margaret Tomalin, (née Baker), remembered her father (born 1888) describing the occasional arrival of a German band in the village. This was usually on a Monday, so the women of the village had a musical accompaniment to their laundry routines. Sometimes the band also brought with them a dancing bear which was a great spectacle for the children. An early, but undated, photograph of a band on the Green:

(Photograph courtesy of Margaret Tomalin)

Children were also absent from school for the Guy Fawkes and Bonfire Night celebrations held on the Green if there was a guy figure to parade around the area. This activity earned some pennies for the fireworks. As the Mistress, Miss Love Jones, recorded in the log book:

5 November 1872
Guy Faux day.
Order interrupted by bringing guys to the school door.

Harry Hodges, who was born in 1898, passed on a memory to his daughter, Jean, of tar barrels being rolled onto the Green before they were set alight as another part of the Bonfire Night festivities in the village.

As befits a village with one of the oldest cricket grounds in the country there was always a ready audience for cricket matches. Maidstone Cricket Week always reduced the attendance figures! The children were given a holiday on 29 April 1929 in order to attend a match on the Green which included a team of cricketers from South Africa. In 1932, one of the Managers, Mr Whitehead, generously provided sufficient tickets for the children to attend a cricket match in Mote Park when the West Indies played All England.

Upon occasion, other local activities impinged upon attendance and resulted in absence. *The History of Bearsted and Thurnham* mentions children who assisted at meets of the local hunt during the week. There was usually a spate of absences when a local shoot was run and beaters were required to flush birds away from the covers. In 1898 the Attendance Committee decided to tackle this problem and resolved to write to Mr Fremlin, a local landowner, to request that boys of school age should not be employed as beaters.[3] Mr Fremlin subsequently advised the Committee that he had spoken to his Head Keeper about this. A decade later the problem still persisted in the area as several boys regularly received cautions for absence for this reason.

Another local custom that resulted in absence from school was recorded in the log book. It took place around May Day[4] when garlands of flowers and leaves were made and displayed:

> 5 May 1876
> Monday being "May Day", several children were permitted by their parents to carry garlands about the parish.

One of the first excursions undertaken by the school took place on 21 July 1864. The children who had passed the government examination, or who were leaving the school, went on a trip to Rosherville Gardens in Gravesend. These had been developed from twenty acres of disused chalk pits. The initial idea was to create zoological gardens but the pleasure aspect soon overcame any philanthropic or educational ideas. Such was the popular attraction of the gardens that one of the houses in the village still bears the name *Rosherville*. At one point, the garden employed professional acts for a limited period during the summer season together with a resident company which provided the music.[5] The attractions that the children would have seen included a bear pit, monkey cages, a maze and some side-shows. This is a transcript of a report in the *Maidstone Telegraph* about the excursion:

> July 23 1864
> **BEARSTED SCHOOL CHILDRENS' HOLIDAY**
> On Thursday last, the Children connected with the Bearsted schools were treated to a journey to Rosherville Gardens. No less than six vans full passed through Maidstone to the station, where a train was in readiness to take them to their destination. They returned in the evening highly delighted with their day's recreation.

There were further trips to the gardens made by the school but at the start of the Twentieth century the attraction was in decline.

It is not recorded whether some of the children from Bearsted visited the Great Exhibition at Hyde Park in 1851. However, the centrepiece of the exhibition was later moved to Sydenham and the Master briefly recorded in the log book:

> 9 August 1865
> Fifty children were taken to see the Crystal Palace.

In 1924, the Empire Exhibition at Wembley was visited by some of the children from Bearsted School. Although the travel arrangements were not recorded, most people that visited the exhibition travelled by train up to London and then used the Underground to arrive at Wembley. Mr Goodman recorded the arrangements made to cover his absence at the school. From the log book:

> 17 July 1924
> As I shall be visiting Wembley Exhibition tomorrow, with ten of the children, the school will be in the charge of Mrs Dibble.

The *Official Guide*[6] to the exhibition described the event as 'a Family Party of the British Empire' on a site of 216 acres. Each colony of the empire was represented by its own building which was called a 'pavilion'. Other buildings showed the achievements of the Empire in the fields of Engineering, Industry and the Arts as well as the work of HM Government. The exhibition was a popular attraction.

There were several friendly societies in the village during the middle years of the Nineteenth century. Amongst these societies were The Ancient Order of Foresters who regularly held fêtes, fairs and other events on the Green. Many children were noted as absent to attend these events.

Through the first hundred years of the school, the children were given entertainments by a variety of religious organisations. An opportunity to spread the word of the Lord was not to be missed. For some time the usual curriculum was adjusted to accommodate addresses by the Church of England Temperance Society on the perils of alcohol. The Temperance Society also gave talks to the children in combination with other occasions. Empire Day, 24 May 1921, was marked with an entertainment which was a departure from the normal lessons. During the morning they listened to an address by one of the teachers, Mrs Dibble, on 'Responsibility', and participated in patriotic songs and recitations. In the afternoon the children listened once more, this time a guest speaker from the Temperance Society addressed the children on 'The Food We Eat'.

Empire Day was normally commemorated with either special lessons or a half-day holiday. In 1924 it fell on a Saturday and so the children were entertained on the preceding afternoon instead. A gramophone was loaned for the event.

In later years before the Second World War, the Empire Day commemorations were expanded into a small concert or entertainment in the early evening at one of the halls in the village. Norah Giles recalled that on at least one occasion it was decided that there would be a different type of pageant and various children would represent aspects of the Empire. Norah was chosen to represent Wales. Her mother made her a special dress and she carried a bunch of daffodils. Two girls chosen to represent England and Scotland were attired in a similar manner.

These two undated photographs show the competition entries for Empire Day celebrations. Note the inclusion of a maypole the first picture:

(Photograph courtesy of Vera Banner)

(Photograph courtesy of Brenda Donn)

In addition to the friendly societies in the village, there were many other societies for specific interests such as gardening. The prizes for the flower and produce shows were always keenly contested and the reports for them regularly featured in the local newspapers. As the *History of Bearsted and Thurnham* mentions, one of these local societies was called 'The Horticultural and Industrial Society'. It was set up in 1906 and held its first show at *Snowfield*.[7] Some of these local society shows had entries by the children. The parish magazine printed reports of the prize winners from the first show: [8]

Horticultural and Industrial Society

Following prizes awarded in the classes for children in Bearsted and Thurnham Schools:

Needlework	Girls over 11 years of age:	
	Equal first	Alice Smith, Dorothy Brown
	Second	Mildred Wilkinson
	Girls under 11	
	Second	Mildred Higgins
Handwriting		
	First	William Thompson
	Second	Vivian Briseley
	Third	Mildred Higgins
	Very Highly Commended	John Marsh
Drawing (Flat)		
	First	Lionel Rideout
	Second	Leonard Brown
	Very Highly Commended	Wilfred Wilkinson, John Marsh
Drawing (Nature)		
	First	Lionel Datson
	Very Highly Commended	John Marsh
Essay		
	First	Charles Hills
	Second	Lionel Datson
	Very Highly Commended	Mildred Wilkinson

On 23 March 1894, the log book recorded a departure from usual lessons:

> Afternoon registers were marked at 12.50pm then work was taken from 1 - 3.10pm. This departure from the usual time table was made in order to allow the girls to go flowering with Miss Scarth. The vicar sanctioned this.

It is possible that this entry about "flowering" was Bearsted's contribution to a Flower Mission. A similar Flower Mission was run in Brenchley, Matfield and Paddock Wood between 1875 and 1905 when bunches of flowers were sent on early trains to children's hospitals in London.[9] Other similar schemes arranged for flowers to be sent to children in the West Kent and Ophthalmic Hospitals in Maidstone.

Around Christmas, Holy Cross church and the Methodist church held separate celebrations for the children of the village. Unfortunately, both events bore the same name for some years of 'A Christmas Tree'. Eventually, Holy Cross church decided to rename their event 'A Christmas Treat' but it still led to some confusion. Both events were arranged around a decorated Christmas tree which had small presents tied to it. There was a substantial tea for everyone and the afternoon concluded with the distribution of the presents. Understandably, it was popular with the children, although Margaret Tomalin's father, Richard Baker, never received the toys he longed-for as a small boy such as a top or a ball: his present always contained socks! She recalled that he also spoke about the occasions, possibly around Christmas, when a cart used to be drawn into the village, and hot farthings were thrown from it for the children to catch. In some parts of the country, this was called *Snap Dragon,* but the tradition has many variations.

Many of the children were members of the church choirs for Bearsted and Thurnham and of their Sunday Schools so the village school was nearly always closed when the annual choir excursion to the seaside took place. The venues for the excursion included Margate, Folkestone and Dover. There were other, rather more secular outings that also took place and reduced the attendance at the school. This is an undated photograph of one excursion by some members of Holy Cross church congregation:

(Photograph courtesy of Margaret Tomalin)

In the first few decades of the Twentieth century a number of national organisations were established for children. The Scarlet Pimpernel troop of the Boy Scouts was opened in Bearsted in 1912. Some of the boys were absent from school to attend camps. After the unexpected death of the first Scoutmaster, Mr Draikes, the troop was run for a time by James Elliott. He had attended the school and was one of the first boys to be enrolled in the Troop.

This photograph shows the Scout Troop at a camp in 1912. James Elliott is in the centre of the front row.

(Photograph courtesy of David and Theresa Elliott)

The Girl Guides and Brownies also ran camps and excursions. Girls were sometimes also absent from school to attend these events. From the log book:

<u>29 July 1925</u>
There are several absentees today owing to the 'Brownies' outing.

The Golf Club in the village was a further distraction from school. The club opened in 1895. The prospect for some children of a small financial reward for carrying a bag of golf clubs for a member resulted in some absences. In 1898 the Attendance Committee gave notice to the Club Secretary that children should not be employed by the Club during school hours. The Attendance Officer for Bearsted School reported to the Committee that matters had not improved. A subsequent suggestion of a system of badges to indicate eligible children failed as the badges were easily transferred!

A stronger approach was clearly needed to resolve the problem. A covert visit to the Club was arranged and resulted in the discovery of several boys in the employ of a member. The Committee advised the Club that boys could only be employed during school hours if the child could produce a certificate confirming that they were exempt from attendance.[10] The matter was then resolved to the Committee's satisfaction.

The annual School Treats given to the children were highly popular as is shown in the following extract from the parish magazine: [11]

February 1875

Our School Treat

The annual treat to the children of our National and Sunday Schools was given on the 23rd of last month in the usual place of meeting - the beautifully situated paddock of H Tasker Esq. They mustered at the schoolroom upwards of 150 in number and proceeded in procession to the Church, singing as they went hymns 366 and 164 and preceded by the parish banner made last year by Mrs Tasker.

After a short and hearty service of praise, the procession reformed and proceeded to the meadow where many flag-bearers were relieved of their burdens. A general rush was made to the swings, and very soon the whole number was engaged in various games, enjoying themselves to their hearts' content; - the numerous amusements being promoted and shared in by their teachers and other active friends.

An excellent tea was provided for them at 5pm enhanced by sieves of cherries and gooseberries kindly presented by Messrs Bridgland and Larking; and after the contents of a brawn pie had been distributed, the sports were resumed and carried on till sunset. We were glad to see so many parents of the children, and other parishioners, present on the ground.

In the course of the day, rewards of handsome books and texts were distributed to every regular attendant at the Sunday School. The proceedings were brought to a close by hearty cheers from the children for Miss Vincent and their Sunday School teachers; for Mr and Mrs Tasker and other promoters of the treat, and for the Vicar, and by their singing the beautiful hymn for children, No 368 beginning:

> *Now the day is over*
> *Night is drawing nigh -*
> *Shadows of the evening*
> *Steal across the sky.*

In 1878, the treat also included a religious service before the celebrations: [12]

August 1878

Our School Treat

Our School Treat took place on June 28th, too late to be notified in our issue for July. We were favoured this year with a fine day, very hot, but tempered by a cool breeze from the north. The children assembled as usual at the school at 1.30pm and then proceeded to the church in procession, headed for the first time, by the Juvenile Drum and Fife Band, which gave much satisfaction and which will, we hope, ripen into a permanent village band. They greatly need better instruments and we hope that as winter comes on, with its dark evenings, giving opportunity for practice, some effort may be made to supply them with what they need.

The service in church consisted as usual of an abbreviated evensong, with some hymns, which were well sung by the children, and after that they proceeded in procession to Mr Tasker's meadow, being joined at this gate by the Infants, who swelled the total number to about 150.

As soon as their ranks were broken up, there was a rush made for the swings, while the bigger boys enjoyed a cricket match. Much regret was felt at the absence of the Mistress, Miss Vincent, not so much on account of the children, who were well amused and cared for, as for her own sake - being prostrated by illness. We must hope that she will return after the holidays quite renovated in health and able to take charge of the school again. As we have implied, there were plenty of friends able and willing to promote the enjoyment of the children and to assist in the distribution of their tea, which took place at 4.30. At 6pm Mrs Tasker gave a present of some toy to every child in the school and then they re-engaged in their various games until dusk. We were glad to see several of the parents come up to the meadow and hope to see their number increased another year. The thanks of the parish are due to Mr Tasker, not only for the loan of his meadow - without which we should have difficulty in finding a suitable place - but also for the heartiness with which he promoted the amusement of the children.

The following year, the entertainment became a little more sophisticated: [13]

September 1879

Our School Treat

Our School Treat came off at last on the 19th of last month after two postponements - and we are happy to say that we did not suffer the usual consequences of postponements, viz.: disappointment and vexation - for we were favoured with a fine day, and everything went off very well, and the children had a thoroughly happy day. We were glad to notice Colonel Knight on the ground, but Mr Tasker was absent for the first time and was greatly missed by many a juvenile to whose amusement he had ministered in former years. Mrs Tasker, however, did her utmost with much success, to fill his place, and her ingenuity had devised a novel amusement, which we will venture to assert has never been seen at any school treat in England before, namely, a maze, made on the pattern of the famous one at Hampton Court, which gave great delight to the children and to many grown persons also; and throughout the day there were some busily engaged in finding their way through its intricate paths, while others, less enterprising, stood by and were amused by the difficulties of the various travellers. The children were indebted to Mr Larking for a large basket of fruit, the contents of which were distributed at the termination of tea. The performances of the Bearsted Drum and Fife Band did much to enliven the proceedings.

During the reign of Queen Victoria, some of the most memorable events for children were the celebrations surrounding the Jubilee in 1887 and the Diamond Jubilee in 1897. For the Jubilee there are two brief entries in the log books which indicate that on 20 June there was a holiday to mark the occasion. On 8 July there was a tea to mark the Jubilee School Treat. There was at least one photograph taken of the children to commemorate the Jubilee, as the mount clearly indicates. This photograph is reproduced below.

THIS PHOTOGRAPH WAS
TAKEN IN THE JUBILEE YEAR
of Her Most Gracious Majesty Queen Victoria, 1887.

(Photograph courtesy of Roseacre School)

The parish magazine carried a report of the local festivities for the Diamond Jubilee: [14]

<u>The Queen's Jubilee</u>

The Jubilee Festivities on June 22 for the joint parishes of Bearsted and Thurnham passed off without a hitch, owing to the energy and forethought of the Committee, aided by the active labours of a large number of volunteer helpers.

There was to have been a Church Parade but owing to the very serious illness of the Vicar of Bearsted, this part of the programme was perforce abandoned. At 1.30pm the actual proceedings began with the singing of the National Anthem and a procession of about 250 children round the Green, headed by the Sutton Valence Band. During the afternoon, various races were run, the sack-races perhaps evoking the greatest interest. A large fire-balloon was let off with great success at each hour except at 5pm (when everyone was busily occupied elsewhere). The Schoolrooms had been placed in the hands of the Committee by the School Managers and the Parish Hall by Mr Marley, and free teas were given to all ticket-holders of the two parishes, young and old. The tables were most tastefully decorated with beautiful flowers and a bountiful meal was provided and we may further say was thoroughly appreciated by about 370 children and about 550 adults.

In the evening 252 Diamond Jubilee mugs were presented to the School Children and oranges and buns to all the children on the Green.

At half-past 9 the whole Green was lit up with coloured fires, which made our picturesque village appear more picturesque than ever, and showed up the decorations which some had taken the trouble to put up, to great advantage. This was followed by a display of fireworks, which lasted until 10, when the Thurnham bonfire and the bonfires all round the country were lighted. From Thurnham Hill, nearly 60 bonfires could be counted, the effect being fine indeed.

This is a photograph of some of the children that was taken to commemorate the Diamond Jubilee:

(Photograph courtesy of Roseacre School)

The children are standing in front of *The White Horse Inn* by a door that is now blocked up, situated on the corner of Yeoman Lane and The Street. Note the slate which says "Bearsted III' and the Union flags!

A ticket for the Jubilee tea:

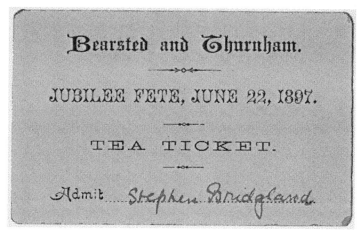

(Reproduced by permission of Norah Giles)

It was agreed by the organisers of the celebrations that tickets would be issued and then surrendered before participation in the events. As Stephen Bridgland did not attend the tea, this ticket is an astonishingly rare survival.

In 1902, with the novel idea of a King on the throne following the death of Queen Victoria, fresh in many children's minds, it looked as if the celebrations for the coronation would proceed smoothly. However, the coronation of Edward VII had to be postponed as the King recovered from an operation and a nation offered prayers for a swift recovery. Once again, the parish magazines carry details of the celebrations but there is no comment in the log book about the occasion. This may be due to the editorial style of the Mistress, Agnes Barclay. It is curious that a cause for national concern is omitted from the log book whilst some of the events of the Boer War are chronicled. To mark the end of the war on 6 June 1902, the log book records a holiday and a tea held in the school grounds, at the behest of the Managers.

The parish magazine reported: [15]

July 1902

The Coronation Festivities which had been so greatly looked forward to, had to take place in a very different spirit to what we anticipated. Owing to the sudden and dangerous illness of our King, which postponed his coronation so abruptly and unexpectedly most of the national rejoicings, especially those in London, had of course, to be put off, but with his usual forethought and consideration for his people so as to avoid inconvenience or disappointment, the King expressed his earnest desire that all Celebrations which had been arranged in the Country, should still be carried through. A Special Committee Meeting was therefore called here, with the result that the Public Dinner and Children's Tea took place on what should have been Coronation Day and the Sports Programme was carried out on a modified scale, much to the joy of the children who took part. In the morning, there was a Special Service of Intercession for the King, at which many people were present. After the Children's Tea in the School, Mr Tasker kindly invited them up to 'Snowfield', where Mrs Tasker presented each child with a book, descriptive of the Realm of our King, and Mrs Whitehead gave away over 100 mugs commemorative of the occasion. Three cheers were given for the donors and Miss Barclay, but perhaps the heartiest were those which Mr Tasker called for the King. It was a hard day for the Committee who all helped so well, and the best thanks of all are due to Mr Whitehead, upon whom as Secretary fell the chief share of organisation. The day passed off very quietly, indeed no one seemed to forget under what anxious circumstances they were gathered together. The cloud of suspense that hung so darkly over us that day seems now, by God's mercy to be dispersing as we read day by day of the King's remarkable progress towards recovery.

For the next coronation, that of George V on 22 June 1911, the school was already closed due to an epidemic of measles in the parish. Two photographs of the King and Queen were received from the Kent Education Committee and were on display when the school re-opened on 30 June. Nevertheless, the village celebrated. It is likely that the photograph featured opposite and on the front cover of this book, of the children in front of the school, was taken on this occasion.

These two photographs of sports events on the Green are undated but it is possible that they were taken at the 1911 Coronation celebrations:

(Both photographs courtesy of Margaret Tomalin)

(Photograph courtesy of Roseacre School)

Other events concerning royalty that encroached upon the time-table of the school included a holiday on 27 July 1921, in order for the children to see the Prince of Wales pass through the village.

There were further holidays to mark the occasion of Princess Mary's wedding on 28 February 1922, and the Duke of York's wedding to Lady Elizabeth Bowes-Lyon on 26 April 1923. The latter was recorded in the log book:

> 26 April 1923
> The school as given a holiday today by the express wish of His Majesty the King to celebrate the wedding of the Duke of York.

Other royal weddings to merit a holiday include those of the Duke of Kent in 1934 and the Duke of Gloucester in 1935.

For the celebrations of the 1935 Silver Jubilee of George V's accession, the parishes of Bearsted and Thurnham combined. There was a two-day closure of the schools. On 6 May, there was a Thanksgiving service at Bearsted church in the morning. In the afternoon sports were held on the Green and a tea at the Women's Institute Hall for children aged between five and fourteen. Violet Hale (née Pollard) remembered that her cup of tea was served in a Jubilee mug. She was then given the mug to keep as a souvenir of the day!

The parish council accounts detail that the total cost of the mugs came to £7 10s and the refreshments cost £10.[16] Later in the day there was dancing on the Green, a beacon was lit at Thurnham castle and there was a display of fireworks.

As part of the Jubilee celebrations, all the children were given tickets for free rides at a fair that was held in Mote Park. There was also a Jubilee Essay competition set by the Member of Parliament for Maidstone, Mr A C Bossom. The winners received Jubilee Medals from Mrs Bossom:

Class 1	Ella Foster, Ernest Guest
Class 2	Thelma Baker, Colin Colebrook
Class 3	Lucy Garrett, Keith Hilton[17]

For the Coronation of George VI on 12 May 1937 there was another two-day closure of the schools as Bearsted and Thurnham combined once more to celebrate. The local festivities were reported in the parish magazine: [18]

Coronation Celebrations

Coronation Day was both a Holy Day and a holiday. The religious significance of the occasion was not lost on Bearsted, nor did we fail to rejoice at the crowning of our King.

Our celebrations were combined with those of Thurnham and a committee representing both parishes planned the various events for the day.

Bearsted bells, rung on many Coronation days, heralded the days proceedings at 6.45am and were heard again in the afternoon.

Holy Communion was celebrated at 7.15am and at 8am at Bearsted church and the morning was free for listening to the broadcast from Westminster Abbey. The broadcast and the inclement weather combined to keep most people indoors until the sports commenced in the afternoon

The Green was gay with colour. Fluttering pennants strung between decorated and beflagged poles encircled the Green. There were two decorated arches whilst the houses round the Green, dressed with flags and bunting, lent colour to the scene. There were prizes for the best decorated houses.

The persistent rain caused a postponement of the start of the sports but in spite of the weather, a start was made soon after 3pm and the whole programme completed. During the afternoon, many people sent off balloons. We have not yet heard of any that have gone prodigious distances but they have got to August Bank Holiday! About 200 Bearsted and Thurnham children had tea at the WI and were presented with Coronation mugs.

In the Fancy Dress parade, the standard of entries was high and in spite of the discouraging weather, the numbers were good. After dusk a bonfire was lit on Thurnham Hill and so despite the poor weather the two villages celebrated the Coronation of His Majesty King George VI.

In addition to the local celebrations, Maidstone Town Council decided to distribute to children of school-age some souvenirs to commemorate the event: Coronation medals for the boys and spoons for the girls.[19]

After the Second World War, the nature of celebrations in the village began to change. Although local events continued to be marked, the school became less directly involved. Fêtes and fairs were moved to Bank Holidays and weekends. Consequently, the occasional holidays that had occurred in term time diminished and then vanished completely.

Chapter 8
The Development of the School & Curriculum:
1914 - 1937

On the day that Britain entered the First World War, 4 August 1914, the school re-opened after a week's holiday. Almost immediately, there was an epidemic of mumps so the school closed! It took some time before the war began to intrude into the life of the school. One of the earliest references in the log book to the war was made on 1 July 1915, when it was recorded that the needlework lessons were now devoted to making garments for the army and hospitals.

As the school was near to the railway, the children saw seen many trains carrying troops travelling to Dover as they made the journey to France and Belgium. By 1915 Maidstone had turned into a kind of transit camp. People moved into the town looking for war work, and as a military base, many men passed through the town en route for other destinations. Hospitals were set up around Maidstone for the wounded[1] so there were plenty of recipients for the clothes the children produced.

The Daylight Saving Act made an impact upon the school during the early years of the war as the afternoon time-table was slightly altered, shortening the Lower School day by twenty minutes. In addition to these measures, the street lighting in Maidstone was dimmed and then extinguished in 1916 because of fears of attack by Zeppelins and other aircraft.[2] However, the only effects recorded in the log book were in October 1917, when a request was received from one mother asking whether children could be sent home if an air-raid took place in school hours. The following month the Master did note that attendance seemed to be rather low due to the effects of the air-raids, so some children were deliberately kept at home.

Early in 1918, the curriculum expanded to include Gardening Instruction for the senior boys. These lessons were very welcome as there had been food shortages since 1915.[3] The lessons were held by Frank Goodman on an allotment a short distance from the school on Thursday afternoons. The gardens were inspected by Mr W P Wright, a Horticultural Superintendent for the Kent Education Committee. From the first annual report filed:

Season	1918
School	Bearsted
Number of Pupils	14
Site and Area of Garden	Allotment near the school, 20 rods.
System	Single and Dual.
Condition of Crops	Excellent: particularly potatoes, beans, carrots and parsnips.
Condition of Tools	Excellent.
Remarks on Fruit	There are a few large trees which have been carefully pruned and will receive further attention. There are some old gooseberries which are hardly perhaps worth the ground they occupy.
Disposal of Produce	Given to the pupils.
Methods of Correlation	Diary, lessons on plant life, plans of the garden and cropping.
General Remarks	The garden is new this year and a very promising start had been made.

Signed W P Wright, Horticultural Superintendent

Prior to this, on 13 August 1918 the gardens were separately inspected by Mr Wright as prizes for the best kept garden had been presented to the school by the Women's Institute. The first proud winners were Edmund Walters, Sydney James and Edward Butler. Several Old Scholars have suggested that the first photograph opposite is actually a gardening group, taken in the grounds of the *White Horse* public house. It is undated but worth noting that all of them are wearing fairly sturdy boots! Amongst the boys are Wilfred Baker, Frank Swift, William Tree and Robin Martin, also some members of the Shorter and Cackett families:

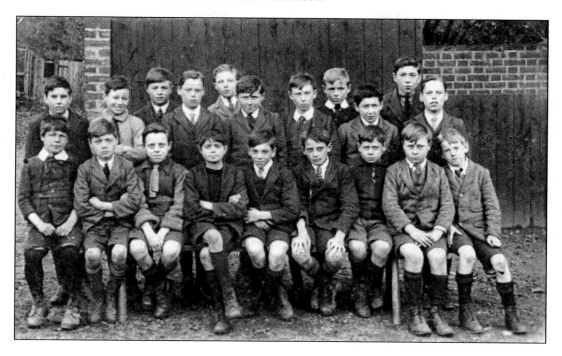

Two photographs of the children that were taken around 1917 to 1918 are in the school records. It is likely that they were taken at the same session which may have commemorated Empire Day as all the children are looking very smart: [4]

(Both photographs courtesy of Roseacre School)

(Photograph courtesy of Roseacre School)

The names for the children shown here (left to right):

Top row   --- Earl, B Smith, E Butler, H Ball,

Next row   P Britcher (standing) , L White, H Webb, G Goodman, P Chapman,
                  D Jeffrey, B Tester, D Martin (standing)

Next row   W Offen (standing), F Colegate, M Corps, W Tree, E Simmonds,
                  R Martin, I Martin (twins),

Front row   P Ball, T Moore, G Jones, D Wickens, O Walkling, B Merrall

By the end of the war in November 1918, the staff were distracted once more from national events by more immediate parochial concerns. Influenza was spreading through the village. This was the 'Spanish Influenza' outbreak that was later calculated to have caused more deaths than the First World War. The school was closed on 4 November and only re-opened on 18 November with a very low attendance. At one of the most important dates in the first two decades of the Twentieth century, 11 November, when the First World War was officially ended, the log book is frustratingly silent.

Although there were many Old Scholars involved in the First World War, one instance of distinguished conduct is particularly noteworthy. Lance Corporal L Datson had won a Wayth's Prize during his time at the school. His family ran the bakery in The Street, a short distance from the *Royal Oak* public house. In February 1918 he was awarded the Military Medal. The citation gives the details of courageous action under fire, driving three times through a village which was being heavily shelled and enabling a dressing station to be cleared of wounded men.[5]

There are twenty-five men named on the village war memorial who probably attended the school. The names of three of them are mentioned in the log books: Reginald Allcorn, Reginald Ball and Albert Croucher. It was appropriate that the next generation of pupils at the school witnessed the dedication of the memorial in the churchyard of Holy Cross.

Normal life at the school and in the village was quickly resumed after the war. The annual diocesan inspection was carried out as usual in February 1919, but bore the following amusing comment on the written work:

> The weakest papers were those on Christ's Death and Resurrection.
> Curiously, nearly all spelt Philistines with two l's...

An architectural survey was undertaken in 1919 but there are no details in the National Society records. This was followed in August 1920 by a visit from Maidstone's Director of Education. Mr Abbott was supported by an Education Committee ready to use the new opportunities provided under the 1918 Education Act.[6] He suggested to the Managers that new subjects such as swimming for the boys and cookery lessons for the girls should be considered for introduction to the curriculum. It was clear that life was changing for many children. Although the basics of reading, writing, mathematics and a thorough knowledge of the Bible continued in good measure, the curriculum began to widen.

In 1926 a report on 'The Education of the Adolescent', was published by part of the government. The committee of the Board of Education was chaired by Sir W H Hadow. Inevitably, it became known as "The Hadow Report". The proposals included the idea of using the age of 11 as a division in education and a comment that became famous:

> There is a tide which begins to rise in the veins of youth at the age of 11 or 12. It is called by the name of adolescence...[7]

One of the committee's main aims was to establish central schools for working-class pupils as an alternative to grammar schools. To achieve this in the Maidstone area, some church schools were converted into junior schools and the Junior Technical school (part of the Technical Institute) was enlarged.[8]

The 11+ examination for entry to Junior Technical and Grammar Schools was introduced. It was intended that the Grammar Schools should become the agency through which children from all social classes would mix together according to their intellectual abilities. Scholarships, which would cover the costs of sending a child to grammar school, were available for the brightest children. Some schools even formed special 'scholarship classes'.[9]

Nell Hodson (née Byam) recalled that Frank Goodman did not really pursue the idea of children working for scholarships. He believed that they should be won on natural ability. However, there were some children who did win scholarships but could not take them up. Their parents needed the money that they could earn on leaving the village school.

Once the 11+ examination was established as the route to secondary education, there was little real change for twenty years in the emphasis upon numeracy and literacy in the curriculum.[10] Although passing the examination did not always mean a child was able to attend secondary school and university, it was a marked change from the situation at the end of the Nineteenth century.[11]

From 1922 there are regular details in the log books of scholarships awarded to children. Amongst the first children that are specifically named were Joseph Webb and John Holmes who were awarded fee-paying scholarships to the Junior Technical School. This early success was consolidated in 1924 by Gordon Blundell winning a scholarship to Maidstone Grammar School. The first girls to be specifically recorded in the log book as winning scholarships to Maidstone Girls Grammar School were Jean Wilkinson and Dora Foster in 1926.

In 1923 the Master received notice that the Board of Education was concerned that the number of Infants seemed to be falling, so the idea of uniting the schools at Bearsted and Thurnham began to be explored. The population figures from the Census taken in 1911 and again in 1921 do not seem to reflect this as Bearsted and Thurnham's population rose by four per cent overall. Nevertheless the Board felt that there was a surplus of staff at Bearsted and terminated the contract of Miss Hearnden, reducing the staff to three.

The amalgamation of Bearsted and Thurnham schools took place on 2 June 1925. The classes were known as 'Standards' by this time. Children eligible for Infants and Standard I attended Thurnham. Children of Standard II and up to the school-leaving age of 14 attended Bearsted.

It took some time for the system to settle. It was not until 1928, following firm instructions from the Board, that a policy of transferring children aged around eight in September of every year from Thurnham into Standard II at Bearsted, began to be implemented. Bearsted School lost Miss Clayton as a member of staff as she transferred to Thurnham, having previously taught the Infants and Standard I at Bearsted.

The early days of the new scheme were predictably chaotic. On the first day, only six of the older children that should have transferred from Thurnham attended Bearsted. Norah Giles, who attended Thurnham, recalled that the first morning of the new arrangements was marked by a near-riot of parents and senior pupils! Some of the older girls were so adamant that they were not going to attend Bearsted School that they decided to go on strike. Fortunately, Police Sergeant Groombridge was in attendance and calmed things down. The girls that had gone on strike eventually agreed to attend school at Grove Green.

Winifred Harris (née Guest), Ella Cardwell (née Foster), Norah Giles and Nell Hodson (née Byam), are four Old Scholars that remember Bearsted School in the first two decades of the Twentieth century. Winifred and Ella particularly recalled the reorganisation of the two schools. Their memories give a good picture of Bearsted School at this time. After the schools were combined, both Winifred and Norah transferred from Thurnham to Bearsted for a short time, before leaving when they were fourteen. Winifred recalled that the two schools had many things in common and so there was not a huge difference in moving down to Bearsted School: both schools used the same desks which faced the teacher at the front. Even the children considered these old-fashioned as the seat was fixed to the desk! The seat was a wooden bench and accommodated six children and was probably similar to the design illustrated in a previous chapter. There were inkwells at intervals at the front which held ceramic inkpots for use by the older children.

Ella attended Thurnham School barely a year after the re-organisation and then moved on to Bearsted in 1929, before leaving when she was fourteen in 1936 to work on the family farm. She recalled that there were many items surreptitiously thrown in class. When a pen-nib fractured (either deliberately or by accident) the boys sometimes threw them at each other. This was especially effective if the nibs still had some ink upon them. Some of the boys also tried to distract the girls with long plaited hair that sat in front of them, so that they could gently push the end of a plait into an ink well. When the girl subsequently turned her head, the ink-soaked plait would come out of the well and land on her clothes. It was not a popular activity with parents!

Winifred recalled that the younger children used slates and had special slate pencils to write upon them. The pencils occasionally squeaked on the slate. If a child misbehaved, the punishment was to stand in a corner of the room with twelve slates balanced on his or her head. Unless the child was very quiet and still, the slates quickly came tumbling down and made the most awful noise!

Winifred usually wore a white pinafore trimmed with frills although she had several pinafores that were trimmed with broderie anglaise. Underneath the pinafore was a dress with a straight skirt. She wore boots that were either laced or fastened with many small buttons. In the winter, the school stove would be surrounded by woollen scarves, gloves and hats all drying out on the fire-guard. The air in the school room would be rather damp as the clothes gently steamed.

Nell was taught by three teachers at the school: Miss Clayton, Mrs Dibble and Mr Goodman, although there were some other women teachers who were employed as temporary staff. Nearly all of the women teachers seemed rather distant to Nell and did not particularly relate to the children. Miss Clayton did not always use the bell to mark the start and finish of the school day. Instead, she used a 'clicker' which was made out of wood and shaped like the handle of a skipping rope to clap the children in and out of the school gate. It made a clicking or 'clacking' sound.

Both Ella and Winifred were taught by Mr Goodman and Mrs Dibble. Frank Goodman lived in the village and even when out of school hours, expected to see his pupils behaving properly. He seemed to be even stricter than Miss Beck, the Mistress at Thurnham, and always insisted on the correct form of address: *Sir*. Ella still wonders whether Mr Goodman ever knew that his strictness earned him the quiet nickname of 'Cosh' from the children as he swished the cane threateningly about in front of them!

As a result of this discipline, there was never any unseemly rush to the door at night. The children came out of school in single file and said 'Good Night, Sir' before leaving. However, Ella recalled that the real threat of physical punishment actually came from the vicar, as he was given to throwing the wooden-backed blackboard rubber at anyone who dared to talk during one of his visits to the school.

Mr Goodman was very keen on mental arithmetic. Winifred recalled that he constantly gave his class sums which they had to remember as they were not allowed to write them down. He then expected the children to give the answer straightaway. George Groombridge sat behind Winifred and used to whisper the answer to her until Frank Goodman saw what was going on and moved the desks a little further apart. Nell also recalled that she used to dread the weekday when *The Teacher's World* was delivered to the school. This publication carried mental arithmetic questions on the inside back page. Mr Goodman used to spread these out before him on his desk and use the questions immediately!

Mrs Dibble lived at a house called Mount Pleasant in Ware Street and taught at the school for some years. Physically, she was very small and slight but this belied her energetic teaching! She taught Winifred and Norah sewing whilst the boys had practical lessons with Mr Goodman in gardening or woodwork. Sewing lessons also included darning, patching, and 'how to turn a man's shirt collar' in addition to knitting and crochet. Norah's knitting lessons started with knitting a baby's vest which she only just finished before she left! Sewing was rather more interesting for Norah and she made a nightdress with a square neck and a scalloped hem. She drew round a halfpenny to achieve the scalloped hem. Mrs Dibble tried to equip the girls with 'all the skills that a girl should know about'. However, this did not include laundry or cookery as it was assumed that a girl would learn about these from her mother.

Winifred also had Drill lessons which involved sets of proper physical exercises including bending the knees and stretching arms rhythmically. In one activity, the pupils had to fold their arms behind their backs and stand very straight for what seemed a long time. The exercises had to be performed simultaneously by all the class. Drill was usually conducted at the back of the school by the railway line or on The Green if the weather permitted.

Ella and her friends played many games in and out of school. The main school playground was The Green. The small area at the back of the school was really used just for netball and hop-scotch games. All the children liked to play with whips and tops, hoops, and skipping. The type of skipping depended upon the number of children who wanted to participate. If there were not enough children to turn both ends of the rope, one end was tied to a fence. There was also 'double skipping' which involved two ropes being twirled at the same time and needed a certain amount of physical co-ordination to be successful.

Nell recalled that many of the village children had hoops and tops that were played with on the way to school and during playtime. Tops were conical pieces of wood with a metal pin in the pointed end. Designs were drawn upon them using coloured chalk. A piece of string attached to a wooden stick was wrapped around the body of the top and then quickly pulled away to set the top spinning.

The boys used straight pieces of metal which were locally called 'guiders' to steer the hoops which were also made of metal. On a good day, with very little traffic about, it was possible to bowl a hoop right down The Street to the school. Nell always envied children who had hoops and tops as she did not possess either — her father said that the road outside their house, Crismill Lane, was far too bumpy for them to be of much use!

Jean Jones (née Hodges) was also very keen on skipping. Rhymes were chanted whilst the rope was twirled. Jean particularly remembered the rhyme shown below. There were spaces for names in the verse which were filled in appropriately:

> All the girls of Lancashire
> Shall lead a happy life
> Especially (*Jean Hodges*)
> And she needs a boy
>
> A boy she shall have
> A-courting she will go
> Along with (*Kenneth Jones*)
> Because she loves him so
>
> She kisses him, she cuddles him
> She sits upon his knee
> She says, 'Dear (*Kenneth*),
> Do you love me?'
>
> 'I love you -
> And you love me'
> Next Sunday morning
> The Wedding will be.

Ella recalled that some enterprising children also used their leisure time to go for walks on the golf course in order to look for lost golf balls. If any were found, the children were hopeful of selling the balls back to the club steward for a penny each. Sometimes the balls were too heavily scored with the impact of the golf club. The rejects were cut open as the elastic was useful for catapults made from a twiggy branch. Some of the catapults were taken to school in a pocket, but only for use after school; they were never used during the day.

It was quite usual for the children to go tree-climbing and look at the bird's nests but they knew never to touch the eggs inside. Playing with conkers was also a favourite seasonal pursuit. On a hot summer's day though, a real treat for Ella was a 'Picnic for One' under a special, very shady oak tree. The picnic food was some sugar sprinkled onto a bread-and-butter sandwich, accompanied by an old Camp Coffee bottle that was full of water.

A distinct feature of everyday life in Bearsted beyond the school at this time was a quietness that is hard to imagine today. Amongst the few sounds to intrude into the schoolroom were those of hooves as cows were walked along The Street for milking twice a day. There was also the noise of the hammer and anvil from the forge by The Green and the rumble of the iron-shod horses and cart-wheels as they regularly passed by the school. Shopping from Maidstone was delivered by carrier, normally by Mr Hickmott with a tilting cart and very patient horse. Later on, Mr Bolton ran a carrier service using his van which bore the name 'Trojan' on the front radiator. Most groceries were either collected from the shops personally or delivered by one of the assistants using a bicycle with an enormous wicker basket on the front. The quietness of the village made the school bell, the wire for which was housed in Mrs Dibble's room at the front of the school near a large map, seem even more resonant. The children rang the bell at the start of the school day, the beginning of the afternoon lessons and at playtime.

The undated photograph shown opposite shows the Green and looks towards the school and Chestnut Place on the right hand side. On the left hand side are part of the *White Horse* premises. Some of the details in the photograph indicate that it taken in the first two decades of the Twentieth century as the shops at Chestnut Place were reduced to one-storey when they were rebuilt following the fire in 1900. Note also the cart-wheels propped up by the forge in the right hand foreground and the cows being driven across the Green! The photograph gives a flavour of everyday life in the village which did not greatly alter for many years.

(Photograph courtesy of Brenda Donn)

In 1927 there was a sad loss for the school and the modification of the curriculum. Early in February, Frank Goodman recorded that it appeared that the school garden plot had been sold for building purposes. A week later, his suspicions were confirmed by Mr Wright, the Horticultural Superintendent. Practical lessons continued in the garden attached to the school.

1927 also saw a new idea in education: lessons broadcast over the wireless. Bearsted was amongst the first junior schools to participate in the lessons which had been developed from an idea by John Reith and funded by the Carnegie Trustees in 1924. Following a successful evaluation and published report, the lessons had been specifically tailored to age ranges for the children.[12]

A typical lesson schedule from the log book in November:

Wireless Lessons

Mondays	*Music*	Division I
Tuesdays	*Children in History*	Division II
Wednesdays	*Language Lessons*	Division I
Thursdays	*Out of Doors*	Division I and II
Fridays	*History of Geography*	Division I
	Before Reading and Writing	Division I

Norah Giles recalled Frank Goodman was not pleased with her dismayed reaction to the wireless lessons when she realised that the lessons were to be on history and poetry. They were amongst her least favourite subjects and in order to listen to the broadcasts the children had to give up some of their playtime. The presenter, Rhoda Power, made her best efforts in the broadcasts, but Norah still loathed poetry!

One wireless lesson on history was particularly memorable: Frank Goodman had promised his class that the broadcast would be about Queen Mary Tudor and her marriage with Philip of Spain. On the day, a relay was set up by Mr Harry Elliott, who was the village expert on electrical items and wirelesses, so that Mrs Dibble's class should also hear the lesson. After much excited anticipation, severe interference rendered the lesson virtually inaudible although a word or two did come through. The radio lesson was abandoned and ordinary history lessons were resumed on the topic of the Great Armada instead! Despite the problems, these lessons proved tremendously popular and in 1929 were used to supplement the Empire Day commemoration.

This photograph was taken in 1928 and shows Mrs Dibble's class:

(Photograph courtesy of Norah Giles)

Norah recalled these names for the children pictured:

Top row	--- Edmed, Rachel Leggat, Kath Playfoot, Eileen Blandford, Eva Boorman, Dorothy Frost, Willy Apps, Reggie Guest, Arthur Croucher
Next row	Steve Cox, Fred Pilbeam, --- Boorman, --- Moorcraft, Frank Hammond, John Feakins, --- Boorman, Fred Martin, Harry Fisher, Mrs Dibble
Next row	Winnie Gravel, Norah Pettipiere, Nellie Giles, Nellie Earl, Doris Cook, Lily Cooper, Peggy Foreman
Front row	Jack Shorter, Stan Forward, Cecil Raggett, Tommy Bolton, Bernie Hurst, Bob Leggat

In 1930 Frank Goodman retired after twenty-five years of service as Master. During his tenure he had seen many changes both in education and the wider world. He had carefully shepherded the school through the difficult and disrupting years of the First World War into the calmer waters of peace time and left it in good shape for his successor, Mr John Sarjeant, who was appointed under the new title of 'Headmaster'.

John Sarjeant commenced his appointment on 6 October 1930 when the school returned from the hop-picking holidays. His tenure of office marked the continuing expansion in the curriculum, educational thought and practice. In January 1931 it was recorded in the log book that the Headmaster had started 'a Milk Club' but it is not clear whether a small fee was charged. Other schools charged a halfpenny a bottle. On the first day, thirty-two children whose parents had expressed an interest in the scheme each received a third of a pint of milk during the morning playtime.

The next year, another report was published which included a recommendation that children should be organised according to their abilities.[13] There is no evidence in the log books to suggest that this recommendation was followed at Bearsted, possibly because an extra thirty-two children had been admitted from outlying areas of Thurnham and Detling. There were 118 children to be taught by just three teachers. John Sarjeant dryly commented in the log book that the seating accommodation seemed rather strained.

Children from outlying areas were carried to school by a daily bus service. It was judged that it was impossible for them to return home for their midday meal, so new arrangements were made to provide hot food for them at lunch time. Initially, this took the form of a hot drink of 'chocolate milk' once a gas meter and cooker had been installed. The installation of these items was achieved following grants made by the Diocesan Education Society and the National Society of £15 and £10 respectively in March 1935.[14] The children paid a halfpenny for the hot drink which was separate to the Milk Club scheme. It is not known where the children ate their lunch but is possible that part of the School House premises was used. Later on, it was noted that the provision of the meals was regarded as a very modern facility for a village school and that 'a committee' had been made responsible for them[15] but there are no further details in the records.

Following the removal of several large trees in 1933, the garden area in front of School House began to be properly cultivated by the boys. A new shed was erected to store the tools separately from the cleaning equipment. Seeds were supplied by the Kent Education Committee and a regular supply of manure was secured locally. Despite various periods of bad weather, storm damage and even raids on the lettuces by ducks during one weekend, it was deemed a success and the lessons were of great interest. The arrival of the shed had been accompanied by the erection of a cycle shelter and this encouraged many children to start cycling to school.

In 1934 the following note was made in the log book:

<u>6 August 1934</u>
Bank Holiday. School Closed. A number of the Children gave a display of Country Dancing on the Green in the afternoon (Annual Fair).

Evidently, country dancing had been introduced to the curriculum prior to this but the precise date is not recorded in the log book. An early photograph of children performing a country dance in the village is shown below. Although the photograph is dated 1933 on the reverse, it was taken at this performance:

(Photograph courtesy of Barbara Foster)

1935 marked the Silver Jubilee of King George V. The village celebrations for the Jubilee are described in another chapter. However, in July, there was a distribution of school prizes at a large house a short distance away. As the log book noted:

31 July 1935
Prize Distribution held in Garden of *The Mount* Mrs Griffiths presented the prizes. The children performed two plays and a Maypole Dance in the presence of many parents.

This is the first time that the log book records that a Maypole Dance was performed. It is interesting, given that Maypole Dancing was to become a regular feature of celebrations and an activity of the school, that there is no mention of the acquisition or the donation of a Maypole in the school records. Many Old Scholars have indicated that it was probably purchased by the next Headmaster, Robert Skinner, so it is possible that a Maypole was borrowed for the display at *The Mount*.[16] The following year the prizes were distributed in the garden of another large house in the village, *Snowfield,* by the invitation of Mrs Lichfield-Speer who became a patron to the school. It was the start of a connection to her family and regular events that were held in the grounds of the house.

This photograph shows part of a folk dancing display held at in the grounds of the *Snowfield* estate in 1936. There are no details about this apart from this note in the log book:

30 July 1936
Prizes provided by the managers were distributed this afternoon in *Snowfield* garden by kind invitation of Mrs Lichfield-Speer.

(Photograph courtesy of Sue Whittaker)

Around this time, the older children started to attend performances of Shakespeare plays that were performed at Maidstone Grammar School. For several years such productions as *A Midsummer Night's Dream* and *Romeo and Juliet* were enjoyed. All of these changes and activities were welcomed by the inspector who visited in 1935 and later commented in the annual report:

> This is in many ways an attractive school building and the recent decorations have given it a pleasant atmosphere of brightness and cleanliness, but the sanitary arrangements are still the open-trough system, the playground needs to be levelled and surfaced and the approach to the playground to be made less rough....

However, the school buildings were now too full. There were difficulties in achieving some space for the regular inspections by the Medical Officer and the School Dentist. These were usually held in the Main Room but now took much longer due to the number of children to be inspected. A temporary arrangement of transferring the inspections to the Women's Institute Hall was disliked as the late arrivals and departures caused even more disruption. The Education Committee deliberated about the matter and decided that children from the outlying Detling and Thurnham were to be re-located and dispersed to Detling and Maidstone schools. The roll was now reduced to 102 children but Physical Training lessons still had to be provided in the Women's Institute. Arrangements were made to use the hall for an hour every week on Monday and Wednesdays. This arrangement was to continue up to the outbreak of the Second World War.

In February 1937 there was a success for the school as a team of Senior Girls entered a Folk Dance Festival held at the Corn Exchange in Maidstone. They were delighted to win a Banner. However, the joy of this success was severely tempered by the sudden and unexpected death of Mr Sarjeant. It is evident from the log book that the staff were shocked at his loss but were determined to keep the school running normally as a tribute to their late colleague. The school was closed for the day after his death and also on the day of his funeral as a mark of respect. Mr Robert Clerk, a temporary appointment from outside the village, was immediately installed until the appointment of Mr Robert Skinner, who initially took up office as Acting Headmaster on 27 September 1937. His appointment was later confirmed to be permanent although there is no record of this in the log book.

The arrival of Robert Skinner marked a new spirit within the school. He had many ideas to develop the school activities and quick to spot potential that would benefit the children. Although he looked fairly stern, there was a rich vein of humour bubbling underneath which some of the children appreciated. Vera Banner (née Croucher) recalled that Mr Skinner seemed so different from Mr Sarjeant: very good-looking and unmarried.

The real novelty to the children was that Mr Skinner never shouted, instead he firmly reasoned. There were many occasions when Vera was unable to find something in her desk. Robert Skinner's response was to walk over, lift out the entire contents of her desk and place the heap on the floor so that she could locate the item! Jean Jones remembered one incident in the early days of Robert Skinner's appointment which greatly amused her class. Robert Skinner had asked a boy to dust the top of a cupboard. The school clock was mounted just above the back of the cupboard and so the hands of the clock could be very easily adjusted. All the children went home rather early that day...

New subjects such as sport and art were introduced. Music was taught with a wonderful enthusiasm recalled by many Old Scholars. The *National Song Book* which had been used in school was replaced with the *Oxford Community Singing Book*. Unison singing became a regular part of lessons. The children learnt the national anthems for nearly every country in Europe, together with many folk songs and sea shanties. Robert Skinner also adopted *Forty Years On!* as the Bearsted School Song.

Doris Britcher (née Bentley) and Violet Hale remembered that there was no formal, prescribed, school uniform. Robert Skinner cajoled the Education Committee into supplying some navy material. He then sold this on to parents at a slightly reduced price of around a shilling a yard. Gym slips were made for the girls by the parents from the material. The dresses were worn with red sashes. Jean Jones recalled that there she had a navy shield-shaped badge on the front of her gymslip. It bore the red embroidered initials of B S, which of course, stood for Bearsted School, in a monogram. Berets bearing this badge were also worn by some of the girls. The photograph overleaf shows four girls wearing the gym slips. Note the girl on the right-hand side is wearing a gym slip with the monogrammed shield upon it.

(Photograph courtesy of Roseacre School)

A games uniform was also devised using the navy material to make rather full knickers and shorts for the children. Together with white shirts, the children could now adopt a rather more formal team identity when taking part in tournaments with other schools. Mr Skinner insisted that this attire should be worn when either a school or team photograph was taken. In this photograph these girls are part of the 1938 netball team:

(Photograph courtesy of Violet Hale)

Regular sports fixtures were arranged and football and cricket teams were assembled. The success of the teams was always celebrated. As a result there was serious competition to win a team place. Regular home and away matches followed and Robert Skinner pioneered the use of the sports matches to impress upon the children that they were ambassadors for the school. Graham Walkling recalled that as a reward for winning a football match, 2-0, against the school at which Robert Skinner had previously taught, the team was taken to the cinema to see the Laurel and Hardy film *Way Out West* at the Granada cinema in Maidstone. The teams were transported to fixtures in Robert Skinner's car. Mr Harry Elliott, who lived locally, also lent his car if it was needed. A formal school Sports day was also introduced and held on The Green.

At some unrecorded point, the idea of organising the children in competitive houses had been discussed in detail by the Managers. During a village social event on 27 October 1937, Mr Whitehead, who was interested in the work of the school, promised the gift of a House Cup. The gift led to the development of the School Houses. Initially the two houses were named Clive and Wolfe but as Robert Skinner wrote in the *Centenary Magazine*:

> The school was arranged into Houses or teams in order to introduce a little refreshing competition into the school work and games. There are captains in every class, those in the top class being the senior captains, upon whom the work largely falls. Each House also has its committees, so that the children receive early training in the correct running of committees and clubs. They make mistakes, but one object of the House system is to give them the opportunity of making mistakes now when the results are not so inconvenient so that later on they may already have had the benefit of the experience that this alone can give. The Houses take their names after two families which have been of some importance in Bearsted years ago: the Berties and the Fludds. The spirit between the Houses is excellent, neither taking the combats between them so seriously as to breed any current of ill-feeling while endeavouring to bring their House out on top if at all possible.[17]

The first formal mention of the School Houses in the log book was made on Armistice Day when the children had attended the service at the War Memorial and laid a wreath as usual:

The school went up and back in Houses...

Later on, a House Points Board was made to accompany the Whitehead Cup. This handsome silver trophy was awarded to the House with the most points at the end of the year.

From the details given in the *Centenary Magazine* the Houses were organised along these lines:

Bertie (Boys)	Leaders: Committee:	Bill Pollard, John Coales, Vincent Widdowson Dennis Swift (Captain) Stanley Bentley (Vice Captain) D Grant (Secretary)
Bertie (Girls)	Leader: Committee:	Evelyn Smith Milly Baker (Captain) Molly Vane (Vice-Captain) Margaret Naylor (Secretary)
Fludd (Boys)	Leader: Committee:	Eddie Keay Maurice James (Captain) Percy White (Vice Captain) E Wingrove (Secretary)
Fludd (Girls)	Leaders: Committee:	Mary Watcham, Margaret Weller Greta Jarrett (Captain) Lily Croucher (Vice-captain) Brenda Hulks (Secretary)

The autumn term of 1937 ended on a high note with the establishment of Robert Skinner as Headmaster. However, the next seven years, 1938 to 1945, would hone the mettle and spirit of the school through his inspired leadership. As the storm clouds of the Second World War began to slowly gather on the adult horizon, it was these qualities that were to stand the school in good stead in the dark days that were to come. In the meantime, a start needed to be made on some of the long-term preparations for the Centenary.

Chapter 9
The Sweet and Bitter Years: 1938 - 1946
Centenary and War-Time

After his first few months as Headmaster, Robert Skinner was keen to introduce practical elements into part of the curriculum. Margaret Tomalin particularly remembered that one morning the science lesson was going to be on 'Sight and the Optic Nerve'. She was then asked by Robert Skinner to go on an errand to Mr Moss, the butcher, as there was an order to be collected. The order turned out to be twenty sheeps' eyes lying on a tray that stared back at her on the return journey! The children then dissected the eyes with horribly-sharp knives and the resulting diagrams were drawn in their science books.

Margaret remembered that Mr Skinner was very fond of Spelling Bees. Margaret and a friend looked up some difficult words to see if Mr Skinner could spell them. They were very impressed when he spelled Ecclesiasticus but had no idea if it was correct! Art lessons now included making pictures with lino cuts and carving blocks of salt into sculptures. Lessons on the quality of various metals were also memorable. One of these included tipping out a small amount of mercury kept in a stone bottle. She wrote down her observations on the behaviour of the metal as it ran into the dust on the desk. Today, these practical science lessons would not be conducted along quite the same lines!

In addition to the science lessons, there were now other good reasons to appreciate school. The Education Committee had arranged for some of the older boys to travel to Harrietsham School once a week. This was to take advantage of woodwork lessons with Mr Jeeves, who was in charge of the workshop there. The boys were supposed to walk up to the Bearsted turning on the Ashford Road and catch the bus to Harrietsham. Graham Walkling clearly recalled that they were all given the 4d bus fare, but sometimes, the boys used to walk through to Leeds village instead. They had worked out that it only cost 2d to travel from Leeds to Harrietsham and so they could benefit from the extra 2d saved!

Mr Skinner was beginning to understand how the village functioned as a community. Some of the local activities seemed rather idiosyncratic though and a good example of this was remembered by Evelyn Fridd (née White). Many of the children, when returning from lunch on a certain day, used to bring back bundles of rags. These bundles were handed over to a rag-and-bone man who was strategically placed on the corner of the Green opposite the school. The rags were exchanged for a goldfish, which was most carefully carried into school to avoid the water slopping over the side of the glass jam-jar. Upon occasion, there was quite a row of jam-jars in the cloakroom awaiting attention at the end of the day.

Another favourite lunch time activity for the children involved visiting Rowland's Bakery. The bakery sold bread in two-pound 'standard loaves'. Rowland Fairbrass recalled that at lunch-time some of the children used to buy half a loaf from the bakery. The staff used to oblige by cutting the large loaves in half with a big bread knife. The half loaf of bread was then taken across to the Green and eaten very quickly. Rowland did not know whether the children were actually allowed to do this or if the headmaster had turned a discretionary 'blind eye'!

From the records, 1938 was relatively quiet for the school. The junior and senior girls teams entered the County Folk Dance competition at the Corn Exchange in Maidstone, and were awarded certificates. One of these is pictured opposite.

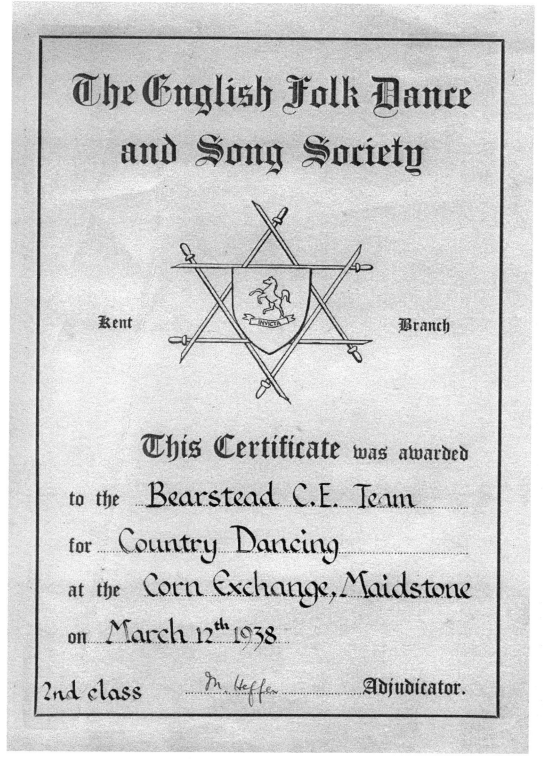

(Reproduced by permission of Roseacre School)

New activities included the formation of a 'Travel Club', which was intended to widen the children's horizons and experience. The children voted for suitable venues for a visit, which would take place on a Saturday. Each child was given a card to record a weekly payment that ranged from 3d to 6d, until approximately half the cost of a child's fare was recorded. The rest of the fare would be paid either from school funds or by Mr Skinner himself. Amongst the first places to be visited were Folkestone, Dover Castle, and the cathedrals at Canterbury and Rochester.

This is a photograph of an early Travel Club visit to Folkestone:

(Photograph courtesy of Sue Whittaker)

Robert Skinner encouraged many people to give short talks to the children on a variety of subjects. Lieutenant Litchfield-Speers accompanied his talk with a film of the Mediterranean. It was shown in the newly-devised 'Lantern Room', the classroom at the back of the school that now had curtains fitted to block out the light. This development had been the result of a successful fund-raising concert given by the newly-formed 'Friends of the School Association'. There were also generous donations from the Monckton family towards the cost of the lantern and silver screen.

Following a talk to the school by Mr Clements about Finland, a link developed with the Legation for Finland. Invitations were issued to both the school Folk Dance team and a team of Finnish students to participate in a display at *Snowfield* to celebrate the August Bank Holiday.

(Photograph courtesy of Doris Britcher)

The previous photograph shows the special costume worn by the girls which they had made in class under Mrs Lattin's careful tuition. The Magyar-shaped sleeves of the dresses were particularly memorable for Evelyn Fridd. The older girls made green tunics and white organdie blouses whilst the younger girls made print dresses.

Among the children in this photograph of maypole dancing are T White, Doris Bentley, B Croucher, Colin Palmer, P Hewitt, P White, T Hallett, M Smith, R Baker, B Green, B Hopwood and V Palmer.

(Photograph courtesy of Doris Britcher)

In October a school prize-giving took place at the Women's Institute Hall. It was to become an annual event. There were speeches from the Chairman of the Managers, the Director of Education for Kent and a report from Mr Skinner about the school. The prizes were presented by the Lord Bishop of Dover. The Bishop gave the children four wooden shields for the School Houses made from a plank of oak from a discarded pew previously in Holy Cross church, Bearsted. This undated photograph of the prize-giving appeared in the *Kent Messenger* newspaper and includes the Bishop of Dover, Josie Simmons and Mr Skinner:

(Photograph courtesy of the Kent Messenger group)

There are two versions of a school Christmas card which was designed and photographed by Robert Skinner in 1938. The first showed a group of children playing in the snow on the Green. The second, pictured here, shows the House Committees. Sue Whittaker (née Millie Baker) identified the children pictured:

(left to right) Molly Vane, John Coales, Millie Baker, Eddie Keay and Lily Croucher

(Photograph courtesy of Sue Whittaker)

The start of 1939, when Britain would once again go to war, also heralded the start of the Centenary year. There are various hints in the log book throughout the previous year that all was not well in the wider world. On 29 March 1938 the headmaster was called away to attend a course on Air Raids run by the Observer Corps. As the international situation hardened to a crisis, and the government worked frantically to preserve peace, the Kent Education Committee was considering arrangements for schools in the event of war. There was a note on this subject made in the log book:

26 September 1938
Preparations are in hand to close the school if deemed necessary, owing to the National Crisis.

Given the subsequent events, this consideration was well-timed. Two days after this, there is a further note in the log book that the children seemed very nervous and pre-occupied with the international situation. The Munich Crisis was resolved and it seemed as if Hitler's hand, for the time being anyway, was stayed. In the meantime, the vision of the school was almost determinedly fixed upon the Centenary celebrations.

It had been decided that although the school would try to celebrate the anniversary throughout the academic year, the main body of the celebrations would be held during the week 11-17 June. The date of the celebration was arbitrary. The log book recorded details of the Centenary week arrangements:

Sunday June 11
3pm: Thanksgiving Service in Bearsted Church, attended by the Bishop of Dover.

Monday June 12
Open day at the school from 1.30pm onwards
The building will be kept open until 9pm so that visitors may see for themselves what needs attention.

Tuesday June 13
7.45pm: Meeting of the *Friends of the School* at *Bell House*, by permission of Mr and Mrs Lance Monckton.

Wednesday June 14
5.30pm: Sports Day on the Green.

Thursday June 15
5pm: Cricket v. Headcorn and Rounders v. Headcorn.
8pm: Old Scholars Meeting at the School.

Friday June 16
Afternoon rehearsal and picnic for the Folk Dancers.

Saturday June 17
3pm: Folk Dance display at *Snowfield* by kind permission of Mrs Lichfield-Speer.

Mr Skinner had spent some time previously researching some of the school's history. He was able to invite two very special senior Old Scholars to the celebrations: Mr Wilkinson, and Mrs Walkling. Mr Wilkinson attended the school in 1861 and had been a School Manager for over forty years. Mrs Walkling attended the school in 1886 but she was able to trace her connections back to when the school first opened as her mother was Grace Golding. Grace had walked from Scragged Oak at Detling every day to attend!

Mr Skinner also published a small booklet about the history of the school. There were short contributions from the Bishop of Dover and the Chairman of the Kent Education Committee. It was called the *Centenary Magazine* and cost 6d. It is a remarkable document, written as the storm clouds of World War II were looming, the contents bear some poignancy. From the Editor's Introduction:

As Centenary Week was approaching, I began, in an idle moment, to glance through three books... From those faded old pages peeped children of years ago, doing the things that children have always done and always will do. They caught my eye, smiled roguishly at some of the entries in the school records, and passed on. There took shape a place of different customs and of different ways, and yet so very much of the same beautiful village which is as dear to our own children now as it was to them. Above all emerged the personalities of those who worked, often against heart-breaking difficulties and in the face of bitter disappointments, to do their share in moulding this world into a better place for those who came after. They worked with flesh and blood as others have worked in bricks and mortar...

The *Centenary Magazine* is a largely accurate rendition of the first hundred years and remains one of the main historical sources for the school. The magazine's forty pages provide a valuable 'snap-shot' of the life at the school and Bearsted in the immediate pre-war period. The beige cover, pictured below, has a simple typical 1930s design and carries advertisements on the inside pages including one for a company based at *Danefield* in Bearsted that supplied fur gloves and another for Datson's bakery.

The front cover of the *Centenary Magazine:*

(*Reproduced courtesy of Violet Hale*)

This is the service sheet from the Thanksgiving Service celebrated at Holy Cross church:

Bearsted School Centenary Week.

1839   June 11th to 17th, 1939.   **1939**

Thanksgiving Service

Holy Cross Church, Sunday, June 11th, at 3 p m.

ORDER OF SERVICE.

The Divine Praises :

> Blessed be God ;
> Blessed be the Name of Jesus ;
> Blessed be Jesus Christ, true God and true Man ;
> Blessed be the Name of Mary, Virgin and Mother ;
> Blessed be God in His Angels and His Saints.
> Blessed be God.

Hymn 470 : "Praise my Soul, the King of Heaven"

Lesson : Ecclesiasticus xliv. verses 1-15

The Creed

The Lord's Prayer (*School Setting*)

Prayers and Thanksgiving

Hymn 533 : "Now thank we all our God"

Address by The Lord Bishop of Dover

Hymn 545 : "Thy hand O God has guided"
  (During the singing of this Hymn, a Collection will be taken
            for the School Funds).

Blessing.

G. A. M. GRIFFITHS
Vicar.

(Reproduced courtesy of Sheila Foster)

A transcript from the *Kent Messenger,* 17 June 1939:

BEARSTED SCHOOL CELEBRATES 100TH BIRTHDAY

Many Changes Recalled In Centenary Week

Senior scholars to come to Maidstone

This week Bearsted School is celebrating its centenary. The school was built in the year 1839. The actual deed (which has been on view in the school during this week) says:

> 'The school is to be used for the education of such poor children residing in or belonging to the several parishes of Detling, Thurnham, Boxley and Bearsted, some or one of them as aforesaid in the principles of the Christian religion'

The first Master was John Peirce: the school consisted of one room into which 69 boys and 72 girls were packed. In 1856 a school was opened at Detling and Mr Peirce left Bearsted to take charge of it; he was the first, and only schoolmaster at Detling, as all his successors have been women.

THEN BOXLEY SCHOOL OPENED

Samuel John Taylor succeeded Mr Peirce at Bearsted. In 1864 a school was opened at Boxley and the children of that parish left Bearsted. Richard Seton Johnson followed Mr Taylor in 1870 and the first Mistress, Miss Love Jones, came in 1872. In that year a school was built at Thurnham and those children left for their own school. Miss Elizabeth Vincent was Mistress in 1874, Mr E R Barnacle Master in 1879, Mr William Smith in 1881 and in 1883, (the year of the railway line coming through Bearsted, which took half of the school playing ground) Mr John Day was Master and there are many living in Bearsted today who affectionately refer to him as 'Johnny' Day. He was followed by another Mistress, Miss Agnes Barclay in 1897.

DAMAGED BY FIRE

Many residents recall the fire which destroyed Mr John Perrin's shop in 1900 causing considerable damage to the school.
Mr J C Cripps was Master for only six months in 1905 and he was followed by Mr F C Goodman who is still living in Bearsted, and remained Master until 1930. The late Mr John H Sarjeant served the school for the next seven years and in 1937 Mr Robert Skinner (the present Headmaster) took charge of the school and it is from him the idea of a Centenary Week emanated.

IMPORTANT CHANGES

The celebrations opened with a Thanksgiving Service in Bearsted Church on Sunday, at which the Bishop of Dover gave an address to a crowded congregation. There has also been an open day at the school, an exhibition of Finnish Craft, a meeting in the studio of Bell House to elect officers for the Friends of the School Association.

At this meeting Mr W H Whitehead spoke of the changes expected to take place in the school in September when the senior scholars will be transferred to East Borough Central School in Maidstone, and Bearsted School will be for juniors only.

Mr Whitehead also spoke of the enormous amount of work Robert Skinner has done for the school and scholars. A lantern lecture and talk on Young Farmers' Clubs in Schools by Mr Voysey, of the Kent Education Committee staff, proved interesting and a splendid film of the scholars and staff of the school, taken by Mrs Lance Monckton, was shown by her.

PRESENTATIONS

The two senior old scholars, Mr C Wilkinson and Mrs W Walkling were presented with autographed photos of the present scholars.
Mr C Wilkinson, who carries on a business of builder and undertaker at Mote Hall Villas, Bearsted, is not the oldest boy, first attending Bearsted School in 1861, but he has been a Manager of the school for over 40 years. After being presented with a framed photo of the scholars of today, Mr Wilkinson said he had vivid recollections of the old school and he must tell the children present that the conditions today were much better than in his school days. He hoped they appreciated what has been done for them by their Headmaster and teachers.
Mrs Walkling, who lives at West View Villas, Bearsted, first attended the school in 1886 at the age of five and previously attended an infants school in Smarts Cottages. She has revisited the school this week and noticed many improvements compared with her school days. Mrs Walkling is a daughter of Grace Golding who was one of the first scholars a hundred years ago and walked daily from Scragged Oak at the top of Detling Hill to Bearsted. Mrs Walkling was also presented with a framed photo.
Addressing a large congregation at a thanksgiving service in Holy Cross Church, Bearsted, on Sunday, to commemorate the Centenary Year of Bearsted Day School, the Bishop of Dover said the church-people of Bearsted built the school because they thought it was their duty to educate the children and teach them what God had done for them and what they could do for God.
Centenary week includes School Sports on the village green and a Folk Dance Display at '*Snowfield*' on Saturday afternoon.

This photograph, of the whole school was taken in the grounds of *Bell House* by kind permission of Mr and Mrs Monckton. The numbers for the dates came from a cricket scoreboard.

(Photograph courtesy of Jean Jones)

The following scholars and teachers signed the original of this photograph when it was presented to Mr C Wilkinson, Senior Old Scholar, by Bearsted School children in the following order, as a souvenir of the Centenary:

B Vane, B Hulks, M Naylor, V Pearce, E White, J Simmonds, L Brown, P Noble, V Pollard, T Baker, D Brown, S Curtis, A Waller, E Wingrove, D Grant, L Fox, A Cole, G White, F Datson, E Beer, A Nobb, G Cannon, P White, A Humphrey, G Walkling, B Croucher, T White, C Palmer, E Seagar, P Hewitt, F Hallett, B Savage, D Green, G Williams, B White, C Panting, B Pollard, M Craig, D Baker, E Rumble, D Green, J Drake, Pearl Fairbrass, C Beer, D Finnis, Ken Sayer, M Hynds, P Redman, P Godfrey, G Keay, H Whiting, E Groves, R Yuill, R Fox, R Tree, S Attwood, P Hayman, T Martin, G Stripple, R Goble, R Longstaff, A Sayer, G Attwood, B Baker, P Town, V Atkinson, F Carman, I Datson, J Carr, A Humphrey, J Waters, D Bentley, M Smith, B Hopwood, Milly Baker, Greta Jarrett, Lilian Croucher, M G Ling, Molly Vane, R Skinner, S Bentley, M James, E W Horsman, D Swift, P White.

Naturally, full details of the week were recorded in the log book. A copy of these entries can be found in Appendix Four. The crowning touch to the school celebrations was the news received on June 26, that Marion Smith had won a scholarship to Maidstone Grammar School for Girls.

Once the Centenary celebrations were over, for the children there was a sense of anti-climax. For the adults, there was little to concentrate upon other than the possibility of war. It was recorded in the log book:

> <u>10 July 1939</u>
> The children are extremely tired this morning, probably due to the Air Raid precautions during the weekend. Two of them had been used as casualties at midnight.

Pat Grimes (née Robbins) remembered visiting Mr Johnson at *Bearsted House* to collect her gas mask, as a supply had been delivered there. This was a few days after the air raid exercise. Further supplies of gas masks were also distributed at the school to some of the children. Despite the growing menace of war, normal life continued with some staff attending a course in teaching English in London before the summer holidays commenced.

As war looked imminent, the government produced a report which gave guidelines for evacuation arrangements. The Board of Education, after consultation with the Air Ministry, had issued advice on air raid precautions for schools in April 1939. Education authorities were urged to make every effort to secure additional accommodation through hiring such premises as village halls and churches so that there was enough space for evacuated children and schools to ensure full-time schooling would be possible. However, it was recognised that a system of double-shifts would often be necessary. To retain the individuality of the visiting school, it was decided that the evacuated children should be taught by the teachers that would accompany them but close collaboration with the host school was to be pursued.[1]

Following the declaration of war on 3 September, the village received some evacuees from Plumstead. The evacuees arrived at Maidstone by rail and were then taken in a charabanc to the Red Cross centre at *Bearsted House* so that the accommodation officer could sort out the local billeting arrangements. Some of the evacuees later travelled around the village in an open truck prior to their distribution. Jessie Page (née Brook) took this photograph of their arrival:

(Photograph courtesy of Jessie Page)

Unfortunately confusion and a lack of information at the main railway stations led to many problems with the evacuation. Matters which were not helped by the senior billeting officers arbitrarily dividing many family groups and schools.[2] As a result of this, Bearsted received many more families than could be accommodated. The school was allocated the children and teachers from Purrett Road School, Plumstead. Initially, Bearsted also received the children and staff from another school from the High Street, Plumstead, but they were sent on to other localities. As the Autumn Term commenced Mr Skinner noted:

> <u>19 September 1939</u>
> School re-commences today.
> War has broken out with Germany, and Purrett Road School, Plumstead are billeted in the village.

At the start of the war, the Purrett Road School numbered 90 children with nine supervising staff whereas Bearsted School stood at 130 children with three members of staff. It is hardly surprising that Mr Skinner felt that Bearsted had the disadvantage of the situation. The regulations stated that no more than 60 children could be in one place at the same time. Mr Skinner particularly commented in the log book that in regard to this regulation, his staff felt that the complaints of the Purrett Road staff were unjustified. Only two teachers from the Purrett Road School are specifically named in the log book: Mr Tonkin and Mr Fyfe.

Although the arrangements for accommodating Purrett Road School varied throughout the war years, it was initially decided the available space would have to be shared on an alternate basis. This meant that in order to teach the children in premises other than the main buildings of the school, there was a constant traffic of staff, children and resources taking place in The Street and Ware Street.

The extra accommodation included using part of the Memorial Hall and the Men's Institute. A scheme to use a garden room on the lawn of *Snowfield* donated for use by Mrs Litchfield-Speers had to be abandoned due to the cold weather. The schedule for the accommodation was noted in the log book:

> Memorial Hall to be used for general activities.
> A large room at the Men's Institute to be used for Craft Work.
> A small room at the Men's Institute to be used for a new 4th class for Bearsted School.

The new fourth class was devised for Bearsted School as the roll totalled 125 children. By this time the Board of Education had realised that the new scheme of converting all-age village schools into Junior Schools would have to be abandoned due to the wartime conditions. In order to deliver effective teaching, the existing all-age schools now had extra classes instead.

It took some time for the children from Plumstead to settle down to life in the village. Many children were taken back to London by their parents during the period of the "Phoney War" when it was realised that there was no immediate danger. For the children that remained, much of what seemed quite ordinary to the village children was a source of wonder and amazement. The spectacle of cows being walked through the village twice a day to be milked was constantly commented upon!

Another good example of differing cultures followed the heavy snowfall in January 1940. The Plumstead children regarded the snow as a novelty. A boisterous game of snowballing resulted in the following log book entry:

> <u>18 January 1940</u>
> The London boys have continually run onto the school gardens and the ground has been trampled down terribly. Today it happened to snow and the London children just ran wild. They ran all over the rockery and the rest of the garden and have done a lot of damage. Mr Tonkin has promised to keep them off three times, but it has had little effect and so today we were forced to erect a fence around the garden to keep them off.

Eventually the evacuated children came to realise that what seemed extraordinary was really quite normal outside London.

There were only two incidences of trouble with the London children during their stay in Bearsted. In March 1940, several boys from both London and Bearsted had been apprehended whilst interfering with a cigarette machine. Robert Skinner attended the Juvenile Court to assist in a probation order which resolved the matter. In May it was recorded in the log book that the school roof had been damaged by some of the evacuees but there are no further details.

To help both schools acclimatise to life in war-time some rules were drawn up for air-raids:

> The following definite instructions for the air raid warning have been received from Maidstone and are approved by police.
>
> 1. No children to leave the building they are in at the time of warning.
> 2. All children to be removed as far from glass as possible.
> 3. Should parents come for children they take them on their own responsibility.
>
> This holds good until and unless further instructions are issued.

Some of the problems of sharing accommodation under the regimes of wartime were briefly forgotten in the excitement of a visit from the Archbishop of Canterbury, Cosmo Lang. The Archbishop presented the House Trophies and the Whitehead Cup to the winners. Several Old Scholars particularly remembered how special it felt to be individually blessed by an archbishop! He gave the school a present of a motto board. It was unveiled on 24 May by the four youngest house captains:

Courtesy, Fidelity & Courage to endure.

These were brave words to inspire the morale of the children in the difficult days to come as the British Army were evacuated from Dunkirk. Robert Skinner noted the next week:

31 May 1940
This has been a ghastly week…. The British Expeditionary Force seemed trapped in Flanders and everyone expected the whole half million to be cut to pieces. The children have been on edge all week and very difficult to deal with.

Other signs of the hostilities were becoming evident: the school windows now had fine-gauge wire netting placed over them to prevent splinters from bomb bursts in the locality injuring the children. The windows at the Memorial Hall were personally painted by Mr Skinner for the same reason and buckets of sand readied. Following his appointment as Head Observer of Bearsted Observer Post 22, it is evident that he was quite determined to defend the school in every eventuality. From the log book:

19 June 1940
The news seems rather depressing, on account of the complete collapse of the French Army. This country is now left alone with a great part of the world against it - a position not entirely new to us or in our history.

The need for some sort of protection for the children was early recognised in the war as there were obvious targets near the village that could attract enemy attention. There was an airfield at Detling, Maidstone was deemed a closed military town, and the very proximity of the railway to the school buildings caused grave concern. Jean Jones (née Hodges) confirmed that many people in the village were concerned about the fact that a train engine had to be fully stoked in order for it to climb the gradient, before arriving at the railway station. It was always possible that the German pilots could spot the red glow of the engine fire and use it as a target, as a railway line always led to somewhere.

This theory was proved for the Hodges family one night, when a bomb embedded itself in the far side of the railway embankment before detonating. It was less than thirty yards from her family's house in Ware Street. Fortunately, there was no damage caused other than to the embankment and the metal rails which had twisted and buckled. Robert Skinner had been on Observer duty that night. Ella Cardwell confirmed that the Observer post had been situated on part of Mr Bradley's land, (it is now part of Hillbrow on the Landway estate), which was quite high up and so a good view encompassing part of the railway line and bridge was therefore obtained. Robert Skinner was very relieved to see Jean walking in to school the next morning.

Some Old Scholars have mentioned that there was cause for concern much closer to home for the headmaster. One of the Bearsted school staff had a German father and was known to have pro-German sympathies. There were many rumours about the teacher in the village, including the knowledge that a close friend was a member of the Nazi party. Matters were not helped by the teacher's class forming a link with a school in Germany. As Doris Britcher quite clearly recalled, the whole activity seemed rather odd at the time. The children were given some ideas to put into their letters about the usual leisure activities for young people in the village but they were to give some geographical facts about the area too. This information included details that there was a railway line nearby, the proximity of an airfield and the distances to Canterbury and Maidstone. Some replies were received from the German school but Doris was sufficiently worried about the matter to destroy her correspondence when war was declared.

Whatever the truth of the situation, Robert Skinner was evidently aware of the difficulty. The official records of the matter are some very brief notes in the log book about separate meetings for the teacher and himself with the Director of Education at Springfield. This is followed ten days later by a fairly cryptic note in the log book, dated 1 July 1940, that the member of staff had left rather suddenly. Fortunately, another teacher, although coming straight from college, was able to fill the vacancy immediately. Many Old Scholars have expressed the view that the abrupt departure was caused by compulsory internment.

Early in August 1940 there was a heavy air raid on Detling airfield. Fortunately, as it took place in the summer holiday, the school was closed and the buildings were unscathed but it showed that the proximity of the airfield could render the school vulnerable. As Doris Britcher recalled:

> We had decided to have a family picnic on the Green that day. We played lots of games and had spread a blanket on the grass. We had just started to eat our sandwiches when a terrific roaring sound approached from the direction of the church (it certainly didn't sound like Spitfires or Lancaster air planes) came over the Green and straight over our heads just as the Air Raid siren sounded. It was unusual for an attack to take place on a cloudy day as we had heard that the German pilots preferred to see the ground that they intended to bomb. Somehow the planes had avoided the radar system: the air was black with them. We later estimated that there must have been around forty planes. We were terrified and threw everything into the baby's pram whilst we tried to think where we could shelter as there did not seem to be anyone else around. Almost miraculously, Mrs Pellet appeared at the front door of her house, which was near the Men's Institute, and frantically beckoned us to come in. We stayed at her house for hours whilst the raid took place at the airfield. The sound of the raid carried straight over the hills from Detling and we could hear it so clearly.

Later enemy action involving aircraft in the vicinity of the village included the crash landing of a Messerschmitt 109 and another aeroplane crashing near to Bearsted Golf Course.[3]

The majority of the traffic that regularly passed through the village comprised army vehicles as sections of the army were posted nearby in Mote Park, although no-one officially knew anything about it. However, this did not stop Rowland Fairbrass and his friends visiting them. They regularly asked the American soldiers that were stationed there later on, 'Got any gum, chum?' as they were known to be very generous with their rations, as were the New Zealand soldiers that were also temporarily billeted nearby. Some of the children were even taken for rides on the pontoons that had been constructed across the lake in Mote Park.

Naturally, the children had to be careful with the heavy army vehicles passing through the village. Margaret Peat (née Lang) recalled one occasion when she was asked to take a message from the Memorial Hall class back to the main buildings. On the way down to the school, she fell off Brenda Mercer's bicycle, just as an army lorry headed towards her. Fortunately, the driver was able to stop in time. It was a further reminder to the children about some of the dangers of wartime as they travelled around the village to the various venues for lessons.

As the war progressed, further adjustments had to be made to the timetables and accommodation used by the schools. Half-time teaching was introduced due to the perceived danger of air-raids but this was found to be disruptive and disliked by both staff and children. Margaret Peat recalled that some of the older children attended first aid courses held at the Red Cross Centre. The courses included treatment of cuts and bruises and fractures. The children used each other as models upon which to practise the many different types of bandaging. Evelyn Fridd recalled that she won a first aid kit in a big blue box when the children had a subsequent first aid test. Several Old Scholars have commented that they thought it likely by teaching some of the children these skills, in the event of a bomb falling on the school, Mr Skinner would then have been able to rely upon some of the children being able to administer basic first aid to each other.

For a time, the Mission Hut by Foster's farm and the Methodist Chapel which were both in Ware Street were used for teaching, after the rooms in the Men's Institute were deemed unsuitable by the Kent Education Committee inspectors. However, both of these venues presented different problems that needed to be remedied before use. Use of the Mission Hut would have to be shared with Thurnham School and Mr Skinner noted with concern that the flue for the stove in the Mission Room needed alteration. The Chapel classroom merely needed some additional coat pegs. There were no air raid shelters at either venue. Despite these drawbacks and his own misgivings, Mr Skinner had little choice but to abide by the directives issued by the Education Committee to use what resources were available.

This undated photograph of Ware Street was taken looking down the street towards the railway bridge. It clearly shows the Mission Hut on the left hand side of the road:

(Photograph courtesy of Michael Perring)

Miriam Stevens (née Gardner) recalled that it seemed appropriate that singing lessons were held at the Chapel but energetic classes like drama and country dancing were conducted in the Memorial Hall. In the playtimes between lessons the boys would chase the girls around the outside of the hall on the surrounding grass.

Whilst using these 'satellites' for teaching, the children were able to use the oast house also in Ware Street for an air raid shelter. At the main school buildings, air raid shelters (which included a decontamination unit for gas attacks) were finally installed in November 1940. Margaret Plowright (née White) recalled that the shelter always seemed to be very dark! Up until this time, the children and staff would dive for shelter under whatever protection was available. More often than not, it was a school desk. Robert Skinner recorded that whilst he was grateful the children would have some degree of protection, he would have preferred trenches. Children who lived in very close proximity to the school were still allowed to go home if the air-raid siren sounded.

Despite all the accommodation arrangements and disruption to the curriculum and normal running of the school, scholarships to the Maidstone Grammar and Technical Schools were still won by some of the children during the war.

There was enthusiastic participation in the end-of-term Christmas parties which usually included a fancy dress event. Robert Skinner recorded that considerable help was given by his staff to the children in order that the celebrations were successful and boosted everyone's morale. A puppet show devised and produced by the children was a considerable success. A transcript of the programme is shown below as the original was too fragile to reproduce:

```
                    Programme.
SNOWHITE   -  a Puppet Show.
Produced by the Juniors of Bearsted
School in aid of School Funds.

Narrator:-  Pamela Snell.

Puppets worked by:-

Herald:-              Alec Nourse.
The First Queen:-     Marjorie Green.
Snowhite:-            Margaret Baker.
Second Queen:-        Colyn Elswood.
Huntsman:-            Sidney Walters.
Grumpy:-              Marion Shepherd.
Doc:-                 Edith Horton.
Dopey:-              Eric Hulks.
Bashful:-            Brenda Baldwin.
Sleepy:-             Barnaby Holliday.
Sneezy:-            Henry Lavender.
Happy:-             Marion Shales.
Witch:-            Ann Coveney.
Prince:-          Maureen Monaghan.
       _____

All the Puppets have been entirely
made by the children.  Puppetry is
recognised generally as an excellent
Introduction to play production and
as a means of teaching stagecraft.
It is used for this purpose in the
Junior Classes of the School.

Production by Miss I. Hilton.
Music by Mrs M.G. Ling.
```

(Original courtesy of Margaret Tomalin)

Wherever possible, life in the village and school went on as normally as could be permitted under the circumstances. Several of the senior children participated in the annual beating-of-the-bounds ceremony that took place in the village. The photograph below shows people gathering in front of the school beforehand. Note that the foundation stone has been covered up, presumably as a precaution in the event of an invasion.

(Photograph courtesy of the Kent Messenger group)

The school participated in the War Effort launched by the government. Paper was salvaged despite the total amount available for stationery being reduced to less than half that normally used in peacetime.[4] Other fund raising for charities included the children collecting rose hips and conkers. These were then sold on to factories and the proceeds passed to Bearsted Red Cross. In 1942, £42 was raised in December through the sale of toys and dolls made and dressed by the children, at a Red Cross event at *Bearsted House*. This photograph of some of the children with their work before the sale was taken by the air raid shelter:

(Photograph courtesy of Roseacre School)

As part of the 'Dig for Victory' campaign, a piece of land adjacent to the back of the school and behind the parade of shops at Chestnut Place called 'The Spinney' was cultivated by the children. This was a generous donation of land from part of the *Snowfield* estate by Mrs Litchfield-Speers in 1942. Many of the village children already possessed gardening skills. They were also able to use their experiences from cultivating another piece of land in the village which had been previously provided by Mr Swain. The children had used this to grow potatoes and other vegetables. Margaret Peat recalled that it did not take Robert Skinner long to organise groups of children to undertake gardening and weeding duties. An old sink was donated and installed as a pond. In the spring, the children would watch and record the frog spawn developing into frogs as part of their nature studies. This photograph of some of the children by the Spinney was taken just after it had been cleared and planted.

(Photograph courtesy of Roseacre School)

The first harvest of potatoes from the new land in The Spinney totalled half a bushel. The crop raised 18 shillings in an auction following a horticultural show held at the Men's Institute.

Mrs Litchfield-Speers died the following year and Mr Skinner paid fulsome tribute to her in the log book:

6 April 1943
...in her passing the school has lost a very good friend, in the five years which I have been here she has been like a fairy godmother to these children...

The land was formally presented to the school in June 1943 by Mr Litchfield-Speers although there are no documents recording this acquisition in the Centre for Kentish Studies. Shortly afterwards, it was felt that the part of the land that steeply dropped down to Thurnham Lane was not safe for the children to use so it was fenced off. This fenced-off portion was named 'Dingley Dell' by some of the children. The rest of the package of land was extensively used until the re-location in 1972. Many children had reason to be grateful to Mr and Mrs Litchfield-Speers as their gift resulted in early memories of shady places under the trees to sit on sunny days.

The formal introduction of school meals took place during the war. By June 1940, the Ministry of Food had investigated the provision of food to children in wartime. The government was agreeable to the idea, providing it was part of a tightly-controlled national food policy. The school meals service was properly implemented in October 1941 after an agreement that the granting of free meals and milk would no longer need evidence of malnutrition, and would be assessed on financial need.[5]

In Bearsted, an informal facility for school meals had been provided from the time that the children from Detling had briefly attended the school. During wartime, the meals were cooked by ladies from the village at the Women's Institute[6] and were initially only offered to the evacuees so that they could have hot food at least once a day. As the war progressed, other groups within the village took advantage of this service.

These anonymous memories give an excellent picture of life at the school and in the village during the war: [7]

During the Second World War, I attended a little church school in the village of Bearsted. It only had three classrooms. In each was a tall black, coke burning stove. This was fine for the children sitting in the front of the class, but the ceiling and windows were high, and the back of the room was cold. There was an ink well in each desk, and when it was very cold the ink used to freeze. Each child was allowed a small bottle of milk a day, the cost being one halfpenny. I enjoyed it in the summer, but it was warmed by the stove in the winter, which was horrid.

We walked to school. I lived about three miles away and we always went, whatever the weather. Sometimes we skipped, if skipping was in, or maybe played hopscotch, or two-ball. When marbles were the rage we were often late. School started at 9am and finished at 4pm.

There wasn't room at the school to cook or eat school dinners. It had no kitchen or staff room. The cloakrooms had hand basins with only cold water, which we used for drinking, washing, mixing paint, and whatever water was needed for. The toilets were in the school yard. But we did have school dinners, and how good they were. They were cooked by the ladies of the Women's Institute. The WI Hall was a few yards away from the school. Their stew and jam tart and custard, were out of this world. It always impressed me to think that the president of the WI had cooked my dinner.

One of the dinner ladies used to rush around the village on her bike, making sure that we all attended Sunday school. This wasn't easy as the venue often changed due to air raids. On one of her trips a chicken ran in front of her bike. I am glad to say she wasn't hurt but we all enjoyed chicken casserole the next day.

At the beginning of the war many evacuees from London came to our village. The school was much too small to house them and us all together, so a plan was devised. We all had to have a timetable. This was written on the blackboard. Those capable copied it, plus an extra one for the children that couldn't manage it. Woe betide the children that lost their timetables, they lost house points.

It worked out that on some days we only attended for half a day. On another day our class would meet at the 'mission room'. This was just a large wooden hut in a field. It stood a little higher than the main village street. It was fitted out with desks, the idea being that we achieved some written work, but the windows were low and there was so much to see. The milk lady came by with her churns and ladles, which she swished in the milk to make sure the cream was well distributed for the housewife waiting with her jug. The baker's boy would ride by, with the bread piled in a basket on the front of his bike. None of it was wrapped, but if it rained hard he had a mackintosh cover to put over it. Sometimes we could see a horse being led to the forge so that the blacksmith could make a shoe. One day an army convoy came one way, as the farmer drove his cows the other way. Only the really dedicated finished their work that day.

Once a week our class went to the oast house. This was a round building with a rough brick wall. No desks here, just a circle of chairs. There we would learn our spellings or maybe have a general knowledge quiz. We would spend another half day in the Chapel rooms. This was a dreary place, with no outlook, no reason to daydream, and only the noise of the steam train to disturb us.

There were certain places that we had to pass, where it was imperative that we held our breath until well by. Any house where the occupant had TB was a great fear, and we didn't dare breathe any air nearby. The same applied to another very large house for unmarried mothers!

My favourite half day was taken, when we went to the King George Memorial Hall. It was large, bright, and the newest building that we used, with shiny red oilcloth curtains and a polished floor. Here we had singing, play reading or Physical Training. The girls wore navy blue knickers with a vest or blouse, the boys just took off their shirts, as they all wore short trousers, winter and summer, until they left school at 14.

We never minded walking to school as there were many routes that we could take, with lots to see and do. In the spring and summer we looked for wild flowers. Each week our teacher would list six for us and we gained a house point for each one we found. We nibbled the new leaves of the 'Bread and Cheese' tree (hawthorn), we sucked the nectar from the dead-nettle flower, and chewed the stem of the fresh tall grass. In the autumn conkers kept us busy for hours. We collected chestnuts, hazelnuts, cobnuts and walnuts. We would roast the chestnuts in the ashes of our open fire and enjoy them while we listened to the wireless in the evening.

In the winter we couldn't wait for the village pond to freeze over. It wasn't very big, but large enough to make a grand slide and deep enough to fill your wellingtons when the ice gave way.

We also passed the village laundry, which had an air raid siren on its roof. We would rush by and hope that it would not go off. The noise at close quarters was more frightening than the raid.

It has been estimated that much of the damage to schools in the war occurred in 1940 and 1941.[8] Mr Robbins, father of Pat Grimes, later wrote that he remembered reading an article about the amount of bombs that had fallen. He included the information that around 2,000 bombs were estimated to have been dropped within three miles of Bearsted. Despite the close proximity of Detling airfield and the earlier extensive air raids in August and September 1940 in the vicinity, the main school building was virtually undamaged. The Chapel classroom sustained some damage, though, in March 1943 when a stick of bombs dropped nearby. It was rendered unoccupiable for several days but normal classes were quickly resumed.

By 1944 Robert Skinner had organised several clubs that were appropriate for war time - a Rifle Club for both boys and girls which used the shooting range in the village and a 'Spotters' club through which the children learnt the shape and markings of enemy aircraft. Graham Walkling remembered that it was possible to divert the headmaster from mental arithmetic lessons quite satisfactorily by asking questions about aircraft markings!

In July 1944 the 'Spotters' club was particularly useful to the school during the period of flying bombs. Rowland Fairbrass recalled that several dependable boys were deployed to go onto the roof of the air-raid shelters. There were two chairs for them if they wanted to sit down. When a bomb was sighted heading towards the buildings, a whistle was blown. Several weeks after the start of the flying bomb offensive, a bomb was spotted flying toward the school accompanied by two Tempest fighters that were firing machine guns at it. The defensive action by the Tempests was to no avail but fortunately the bomb passed over. By this time Robert Skinner was able to record in the log book:

11 August 1944
Children are now getting used to the flying bombs and are not in the slightest nervous. They are splendid in school and we can depend absolutely upon the children keeping their heads.

On 8 May 1945, there came the long-awaited announcement of victory in Europe. There is a very brief note in the log book of this - to the effect that Victory in Europe was announced and that the school would be closed for two days to celebrate. Rowland Fairbrass remembered that there was at least one enormous bonfire assembled in Shirley Way that was lit as part of the village celebrations.

Almost immediately, life began to return to normal in the village. The air raid shelters were used for storage purposes and on 2 June the wire netting was taken off the school windows. A week later, the playing space at the back of the school was finally tarred: Robert Skinner wryly noted in the log book that it had taken 106 years! The Annual Sports Day for 1945 was eagerly anticipated and the special nature of the event that year was commemorated with souvenir certificates, as shown below:

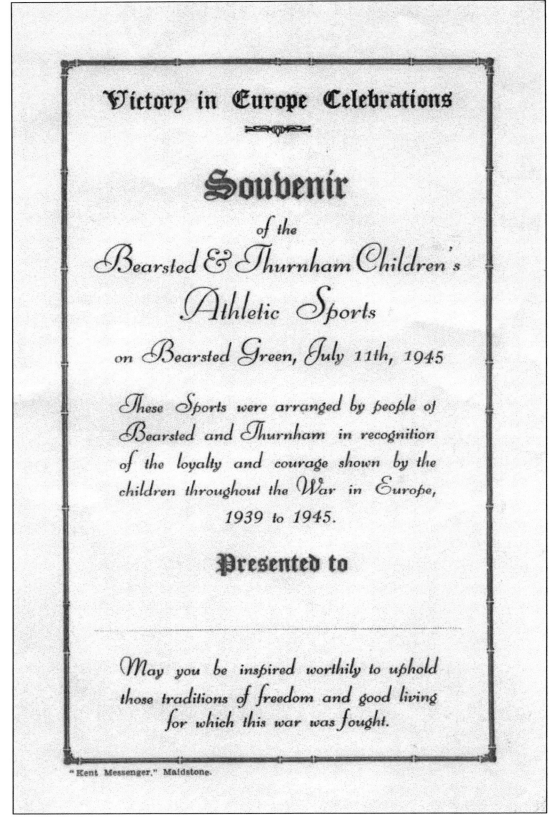

(Reproduced courtesy of Roseacre School)

Sports Day was also marked by the visit of Sergeant-Pilot John Coales. He was an Old Scholar and former School Captain in 1938-1939. He was in the Royal Air Force Volunteer Reserve, and was serving in the Middle East with 35 Squadron. He was a regular visitor to the school when he was on leave.

The happy visit of John to his old school was rather diminished the next day by news of Eddie Keay, another Old Scholar. Mrs Keay advised Robert Skinner she had received notification from the Red Cross that there was little hope for left for the safe return of her son, who had been posted as 'Missing' since November 1944.[9] Robert Skinner, as former headmaster and a friend to Eddie, wrote a tribute which was printed in Holy Cross church parish magazine. This is shown below. John Coales later died whilst on active service.[10] Both John and Eddie's names were included in the list of names on the sun-dial war memorial that was subsequently erected in 1949.

EDDIE KEAY - A TRIBUTE

Eddie Keay, one of the most popular of Bearsted school head boys and captains, is reported missing from an operational flight over enemy territory.

Eddie Keay was one of the finest and most likeable characters at Bearsted school, which he attended from 1933 to 1939. Always courteous and considerate, and as captain for two very successful pre-war years, he was an inspiration to the school and a great help to the staff. A terrific worker, and with a magnificent physique, at the age of 13, he led his sports teams to victory, and during those two years Bearsted School more than held its own with the schools in the district.

His school work was as outstanding as his physical activities. Always thorough and painstaking, he was quick to grasp new matters, and was one of the best scholars. It was no surprise to us who knew him that he was able to pass all his difficult Flight Engineer's examinations and pass into the Air Force a member of an air crew. Eddie never lost contact with us; on every leave he would visit the school to glance at the old groups in which he was such a prominent figure and to take his cheerful and confident smile through the rooms. His old fellow scholars will always remember that smile and the quiet confidence behind it.

The school prays that he may be returned to continue a life which is so full of promise. If that cannot be, we know that Eddie met whatever happened as he always met other things with a quiet calm - and without complaint.

R.S.

Now that peace had been won in Europe, the suspended plan to convert Bearsted into a junior school was re-considered. The roll looked as if it was set to rise to the alarming number of 170 children for 1946. This number of children was more than could ever be safely accommodated in the school buildings. It was decided by the Kent Education Committee that the seniors would be sent on to East Borough central school. From the log book:

24 August 1945
During the summer holiday it was decided to reorganise the school. We are all very sorry to lose the seniors, and to see broken up a school which has earned the regard of those who know it. It has been a really 'Happy family' and the Old Scholars would be a source of pride for any school.

The war had many effects upon both education and Bearsted School. The immediate post-war period was one of recovery, rebuilding, and change. New opportunities were about to emerge as the result of the 1944 Butler Education Act. How would the school meet the challenges of yet another changed world and social order? The immediate need was for Bearsted School to acclimatise to becoming a Junior School. Ahead would lie more change and further growth in and around the village of Bearsted.

Chapter 10
Chance, Change and Two Anniversaries
After the Second World War to 1959

The new method of transfer to secondary school took some time to establish. All children aged eleven and above took an examination to determine the secondary school that was appropriate for their intellectual needs. The examination took the form of a timed intelligence test. The children who did not sit the examination enjoyed a day's holiday. The majority of the older children from Bearsted that did not transfer to either the Technical or Grammar Schools in Maidstone went on to East Borough School.

There were several changes in the administration and status during the process of becoming a junior school. The official date for re-organisation was recorded as 1 October 1945. Shortly after this, the church authorities discussed the possibility of applying for 'controlled' status. This meant that the Church of England would finally relinquish financial responsibility for the building. Although the rules governing the delivery of religious education would also be loosened, the diocesan authorities were favourable to reducing their financial burden.

In September 1946, the vicar of Bearsted, the Rev Walter Yeandle together with the churchwardens, in their capacity as Trustees of the school, wrote to the Minister of Education, to express their approval of the Managers' application for 'controlled' status. It was formally approved on 14 November 1946.[1] Mr Skinner made a note in the log book that it was the first school in Kent to obtain the status. The name of the school was altered:

Bearsted Church of England School (Controlled)

As a result of the change in status, religious studies lessons had to be separately authorised by parents when their children were admitted to the school. The lessons were still subject to regular inspection by Canterbury Diocesan Education Committee. In 1947 Miss Daphne Clement was employed with this subject as her specialism. Shortly afterwards, her duties expanded to include much of the core curriculum delivered by the school and she became a much-loved member of staff. Many Old Scholars may remember that she was very small in stature and so consequently many children were actually taller than her but she did not tolerate any bad behaviour. She also had a habit of jumping up and down saying 'Goody, goody, gumdrops' to express pleasure! Daphne Clement is amongst the long-serving full time members of staff whose careers encompassed both Bearsted and Roseacre locations.

The winter of 1947 was severe but as the weather improved, efforts to encourage the process of a return to normal life in school continued. Just after the term ended in December, the school received some food parcels from a school in Canada. After consultation with the Managers, it was decided that they would be divided into seven smaller parcels and presented to mothers who had been widowed and foster mothers who had children at the school. There was a small ceremony of presentation held in order that the Canadian school would feel that their efforts had been appreciated but there is no record of this in the local press or in the log book.

The Travel Club, suspended for the duration of the war, re-commenced with a visit to Canterbury. Other activities were started including a stamp club and camera club. The members of the camera club developed their own photographs. Swimming classes for the children at the baths in Maidstone were reinstated. Sheila Foster (née Gould) recalled that the highlight of the week was actually after the swimming lesson. If the weather was fine, Mr Skinner allowed the children to climb up onto the roof of the air raid shelter and spread their swimming costumes and towels out to dry! The Parents Association was also revived and placed on a proper footing with an elected President and officers.

Despite these welcome diversions, the accommodation for the children remained cramped. The school was still using the separate buildings of the Chapel classroom and the Memorial Hall for lessons. A development plan had been agreed with the local education authority in 1947 which recognised the need for a new school building as the use of the separate buildings was deemed unsatisfactory. Mr Yeandle, concerned about the delays in the provision of adequate accommodation for the school, wrote to the Diocesan Director of Religious Education and the County Education Officer.[2] The reply indicated that no-one had any idea how long it would take to achieve a new building.

Mr Skinner approached the Managers with a plan to record Bearsted School's contribution to the war. They were most favourable to his ideas and with their consent, a flag pole and a sundial were erected at the front of the school. The pillar supporting the sundial was carved from Portland Stone and bore an inscription in the form of the following epitaph;

'When you go home, tell them of us and say,
for their tomorrow, we gave our today' [3]

and the names of the Old Scholars who had been killed in the war:

John William Coales	1946
John Alan Gilbert	1944
Edward Thomas Joseph Keay	1944
Edward Shorter	1940
Herbert Lionel White	1940

In July 1949, it was dedicated by the Bishop of Dover in a simple but appropriate service. A transcript of the service sheet is shown below as the original was too fragile to be reproduced:

A Prayer for the school

A Prayer of Thanks for the school founders and benefactors

A Prayer of General Thanksgiving

Psalm XXIII

The Dedication of the Sundial by the Rt. Rev, the Bishop of Dover

A Prayer for the Fallen

The Lord's Prayer

Hymn 128 from The Children's Hymn Book: *Land of our Birth,*

(words by Rudyard Kipling, Tune: Psalmodia Evangelica, 1790)

The National Anthem (verses 1-3)

(Illustration courtesy of Edith Coales)

The log book entry of the proceedings can be found in Appendix Five. The parish magazine recorded:

> On 27 July 1949, the sundial was dedicated by the Bishop of Dover, the Right Reverend A C W Rose. He was assisted by the vicar. Relatives, 120 present-day scholars, many parents and the churchwardens, Mr S Mendel and Mr E A Abery, were present. After prayers for the school, the founders and benefactors, the children chanted the 23rd psalm and then Michael Miller, Derek Rowland, Pamela Wheeler and Judith Merritt unveiled the memorial and it was dedicated by the Bishop.[4]

The children marked Armistice Day in 1949 by laying a wreath at the sundial and in 1958 a flagpole was erected by the sundial for raising and lowering the Union flag at appropriate moments throughout the school year. Since that unveiling ceremony in 1949, many further generations of children from the families of the Old Scholars named on the memorial have been educated at both Bearsted and Roseacre Schools.

The illustration below shows the format of school reports in 1948. Mr Skinner typed every report as he had no secretarial assistance!

KENT EDUCATION COMMITTEE.

BEARSTED C.E. PRIMARY SCHOOL.

Report on Pat Robbins

Form 4. House................ Attendance...... Good

Summer Term, 19 48

	Grade*	Remarks
Scripture ...	C	
English ...	A	94/100, 2nd in exams. Good results which follow a hard term's work.
Reading. ...	A	Very fluent reader and speaker.
History ...	D	44/100, 10th in exams.
Geography	B	72/100, 5th in exams.
Mathematics ...	B	77/100, 3rd in exams. Pat has worked very hard and her position in the class is a good result.
Science / Nature study.	B	76/100, 6th in exams.
Arts and Crafts ...	B	Embroidery good, uses machine well.

[P.T.O.]

	Grade*	Remarks
Physical Education	A	Always vitally interested, and good at games.
Dancing	A	
Handicrafts ...	A	
Domestic Science	A	Pat has shown great initiative at gardening, and has worked well.
Gardening...	A	

* A=Excellent. B=Good. C=Satisfactory. D=Weak. E=Unsatisfactory.

GENERAL (including out of class activities)

2nd in English and Arithmetic.
8th in oral subjects.
4th in all subjects.
Number in class:-26.

Pat has worked well, and has her reward in having passed the Grammar School entrance examination. All her work is at a good level, and I am expecting her to hold her own at the Grammar School and to do well. Pat is also one of the leaders where games and physical matters are concerned, and should be a useful "all rounder".

She has been an extremely helpful member of the class and a very cheerful one, and has been deservedly popular.

I was very pleased with the way in which Pat took her common entrance success. She did not let it go to her head, and this is a good sign for the future.

.... Form Master or Mistress.

.... Head Master or Mistress.

(Reproduced by permission of Pat Grimes (née Robbins)

In May 1949 there was an inspection that lasted two days. The report gives a picture of the school. A copy was made in the log book:

> Although since the last report the senior children have been transferred to the Maidstone, East Borough County Secondary School, the 119 Juniors on the Roll grouped in four classes are already too many for the present building and one class works in a Chapel Hall some distance from the school. The Village Hall is also used for Physical Training, Dancing, and Dramatics.
>
> The Headmaster who commenced duties in 1937 and his three full-time and one part-time qualified assistants, are to be congratulated on the happy atmosphere, good tone, and the spirit of industry which are noticeable throughout the school. The flower garden constructed out of the waste land at the rear of the building is a very commendable feature.
>
> Much of the work in the school, though stereotyped and formal in character, produces reasonable results in written English, Reading and Arithmetic. Good use is made of the County Mobile Library. Oral expression is less satisfactory, even with the present dramatic work, and some of the History and Geography is somewhat unrealistic. Little use is being made of the wealth of local history. Craftwork is very limited in range and while the girls of Class 4 and 3 have needlework, there is no provision for this in Class 1 and 2. Some of the Art in the school shows promise and there is some tuneful singing. There is a sensible approach to the Gardening undertaken by the boys in the Two Top Classes.
>
> Physical activities, which include Organised Games on the Village Green opposite the school, are thoroughly enjoyed and so is the instruction in swimming one morning a week at the Maidstone Baths. The sports equipment is well used both in the recreational periods and in the mid-day break.
>
> The school plays an active part in the life of the village. There is a Parents Association with a Committee which meets once a month and works in close co-operation with the school.
>
> No provision is made for mid-day meals.

(Reproduced by permission of Roseacre School)

This report showed that Bearsted School had not found it easy to adapt to becoming a Junior School. There were many other village schools in the same situation.

In 1950 the Headmaster began to lay plans to celebrate 110 years of the foundation. Mr Skinner wrote to the College of Arms. He enquired whether there was any possibility of the school using the coat of arms of the Rev Charles Cage, who had been one of the original trustees. He thought that the adoption of the heraldry would provide a good central point for the celebrations.

However, the anniversary plans had to be revised when the College indicated that they could not agree to the school using the Cage arms. There was also limited success for the rest of planned celebrations. An intended 'Festival Week' had to be abandoned through to staff shortages. A service of thanksgiving was still held at Holy Cross church, but the log book entries indicate the staff felt that the attendance of parents was rather poor. Overall, the impression gained by Robert Skinner was that of a decided lack of enthusiasm that was in direct contrast to the Centenary commemorations.

A few months after the anniversary, a technical report was submitted to the Kent County Council. This included an assessment of land at Roseacre which was under consideration as the site for the new school. The four and a half acre site, bordered by the residential areas of Roseacre Lane and Ware Street, was described as verging on the rural but generally suitable for development. The cost of acquiring the site was estimated to be around £695.

The conveyance of the land was agreed on 27 October 1950 between the Kent County Council and Mr F C Bradley. At a price of £640 the council acquired: [5]

ALL THAT piece or parcel of land situate on the North West side of Roseacre Lane in the parish of Thurnham in the County of Kent containing an area of four decimal four five acres or thereabouts which said land has hitherto formed part of the Vendor's property known as Roseacre Farm.

Although the land was now purchased, the question of how long it would take to build a new school for the children of Bearsted continued to concern many people. A brief outline of the early history of the Roseacre area can be found in Appendix Seven.

In contrast, 1951 was a year made brilliant by the Festival of Britain. The older children visited the Festival at the South Bank Exhibition Centre whilst the younger classes visited a zoo. Locally, the children were able to play underneath the new village sign, designed by Mr Warland, which had been erected by the parish council on the Green to commemorate the Festival.

Later, the school participated in a Pageant of Britain that was produced at *Snowfield* in celebration of the Festival of Britain. As it has not been possible to reproduce the original report, the following is a transcript from the *Kent Messenger*, 27 July 1951:

PAGEANT AT BEARSTED

Schoolchildren's fine performance

The children of Bearsted School presented a wonderful pageant of Britain in celebration of the Festival to more than 300 parents and friends in the gardens of *Snowfield* on Wednesday.

Commencing with the traditional maypole and country dancing, the pageant, which lasted more than two hours, covered incidents in English history from the sixth to the 16th centuries.

Gregory was depicted in the slave market in Rome and the incidents leading up to the visit of St. Augustine were well illustrated. King Alfred then appeared at the head of his Saxons and the scenes following showed his troubles with the Danes.

Henry II's quarrel with Archbishop Thomas Becket, the murder in the cathedral and subsequent enshrinement were effectively shown together with one of the miracles attributed to the Shrine.

Then followed Henry VIII, a proud father at the christening of his daughter Elizabeth who was later seen in several picturesque scenes.

Over 100 performers took part in magnificent costumes, many of which were made by parents and others at the school. The 16 scenes had obviously been well rehearsed

and presented most capably by the young children.

"FINE SHOW"

The Reverend W. H. Yeandle, Vicar of Bearsted, congratulated the youngsters on a splendid performance, and he introduced Colonel S. E. Thomas who presented the house shields and cups.

A vote of thanks was proposed by Mr R. Skinner, Headmaster, to Captain and Mrs Litchfield for the use of *Snowfield*, to the parents and all who had helped to produce the pageant.

Awards were: Fludd House for schoolwork, swimming and the Whitehead Cup for school tests; Bartie House for games, sports and competitions, and the swimming cup to J. Cavell.

Following concerns expressed in the 1949 Inspectors' report, permission was granted on 28 September 1950 for an additional temporary classroom known as a Rochester Hut. It took some time for the paperwork to wend through Whitehall, so it was not until 16 July 1951 that approval and strict instructions were finally given for work. It was not to exceed £1,780 and a requisite Timber Licence was allowed.[6]

The new classroom was to be erected at the back of the premises. Once the classroom was built it was intended to be used for Class 1, which was still receiving lessons in the Chapel classroom and the Memorial Hall. As a result of various delays, building work did not commence until the last week of the summer holiday. When the children returned in September for the Autumn term the playground was full of building materials. There were further problems with the erection of the building, too, as the wrong-roof trusses had been supplied. Work temporarily halted and heavy rain poured onto the floor of the hut one stormy night!

There is no record of when the Rochester Hut was finished and opened for use as a classroom as Robert Skinner was thoroughly distracted by a severe staff shortage caused by illness and a lack of supply teachers. After the hut had been constructed, Mr Skinner appropriated one of the two walk-in cupboards at the back for a small office. Previously, there was nowhere separate in the school buildings that he could use as an office area to tackle paperwork, use a typewriter and receive visitors to the school. Although the cupboard was quite generously-sized, once a desk, filing cabinet and bookcase were installed there was very little room for anything else.

The construction of the Rochester Hut inadvertently caused its own problems in later years as Vernon Finch, who succeeded Mr Skinner as Headmaster, wrote in an article about the school: [7]

> [the hut] ...was sited adjacent to the railway embankment...Being only a few yards from the track, every passing train registered its presence as it thundered by...many of the passing [steam] trains showered red hot cinders upon the heads of the younger generation of Bearsted. However, precautions had been taken and the hut roofing was in the form of asbestos sheeting. The hut was therefore protected against a rain of fire, but not against the asbestos itself.
>
> The weight of such a roof took its toll on our Assembly Hall for with the passing of a comparatively short period, the supporting walls began to take on a most fascinating elevation - all vertical lines to the eye taking on the appearance of the archer's bow! We had our own unique 'bulge'.
>
> Reinforcing 4 x 3 timbers were introduced to hold the walls and roof up, and these in turn rotted away under the flooring, and were then replaced by 4 x 4 timbers. But still the walls bulged ominously. Metal tie-bars were then fastened across the hut at about seven feet from floor level.
>
> ..A child jumping onto a vaulting horse in PE with the intention of jumping off again usually found him or herself unintentionally suspended in mid-air draped across one of the rods. Needless to say, strict instructions were given to prevent enthusiastic gymnasts from swinging from the tie-bars.

(Reproduced courtesy of Vernon Finch)

For children who adored watching trains, being able to do this whilst at school was very convenient! When the trains rumbled by, a certain amount of vibration was set up. Bruce Graham particularly remembered that *The Golden Arrow* train sped by at around 70 miles an hour on the way down to the station at Dover. On hot days in the summer there was even greater excitement for the children as sparks from the steam engines sometimes set fire to the dry long grass on the bank. On several occasions the fire spread to the hedges in the Spinney. Several Old Scholars remembered their friends excitedly shouting that the bank was on fire. It did not take long for Mr Skinner to quickly extinguish the flames with water and a hose pipe that was kept nearby.

The school was thoroughly involved with the Coronation celebrations of Queen Elizabeth II in 1953. The children were given the responsibility for supervising the village sports on the Green. The parish council gave the children china mugs as a souvenir. Some Old Scholars have recalled children from Miss Clement's class commemorating the Coronation by planting bundles of reed mace in the village pond on the Green. As there is no mention of this in the school records, it is not clear whether this was part of a lesson or a Brownie activity. Miss Clement ran a Brownie pack in the village for many years.

At Christmas a large bible for use in Assembly was presented by the Parents and Friends of the School as a Coronation gift. The staff gave an oak reading lectern for use with the bible. They were formally handed over by the Chairman of the Managers, Mr Monckton, to the House Captains: James Bartle, Simon Braidwood, Godfrey Collins, Sheila Collins and Nancy Shepherd. An undated press cutting from the *Kent Messenger* is shown overleaf.

This photograph was taken at the presentation:

(Photograph courtesy of the Kent Messenger group)

This is a transcript of the accompanying report from the *Kent Messenger*:

Coronation gift for school

Bible and lectern adds to Bearsted tradition

Another milestone in the 114 years' history of Bearsted School was reached on Monday. In the presence of Managers, parents and friends and the children, a Bible and lectern were handed to the school by Mr. L. R. Monckton, Chairman of the Managers, to commemorate the Coronation of Queen Elizabeth.

The Bible was the gift of parents and friends of the school, and the lectern, made by Mr. F. Bevis, was presented by members of the staff. Mr. R. Skinner, the Headmaster, said during recent years several gifts had been made to the school.

These included an Inter-house cup by Mr. and Mrs. W.H. Whitehead, four house shields by the Bishop of Dover and the school motto, 'Courtesy, Fidelity, Courage', by the late Archbishop Lang.

'We feel that these two new gifts form a fitting addition to those already made and that they will enrich the school tradition' said Mr. Skinner.

LUCKY CHILDREN

He had often heard it said that their children were lucky to live in Bearsted. One of the things in which they were lucky was in their parents and friends, and he believed they realised it to the full.

Whenever they, as a school, set out to do something or obtain something really worth while, they could always count upon the support and interest of a sufficient number of parents and friends to carry it through.

Another thing in which the children were lucky were the teachers whom he, as Headmaster had as colleagues on the staff.

Whenever they discussed matters concerning the school, the real interest of the children was always the deciding factor.

RECEIVED BY SCHOOL CAPTAINS

The Bible and lectern were received from Mr. Monckton on behalf of the school by Simon Braidwood, Geoffrey Collins, James Bartle, Nancy Shepherd and Sheila Collins, the school captains.

A passage from the Scriptures was read by Frances Old.

Making the presentation, Mr. Monckton said to the children:' You will always find a bit in the Bible or in an old hymn that sticks, and it is the things that stick in your mind that will help you later on. They will provide something for you to fall back on when you are in a jam.'

The Bible and lectern were dedicated by the Vicar the Rev. J.S. Long.

Among those present were Mr. W. Moore (assistant county education officer) and Mr. A. W. Peacock (divisional education officer).

Although the school was closed over the three days designated for the Coronation, and the sports day was washed out by rain in a typically British fashion, there was a very successful carnival procession. The school won a small shield for first place in the Topical Section and a small bowl for one of the three best kept gardens in the village.

This is the Coronation Souvenir Programme printed for the Bearsted and Thurnham festivities:

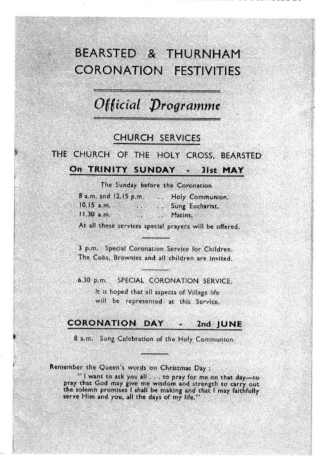

(Reproduced courtesy of Norah Giles)

On June 12, Mr Skinner and several other members of staff accompanied seventy-two children on a visit to London to see all the Coronation decorations. British Railways ran an express train and as a result of the speedy service, the children arrived at Charing Cross in time to see the Queen drive past to Guildhall in an open coach. In the afternoon they embarked upon a three-hour coach tour of the streets. They returned very tired, but happy to have participated in a very small way in a national event. Eileen Jakes (née Young) was a teacher at Bearsted during this time and recalled:

> In 1953, a week after the Coronation, a trip was arranged to see the London decorations. A special train from Folkestone picked us up at Bearsted station and took us to Charing Cross. I remember that we were responsible for ten children each. They were well drilled about safety and were extremely good. The crowds were enormous and quite terrifying. At one point we managed to climb to a stand near Admiralty Arch and there we saw the Queen and the Duke ride by in an open carriage on one of their state drives. Some of the children were disappointed that the Queen was not wearing her crown but wore an ordinary coat and hat!
>
> Getting back to Charing Cross was truly a nightmare and as a young teacher I was quite frightened. I instructed my ten children to hold hands in a line and I took the hand of the first child and pulled him through the dense crowds. I warned them not to let go or they would be lost. As I pulled, I continually looked behind and saw their little white faces coming along. All went well and we arrived safely on the station platform where Mr Skinner counted everyone on to the train.

Building work on further classrooms for the school began shortly after the festivities. Formal permission to acquire extra land in order to build classrooms was given on 29 August 1952 as the school roll had risen again.

Negotiations with various owners of land adjacent to the school resulted in a deed of conveyance dated 14 April 1953 between the Kent County Council and Jack and Dorothy Rowland to acquire 0.26 of an acre on which to erect another Rochester Hut for classrooms: [8]

> all the ground on the north side of Bearsted Green adjacent to the
> north eastern boundary of Bearsted Church of England Primary School.

By another odd quirk of history, the land had been owned around 1899 by the Tomsett family who had run the bakery by Bearsted Green and whose children had attended the school. Although barely finished in September when the school re-opened, the new classes were safely accommodated in proper classrooms parallel with the railway line.

Now the new classrooms had been built, the original hut could serve as both hall and canteen. A Canteen Service was started for those children who did not go home for lunch. Kay Claiborn (née Bruce), recalled that the meals were cooked at the Infants school. They were transported from Thurnham in big metal containers but either the journey or the containers did not improve the taste of the meals for some children! The first Christmas Party to be held in the hall was a thoroughly enjoyable event.

In September 1953, the headmaster was joined by another male member of staff: Mr Roland Tomalin. He recalled that Mr Skinner had many qualities that made him not only a natural teacher but also an excellent manager. Roland benefited from his headmaster's confidence in his abilities as a teacher and encouraged all his staff to develop their particular strengths to benefit the children. For Roland, this meant exploring art and drama with the children: the puppet theatre he designed and made was very popular with the children. He described the construction of the puppets as involving plasticine and papier mâché. Costumes for the puppets were sewn under Mrs Rayner's guidance. The first production was Hans Andersen's *The Little Mermaid*.

A photograph of Mr Tomalin's puppet theatre:

(Photograph courtesy of Roland Tomalin)

Roland also recalled that Mr Skinner would sometimes wear a rather battered brown coat (perhaps at one time it had been a laboratory coat), in order to carry out practical jobs around the school. If an important visitor arrived whilst Robert Skinner was still in this garb he would direct them to the front of the school. This was in order to give himself the time to restore his appearance. Many of the visitors never guessed the identity of the 'caretaker'!

In 1954 some of the surroundings of the school were laid out as garden plots by the side of the new class-rooms. The finishing touch was an ornamental iron gate made by Mr Thwaites of Bearsted Forge. The bill was paid with the proceeds from a Beetle Drive. These improvements were celebrated with an Open Day in July. There was an Arts and Craft exhibition, displays of Maypole and Folk Dancing, a Marionette show, and the new gardens could be inspected through tours given by the older children. The programme for the Open Day featured an attractive lino print of the main school building which was designed by Roland Tomalin and is shown below.

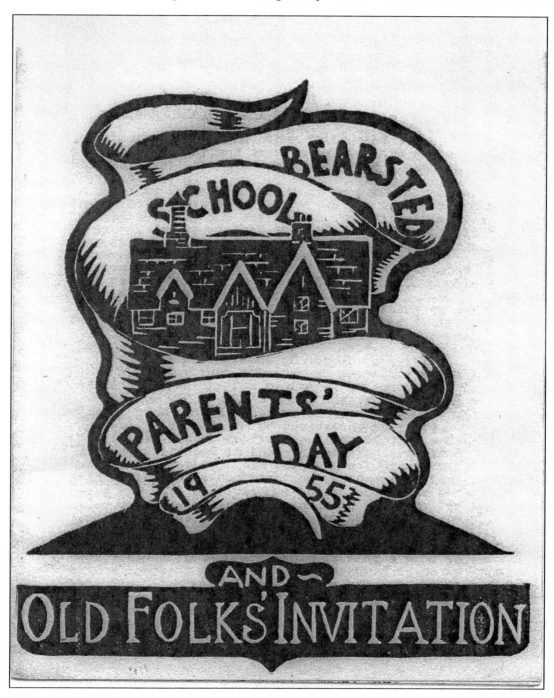

(Reproduced courtesy of Roland Tomalin)

Rosemary Pearce (née Hardy) recalled that the school staff always encouraged children to work on their own initiative, although at times this brought slight problems. On one occasion, she was encouraged to tidy the stock cupboard and help to check off a delivery from County supplies. The latter seemed rather more complicated than at first thought, as the loose paper came in ream packs. She was not sure whether to count every sheet in each pack!

This photograph of Maypole practice was taken in 1957 and shows many details of the buildings that Old Scholars may remember:

Old ties were renewed in June of 1958 when an Old Scholar, June Drake, contacted the school. She had previously emigrated to New Zealand. A flag of St George was sent to Eltham Primary School in New Zealand during the Folk Dance Festival at *Snowfield*. The small ceremony was observed by an officer from New Zealand House and the editor of the New Zealand Associated News service also attended. This photograph shows some of the children with the flags during the ceremony:

(Both photographs courtesy of Roseacre School)

Part of the official correspondence is shown below. For the purposes of this document, Bearsted was deemed as a sub-district of Eltham!

ELTHAM COUNTY COUNCIL

All Correspondence
must be addressed
to the Clerk

TELEPHONE X096
P. O. BOX 40

GREETINGS from the ELTHAM COUNTY COUNCIL, in the Province of Taranaki, NEW-ZEALAND.

The Eltham County Council desires to commemorate the occasion of the presentation by the Bearsted Public School, of a St. George's flag to the Eltham Public School.

The Presentation Ceremony was held at the Eltham Public School on St. George's Day 1959, and we have taken this opportunity of extending greetings from this County to the local authority having jurisdiction over the Eltham District in England.

Many pupils attending the Eltham Public School live in the Eltham County area and we are pleased on this occasion to be associated with the Eltham Borough Council and all local organisations in extending greetings.

COUNTY CHAIRMAN,

COUNTY CLERK.

(Reproduced courtesy of Roseacre School)

133

Attendance numbers began to rise again. In 1958, 172 children were confirmed for attendance in September. The Managers felt that the accommodation at the Memorial Hall would be needed once more for classrooms. They also approached Mr and Mrs Reatchlous who lived at Knowle Cottage to see if they would agree to sell some of their land which was next to the school. Although Mr and Mrs Reatchlous agreed to this by December 1959, the protracted nature of the negotiations took the Divisional Education Office until 1961 to complete.

Meanwhile, the 120th anniversary of the foundation was commemorated by a week of celebrations. The events took place in the summer as Robert Skinner felt that the weather should be more suitable for the activities planned. From the front of the anniversary programme:

Church of England

Primary School

Bearsted.

Service of Commemoration and Thanksgiving

1839   –   1959

In the Church of the Holy Cross

Bearsted.

The Address will be given by

The Lord Bishop of Dover

The Right Reverend Lewis E. Meredith.

Wednesday, July 1st· 1959.

10.a.m.

(Reproduced courtesy of Roseacre School)

This notice shows the details of the anniversary events and concerts. Full details of the anniversary events can be found in Appendix Six.

BEARSTED SCHOOL

120th ANNIVERSARY WEEK CONCERTS, 1959.

Tuesday, July 7th at 6.30 p.m.

Wednesday, July 8th at 7.30 p.m.

PROGRAMME

GOD SAVE THE QUEEN.

1.	POEMS.	CLASS 1.
2.	POCAHONTAS.	CLASS 5B.
	Una Broadbent.	
3.	THE ELVES AND THE SHOEMAKER.	CLASS 1.
	Linda Chesterman.	
4.	THE THREE WISHES.	CLASS 3.
5.	THE MASQUE OF THE SHOE.	CLASSES 4, 5B, 5A.
	Thomas F. Dunhill.	

INTERVAL

6.	THE PIED PIPER (Adapted)	CLASS 4.
7.	PERCUSSION BAND.	CLASS 2.
	Tunes From A Toyshop.	
	Eccossaises by Beethoven.	
8.	ONCE IN SPRINGTIME.	CLASS 5A.
	Winifride Trentham.	

PRICE 3d.

(Reproduced courtesy of Roseacre School)

135

A commemorative certificate was also given to the children. A copy is shown below:

BEARSTED SCHOOL
120th ANNIVERSARY CELEBRATIONS
1st July to 8th July, 1959

FOUNDERS DAY—WEDNESDAY, 1st JULY

10 a.m.	Commemoration Service in Bearsted Church. Address by the Bishop of Dover.
* 2.10 p.m.	Unveiling of commemorative plaque in the school by Sir William Rolfe Nottidge.
* 2.30 p.m.	Presentation of Inter-House trophies in the Women's Institute Hall by Sir William Rolfe Nottidge, who will also present, on behalf of the donors—
	(a) Books for the Wayth Library.
	(b) The school's " 120th birthday present."
2.30 p.m. to 8.30 p.m.	The school and gardens will be open to visitors. All are welcome. Children's art and craft work, club activities, etc. Exhibition from New Zealand House. Teas in the Spinney at reasonable prices.

* Admission to these two events is by ticket only, owing to limitations of space

SENIOR OLD SCHOLARS' DAY—THURSDAY, 2nd JULY

A visit to the school, followed by a coach trip to Hastings, for Old Scholars who were in the school in 1899 or before.

22nd ANNUAL SPORTS ON THE GREEN—FRIDAY, 3rd JULY, 2.30 p.m.

SCHOOL CONCERTS IN THE WOMEN'S INSTITUTE
Admission by ticket

TUESDAY, 7th JULY at 6.30 p.m.
Children 1/- — Adults 1/6

WEDNESDAY, 8th JULY at 7.30 p.m.
Numbered and reserved 2/6 — Reserved, not numbered 1/6

All donations and proceeds from the week's activities will be given to the "120th birthday present," which will be devoted to developing the school's visual aids. Donations gratefully received and acknowledged

This is to certify that..was a pupil in the school at the time of the 120th Anniversary Week, and took part in the activities.

....(Headmaster)

(Reproduced courtesy of Roseacre School)

During the week, some Old Scholars who had attended sixty years previously (in 1899 or before) were invited to visit. It is interesting to note that nearly every Old Scholar that visited during the week was recorded as still resident in the village. There was a special outing arranged for them on 2 July 1959 which included a visit to Hastings and tea at Sedlescombe.

This is the commemorative photograph taken by Mr Skinner. It was used as the official Christmas card for the school in 1959:

(Reproduced courtesy of Roseacre School)

The inside of the card gave the following details:

Included in this photograph:
Mrs L Ring, Mrs F A Taylor, Mr E J Smith, Mrs E Smith, Mr B Walkling Mr B Watkins, Mr H W A Datson, Mrs E W Hickmott, Mr F Baker, Mr F Pollard, Mr T Walkling, Mr Frank Smith, Mr A J Watcham, Mrs W Watcham, Mr A Watkins, Mrs Pettig

Also invited but unable to attend were:
Miss Freda Brown, Mrs Fuller, Mrs E J Smith, Mrs Baker and Miss Margetts

From the log book and press cuttings, it is apparent that many of the prizes and cups presented during this week were awarded for the first time. Several were donated to commemorate the 120th anniversary although the official records do not make this clear. Monies raised from the week's anniversary events and concerts enabled the purchase of a Sound Projector.

There was very little press coverage as Mr Skinner recorded in the log book:

7 July 1959
The week meant much hard work, but everything went very well indeed. Unfortunately the printers came out on strike at the same time and so there is very little record of it all in the local press.

The following transcript is from a local newspaper but is un-named and undated:

School's 120th Anniversary Celebrations

'It has always been a typical village school. Situated in a wonderful place in a wonderful county, it inspired at the beginning the characteristics and kindliness and friendliness that have spread outside to the inhabitants of Bearsted,' said Sir William Rolfe Nottidge.

He was speaking on Wednesday at Bearsted when the C.E. Primary School commemorated its 120th anniversary and was starting a week of celebrations.

Sir William unveiled a commemorative plaque at the school and later in the Women's Institute Hall he presented inter-house trophies to pupils and, on behalf of the donors, books for the Wayth Library together with a cheque for over £50, the school's 120th birthday present, to which will be added all donations, and proceeds from the week's activities.

Concluding he said: 'I think you are very lucky to be at Bearsted School under Mr Skinner, a great Headmaster. He has retained all his old enthusiasm and fire, which have made your school a live one.'

Bearsted School had witnessed many changes in the twenty years since the Centenary celebrations in 1939. The school had now adapted to become a junior school but an increasing number of children still had to be accommodated. Despite regular maintenance, some of the buildings were not in the best of condition to cope with the increasing pressure of numbers. Mr Skinner felt that the best solution to these problems would be a new school building on a fresh site which had been promised since 1948. However the construction of a new school building was still many years into the future.

Chapter 11
New Opportunities: 1960 - 1972

Following the 120th anniversary, there was a steep rise in the number of children attending the school. There was less room in the playground and so the number of accidents, bumps and scrapes increased. There was no Medical Room in which to treat them and there was no Staff Room either. The staff had to use the kitchen in the school hall for a little privacy during playtimes. At lunch times this arrangement was particularly unsatisfactory as the canteen staff worked to serve meals. Another wooden hut, to be used as the Medical/Staff Room, was eventually built behind the small playground area which was opposite the former air raid shelter. It was opened in January 1962.

In September 1961 Mr Skinner marked twenty-five years as Headmaster. He took the opportunity to reflect upon the changes to the school and village since his appointment, which had initially only been for two years! He was interested to see that Old Scholars that he had taught in the early years of his headship had subsequently emigrated after leaving school including Denzil Brown, who went to Australia and Gordon Keay. Others had gone to Canada and New Zealand. Some of those that remained in England had served in the Armed Forces and the Police. He was particularly proud to record in the log book that since the 11+ examination started in 1945, over one hundred children had gone on to Grammar Schools and to university, including Oxford and Cambridge.

In 1962 there were some further alterations and renovations. The school bell was repaired so that the children could be summoned from the playground and Spinney. In December, a stage was placed in the hall through the acquisition and of a portable platform of trestles and boards with some new curtains. These facilities were developed over several years for the annual productions and Mr Finch later added a set of dimmers with a lighting switchboard.

In the early 1960s much of the school library was replenished and replaced. It had been established as part of the bequest contained in the will of Charles Wayth (a resident of long-standing in Bearsted) made in 1851:

I give and bequeath unto the Trustees for the time being of the National School at Bearsted, the sum of Fifty pounds Upon Trust that they do invest the same in or upon some good Government or real security in England and do and shall pay and apply the annual interest or proceeds arising therefrom and all every other sum or sums of money which I have given in this my Will for the said schools in purchasing books of a useful and scientific nature published by the Society for the Diffusion of Useful Knowledge to be given away every year at the Annual Examination the said schools as prizes and rewards for merit and good conduct. [1]

The records do not directly state that some of the money from the bequest had been used to establish a small repository of books. However, entries in the log book that commences in 1863, refer to a set of books that were informally deemed to be the school library.[2] The remainder of the bequest was invested to provide the funds to purchase books which were then distributed as school prizes. There was no discrimination in Charles Wayth's will. The lists of boys and girls that received the prizes can be found in the log books. Pamela Osbourne (née Town), who was School Captain 1941-1942, won a copy of *The Old Curiosity Shop* by Charles Dickens. The book plate from inside the front cover is shown overleaf:

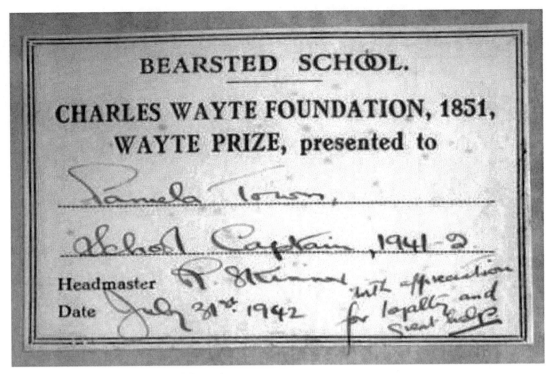

(Reproduced by permission of Pamela Osbourne)

It is not clear when the prizes ceased to be awarded but there are no records of presentation after the Second World War. Once discontinued, the funds may have become consolidated into the finance for what became called 'The Wayth Library': a large central reference and fiction library which was additional to the reference and reading books held in each classroom. Children qualified to use the library by completing the school reading scheme of *Wide Range Readers*. By 1966 this specific bequest had certainly ceased.

The library was also used for additional research and quiet study. It was located in different parts of the school at different times, including the main building, part of the hall and latterly in part of the converted air-raid shelter. Some Old Scholars may remember the shared accommodation with Mrs Coveney, the school secretary, just outside the Headmaster's office. The Wayth library holdings were supplemented by the County Library which provided books that were regularly exchanged. The library van visits were always greatly anticipated.

On 4 September 1961 the railway line, which passed very close to the school, was electrified. The trains up until this time had been powered by steam, so it was relatively safe to be near the line, which had been open and unfenced. However, with the arrival of the electric rail, all this changed. A fence was soon erected along with warning signs about the perils of playing on the line and electrocution. The class rooms and the hall still seemed to shake just as much when the electric trains began to run on the line. Jackie Stewart (née Hirst) clearly recalled that the police and railway officials visited the school to talk to the children about the dangers of trespassing on the railway once it became electrified. This made such a huge impression upon her that she was very reluctant to even wait at Bearsted Station for the trains to arrive!

Reproduced opposite is a school report for 1962. The comments are notably briefer than that from 1948 as shown in the previous chapter. The format had slightly changed too. Due to the increase in school numbers, Mr Skinner no longer typed the reports!

A report for 1962:

KENT EDUCATION COMMITTEE

BEARSTED C.E. PRIMARY SCHOOL

Report on.....Clive....Britcher..... for.....Summer....... Year / Term 196.2.

Class.....4.B...... Age...10...yrs...1...mths. Average age...10...yrs...10...mths.

| ATTAINMENT REACHED | A, B, C, D, E | Where 'C' represents an average grade for the Class | DEGREE OF EFFORT MADE | 1 above average, 2 average, 3 below average |

Subject	Attainment Reached	Effort	Remarks
Reading	A		Very good.
English	A		Good.
Composition	A		Shows imagination.
Geography	A		Very keen.
History	B		
Art	C+		More care needed in details
Craft	C+		
Arithmetic ...Mechan.	B		⎫ A little careless at
Tables or Mental Arithmetic Reas.	B		⎬ times.
Physical Education & Games	C		
Scripture	A.		⎫
Spelling	A		⎬ Good.
Nature Study	A		

General Report. A good term's work.

1000 5/62 cs539

H. N. Meyrick
Class Teacher

R. Skinner
Head Teacher

Next term Commences on......12 SEP 1962......

(Reproduced by permission of Doris Britcher)

By 1964, Robert Skinner was fighting a losing personal battle against arthritis. Several spells of restorative treatment elsewhere in the country were to no avail. He reluctantly tendered his resignation, which was received by the Kent Education Committee with regret. He was presented with many gifts from the Head Teachers Association, the children and staff, and the Old Scholars and Friends of the School Association. He recorded in the log book:

<u>25 March 1964</u>
I completed my Teaching service today, resigning from the post of Headmaster after twenty-six and a half years. They have been extremely happy years and I am very sorry indeed to leave the school community, life and children.

Upon his retirement he left a complete photographic record of his time at the school. Many of these photographs have been of immense assistance in compiling this history. As a parting gift to the children, he presented each of them with a small printed booklet about the School Motto which is shown below:

<table>
<tr><td>

BEARSTED JUNIOR SCHOOL
Near Maidstone

✦

Thoughts on the School Motto:

"COURTESY - FIDELITY
COURAGE"

To: *Miriam Britcher*

From: R. SKINNER - 25TH MARCH, 1964

For Auld Lang Syne

</td><td>

YOUR SCHOOL MOTTO
✦

The rudder of a ship, or the lines of a railway, each help to guide a huge machine and prevent its going astray and meeting with disaster. Your Motto can help you in much the same way if you try to live up to it, as it will help you to be the kind of people we all would like to be.

Our School Motto consists of only three words, but they are very important and will help to guide you on your way. Inside this little leaflet you will find what other people have thought about these words. Think about them yourself, and try to understand how worth while they are.

Above all, try to bring them into your life, not only will they help you, but they will help to make your world a better place for everyone. In particular, your School will be a real " happy family," because you will all be trying to make it one. So, learn the extracts inside, and above all, learn your Motto and make it part of yourself.

One final word—a personal one. The staff of the School have always had a very good opinion of Bearsted children, and this has been shared by all those who have visited us or come in contact with School parties outside. Never do anything to spoil this, either inside or outside the School—its good name is in YOUR keeping.

Goodbye, and Good Luck,

R. Skinner

VIVISH & BAXER LTD., MAIDSTONE

</td></tr>
</table>

(Reproduced by permission of Doris Britcher)

Robert Skinner's final entry in the log book conveys much of his personality: seeking to do the very best for the children but retaining a fine sense of the ridiculous mingling with formality:

<u>13 April 1964</u>
Today I have met Mr V Finch, my successor and formally handed over.
(ink blot here) I very much regret the blot!!

The new Headmaster, Mr Vernon Finch, is doubtless remembered by many of the Old Scholars as a man for whom music was (and remains) an abiding passion. His philosophy was that every child should at least be given the opportunity to learn a musical instrument. The school began to develop an immense reputation for outstanding musical ability coupled with academic achievement. Vernon Finch's leadership oversaw the battle for new accommodation at a different location, but more immediate concerns included the problem of insufficient room for a rising school roll.

This photograph shows the front of the school in the early years of Mr Finch's headship. On the left hand side of the front porch are stacked school milk crates. Every school day, each child received a bottle containing one third of a pint of milk. The school milk service continued until the early 1970s.

(Photograph courtesy of Vernon Finch)

The uniform was now firmly established, although dress fashions had changed and gym-slips were no longer worn. The winter uniform for the boys comprised dark grey trousers, white shirt, a plain maroon tie and a navy jumper or blazer, navy coat and cap. The girls wore a navy blue tunic or skirt, a white blouse, a plain maroon tie and a cardigan, together with a navy coat and beret. One style of tunic that was very popular had a dropped-line skirt that was pleated and a half-belt at the front with a buckle. The beret had a small shield-shaped maroon badge that bore the monogram of the school's initials.

The most important item of uniform for the girls was a leather purse with a long shoulder strap in which to store a handkerchief and other important items such as hopscotch stones. The strap was also very useful to display the People's Dispensary for Sick Animals 'Busy Bee' badges (a charity that the school supported) as they were earned! The tunic or skirt was usually purchased in either Blakes department store, High Street, Maidstone or the school uniform department in Sharps. This shop was located nearby in Gabriel's Hill. During the summer the boys wore grey shorts, a white Aertex shirt and grey socks. The girls wore blue and white striped cotton summer dresses, navy blue cardigans and white socks. The material for the dresses was readily available in fabric shops in Maidstone. It was sewn into several recommended *Simplicity* or *Style* dress patterns by parents.

The hours were now slightly altered to enable the day to finish at 3.30pm so that after-school activities could take place. To take advantage of the school programmes that were now regularly broadcast by the BBC, Mr Finch installed a television in the hall and radios in all the classrooms.

A 'National Savings Group' was started for the children. On the first day of the scheme, 1 October 1965, 107 children purchased stamps to the value of £8 12s 6d. The Group was replaced in September 1972 by a School Bank. Mr Martin Corps, a School Manager and retired bank manager, agreed to be Chief Clerk. Each child was issued with a matchbox in which to bring their funds to be deposited in an account. Every Friday the bank was open in the school hall for transactions, which were recorded by a series of 'junior clerks': one for each school year. At the end of the trading period, all the transaction records and monies deposited were collected by the Chief Clerk for checking. By this means, many children began to learn the real value of regularly saving money.

Vernon Finch had also been quietly observing the children during playtimes and approved of the use of the Green for lunchtimes in summer providing that at least one dinner lady was supervising. However, Sally Hook (née Smith) recalled that Mr Finch warned them in assembly, that they could lose this privilege if it was discovered that they had touched the enormous cast-iron roller that was kept to flatten the cricket square! Behind the main building, some grids were painted on the playground surface so that games of hopscotch could be played. Benches were also introduced into the playground for the children to sit upon. These made quite a change from perching upon the lids of the dustbins and were very popular.

During an "Open Evening" held at the school, Mr Finch gave some details of other changes he proposed to introduce. He included a suggestion that the annual school reports would be discontinued. Instead, there would be a final report for children who were about to leave the school to start their secondary education. For the rest of the school there would be an Open Evening in the Summer Term during which parents could look at the work produced in class. Parents would be welcome to discuss their child's progress with the Headmaster and class teachers at any time during the school year by appointment. The proposal was well received.

The arrangements for Assembly now changed too, as Vernon Finch began to use a record player to play short excerpts from classical music at the start of Assembly. The idea behind this was that the children quietly entered the hall and sat for a few minutes listening to the music. There was then a short explanation about the music that they had just heard.

The Travel Club, which had been instigated by Robert Skinner, had introduced the idea of educational visits by the children to broaden their outlook. Mr Finch was keen to develop the idea. Among the first annual visits was a day out in London for the entire school with children from each year going to a different venue: Regents Park Zoo, the Tower of London, Kew Gardens, the Natural History and Science Museums.

Among the first musical activities that were introduced were lessons on stringed instruments. Before the children began to learn to play, Daphne Clement persuaded other members of staff: Mrs Dean and Mr Finch to take up violins and Miss Stuffins to take up a viola. Her idea was to form 'The Staff Quartet' - as a practical example of musical instrument playing to their charges. The Principal of the Kent Rural Music School, Miss Muriel Anthony, was so intrigued by the audacious idea of junior school staff leading by example, that, for a time, she visited the school to give them lessons! It was not long before the children were formed into a fledgling orchestra. The children's music lessons were further supplemented by tuition from other musicians from the Kent Rural Music School and from Holy Cross church.

An early concert given by the orchestra and choir took place in Holy Cross church for Christmas in 1966 when the performers were given an unexpected surprise. They were supported (unobtrusively, in the back row!) by the international violinist, Hugh Bean who had responded to an invitation from Mr Finch. At the time, Hugh was Leader of the Philharmonia Orchestra and brought along two colleagues who also assisted. The following year, the first Summer Concert was held in the Women's Institute Hall, at which the Staff Quartet, accompanied by Miss Anthony, gave a performance. Although it was nerve-wracking for the musicians, was greeted with enthusiasm by the children. By the time of the next concert, the demand for tickets meant necessitate a change of venue to the assembly hall of the Girls Technical School, Huntsman Lane,

Maidstone. However, at Christmas, it was considered that Holy Cross church was the appropriate setting for the depictions of the Nativity and the story of the First Christmas. Many of these productions were written by Mrs Rayner. All of these activities involved considerable backstage preparations by staff and parents, ably guided by Miss Clement and Mrs Rayner.

Music practise took place throughout the day wherever there was space in the curriculum. This photograph shows Mrs Beryl Dean with a recorder group:

For many years, Mr Trevor Webb, the organist at Holy Cross church, gave unstintingly of his time and assistance to help the musical endeavours of the children. In the summer term it was quite usual to see music group lessons taking place in The Spinney as the photograph below depicts:

(Both photographs courtesy of Vernon Finch)

The rapidly growing musical reputation of the school attracted some reports in the local press. This is a transcript of a typical report about the school carried in a local newspaper, from *The Gazette,* 1 August 1967:

(Photograph courtesy of the Kent Messenger group)

MAKE MINE MUSIC

ONE of the largest orchestras for a school of its size is flourishing at Bearsted Primary School. Started in September last year, it consists of about 40 recorders and 27 violins and one girl is also learning to play the 'cello. Their enthusiasm is infectious: three members of the school staff are now learning to play the violin and one is learning the viola. The orchestra is taught and conducted by Miss Susan Praat, with the assistance of Miss M. Anthony of Kent Rural Music School (at the piano in our picture). Leader is 10-year-old Pamela Marks (front row left of the picture) who attends Kent Junior Music School for specially talented young musicians. The group includes, standing behind the recorders, the school's 40-strong choir.

The buildings and the constant need for maintenance gave cause for concern. After an inspectors visit in 1964 it was calculated that each child had just 13.3 square feet of floor space in the main building. It was minuted by the Managers that it was less than ideal for the accommodation to be so widely dispersed over the grounds - particularly the separate toilet block in the playground, which was less than appealing in bad weather.

It was not until a Managers meeting in October that the staff became properly aware of the difficulties and the prolonged nature of the planning process that might lead to the construction of a new building. Although it was envisaged that the annual intake of children from Thurnham over the next two years would raise the roll up to 200, the Divisional Education Officer was still adamant that new accommodation could still be at least four to five years away.

During meetings between the Education Officers and the Managers, Bearsted's priority in the financial estimates (essential for allocating the money to start building the new school but compiled at least fourteen months in advance) was discussed. It was only these meetings that prevented many people in the village from believing that that the whole planning process had stalled.

It was decided that as an interim solution to the accommodation problems, that the part of the ground purchased from Mr and Mrs Reatchlous, and known as 'The Paddock' would be sacrificed in order to erect two more classrooms. Some of the trees screening the back of the site were retained. Building commenced in May 1965 and was completed on 30 June. Some Old Scholars may remember the peculiarly-thick brown linoleum flooring used in these classrooms! An extra 334 square feet was achieved with the erection of this building which was particularly welcome as the roll now totalled 162.

The next two photographs show the materials assembled for the new classroom in the playground and the construction of the foundations. In the second photograph some of the children are wearing Brownie and Wolf Cub uniforms to mark 'Thinking Day'. [3]

(Both photographs courtesy of Vernon Finch)

Although it was becoming increasingly difficult to teach the children a full curriculum, the school continued to participate in many musical and sporting activities. Swimming lessons continued once a week at the Public Baths in Maidstone. The children also enjoyed considerable success at the annual Weald of Kent Sports Association tournaments. Any sporting achievements were particularly impressive as there was no sports field other than the village green. The first photograph overleaf shows Rounders being played in a games lesson on the Green. The second shows two un-named boys investigating the plant life of the village pond as part of their Science and Nature Studies. Miss Clement is in the background with some other children from her class.

(Both photographs courtesy of Vernon Finch)

Although the Kent Education Committee was responsible for Bearsted School, religious instruction was still separately inspected by the Diocese of Canterbury. Services were held at Holy Cross church each term, which the children attended. This undated photograph shows a typical scene as children returned from a service. The crocodile of children, walking in pairs, which undulated around the Green (carefully avoiding the corner of the cricket square which was guarded by a senior member of staff) during the journeys to and from the church, is remembered by many Old Scholars!

(Photograph courtesy of Vernon Finch)

In the middle years of the 1960s development in and around the village commenced. The school roll continued to rise with the new influx of families to the development of houses around the Memorial Hall and the construction of houses at Foster's farm in Ware Street that became known as Sandy Mount. The extension to The Landway, which became known as the Roseacre Estate and latterly, The Landway Estate, was begun. After the opening of Madginford School in 1967, nine children transferred to that school, but the relief to the roll was only temporary. The Managers for Bearsted were then re-constituted to encompass Thurnham Infants, Bearsted School and Madginford Park County Primary School.

Mr Finch felt it was necessary to add another school house. He decided to call it Culpeper to reflect upon the connections with one of the long-established families from Hollingbourne. The school had children on the roll from the area. The colour for Culpeper house was yellow. He made three small wooden house shields. Each bore the appropriate house colours and initials: green for Barty and blue for Fludd. Every week, when the total number of house points had been calculated, following an announcement in assembly, the relevant numbers were written up on a small blackboard. Both shields and scores were then displayed in descending order on a small pegboard mounted in the school hall. The tradition continues at Roseacre. Two further shields for annual house competition for sports and work were also designed.

Mr Finch decided to extend the nature studies of the school. The children would care for some white Barbary doves in addition to the guinea pigs and rabbits that they already looked after. Later, the doves were joined by some budgerigars. As a special project, and under supervision, the children very carefully built an aviary.

149

This photograph shows three boys involved in the construction process for the aviary. One of the boys is wearing Mr Cecil's brown coat!

(Photograph courtesy of Vernon Finch)

There was a further article about the village in *The Gazette,* October 17, 1967, a transcript of which is shown below:

Bearsted Green - still a 'wonderful spot'

...Just along the road from Mrs Jordan's home is 'The National School for Bearsted, Thornham, Debtling and part of Boxley' erected in 1839 as the stone on its front wall proclaimed.

The astonishing thing about this primary school is the range of extra-mural activities which run every afternoon. When we visited the school the boys were playing football on the Green and the girls' netball team was in training.

Music

At other times the children enjoy music classes - 28 are learning the violin, four children hope to start the 'cello soon and there are already 50 in the recorder group. There are also percussion groups, folk dance teams and a choir. Then there is the school club which looks after the school pets. They have guinea pigs and rabbits and an aviary built by fourth-year boys which contains six budgies and two barbary doves.

All these activities are encouraged by the school's young Headmaster, Mr. Vernon Finch, who came to Bearsted three years ago.

'I think it is a delightful place to work in,' he said, 'I find the parental support most encouraging for all school work and I think the children benefit from the cordial atmosphere which exists between staff and home.

Staff join

'The choir is my particular joy.' he said, 'I am very enthusiastic about the school's music and I like to encourage the children by joining in - I am learning to play the violin now.'

In fact, Mr Finch and three other members of his staff are learning instruments alongside the children.

'We try to give the children both good academic achievements and a well-developed sense of social responsibility,' he said- 'It really boils down to work hard and play hard.'

This photograph accompanied the article. It shows some of the children going home and parents waiting to collect them. This scene virtually unchanged until the relocation of the school.

(Photograph courtesy of Kent Messenger group)

The siting of the school buildings gave grave cause for alarm in 1968. A spate of torrential rain in September led to the accumulation of water in the field on the far side of the railway embankment. During his Sunday lunch, Vernon Finch was alerted by Mrs Rowland, wife of the caretaker, that there was a massive problem at the school. The water had passed through the embankment which was only a few yards away from the Rochester Huts. It then forced its way through the second Rochester Hut, some other school buildings and underneath School House into the road at the front of the buildings. The classrooms were flooded to an overall depth of two inches. Some bricks unconnected with the school buildings also appeared between the two Rochester Huts. As the school had recently raised some considerable funds as a contribution to the Aberfan disaster, the stability of the embankment gave everyone considerable cause for concern.[4]

The school was closed for three days while expert opinion was sought upon the matter from British Rail, which placed a temporary 10 mph speed restriction upon the line. No one could be entirely sure whether there was a weakness in the embankment. Mr Finch feared that a train could topple over onto part of the school. Investigations by British Rail revealed the existence of a brick-built culvert which provided drainage through the embankment. It appeared that the culvert had been blocked by a gradual accumulation of soil and other debris which had given way under the pressure of the water. The flow of water through the culvert after many years caused some of the brickwork to be dislodged, which accounted for the bricks found by the huts. The stability of the embankment was subsequently confirmed after the culvert was reinforced.

This worrying period was followed by further concerns over the state of the school buildings. The fabric of the Rochester Huts had begun to deteriorate as the persistently wet weather led to the establishment of rot in the wood. The poor condition of the buildings became graphically evident when a Manager opened a window frame in one of the huts and it promptly disintegrated.

During this time negotiations continued with the authorities to commence building the new school at the Roseacre site. Matters were not improved by the realisation in a Managers meeting that when the new Madginford infant school opened in 1969, the capacity of both the Madginford schools would stand at 480 pupils. It was noted in the log book that a total of only 201 children attended both Madginford schools. Despite the high expectations of the Education Office that many children from the outlying areas of Bearsted would automatically consider changing to a school closer to home, the parents of only a few children had expressed an interest in transferring to the new Madginford Junior School.

There was a common expectation in the Education Office that the school would be filled by the children of Bearsted who lived on the south side of the Ashford Road. Evidently, when estimating the education provision required, it had not been envisaged that it would take some time for the Madginford development to establish itself and for sufficient families to move into the area, creating the demand for the school. As there was ample capacity at Madginford School, the Education Committee could direct parents towards it, thus giving further justification to delay the start of a new building for Bearsted School. This turn of events was sufficient for Mr Finch to consider his position (and future) at Bearsted.

This plan of the school in 1968 gives a good indication of the cramped nature of the premises:

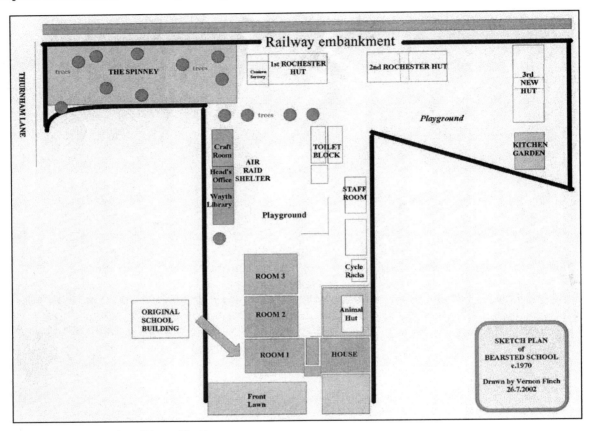

(Reproduced by permission of Vernon Finch)

In November 1967, Mr Finch was finally able to record that he had received notification that the new school scheme had received approval by the Department of Education and Science.[5] The notice meant that the construction of a new school was included in an Approved Programme of building by the council.

A sketch design for the new building was produced by the Architects Department at Springfield. Mr Finch attended a meeting about it in the Divisional Education Offices. He was advised that he was the first headmaster to be involved in design process of a new school.

This illustration is taken from the earliest surviving plan, Draft III, dated November 1967.[6] It shows the proposed layout of the buildings and grounds incorporating a games court, swimming pool and cricket table. It is interesting to see that the pedestrian access is shown from both Roseacre Lane and from the housing estate which became known as The Landway. The proposed new building for Thurnham Infant School is already clearly labelled as sharing the same land.

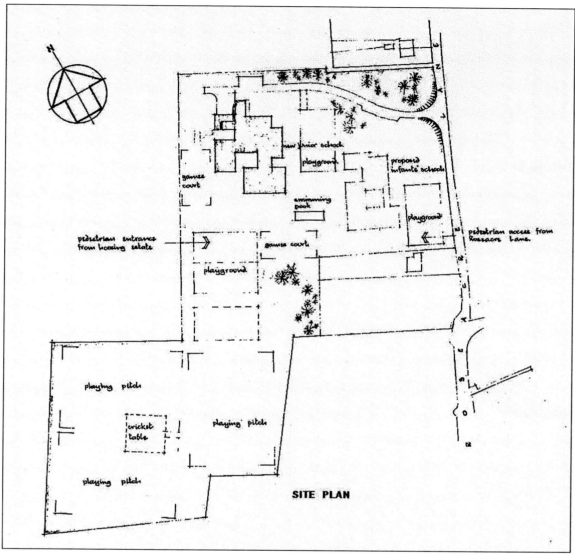

SITE PLAN

(Illustration courtesy of Vernon Finch)

Mr Finch's initial comments upon the third draft of the proposals included the following observations:

> A central library room where individual research could be undertaken and school work exhibited would be preferable to the inadequate space allocated for a library area.
> The space allocated for toilets does not suggest sufficient room for use as changing rooms for games or PE.
> Externally, the boiler house chimney stack will not enhance the outside approach.[7]

Draft IV of the design is shown below.[8] The buildings would have formed a split-level school with a substantial staircase between the two levels. Mr Finch's comments on this draft are dated 11 December 1967. He included the observation that the main working area of Classrooms 7 and 8 had become rather smaller. He also carefully noted that the door entrances to the toilets needed careful siting as the boys toilet adjoining Classroom 1 would give an unimpeded view of the urinals on the facing wall!

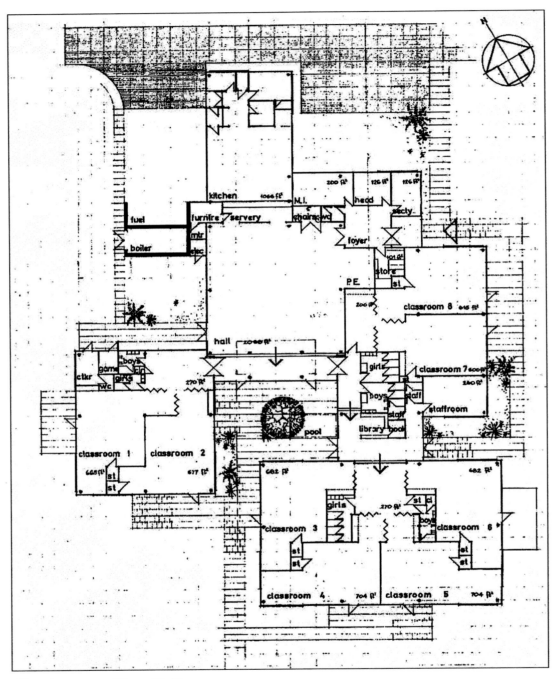

(Illustration courtesy of Vernon Finch)

Other matters under discussion included the height of the proposed new stage to be installed in the hall It was considered that any stage should be no higher than one foot above floor level. There had already been one argument over whether a stage was even required, as productions staged 'in the round' were then favoured by Inspectors. It was quickly realised that this was impracticable for orchestral concerts. Vernon Finch firmly believed for a school in which there was a strong tradition of regular concerts, that a stage at least two feet high would be better for all performers. It was only after some machinations that the battle was won.

This progression of matters was followed months of silence during which it was hoped that all the proposed modifications and adaptations were being considered. However, in a Managers meeting on 16 May 1968, everyone was officially told that the construction of the new school was now envisaged as commencing April 1969 at the very earliest.

Concerned about the lack of action, a letter from Bearsted and Thurnham parish councils was sent to the Kent Education Committee. A reply was received advising that part of the delay had been caused by the Secretary of State's decision to review the 1968-69 building programme. This had resulted in the exclusion of the new Bearsted school project. However, the Education Committee were able to advise that the 1969-70 building programme was now under review and this included Bearsted.[9] It is likely that some of the delay had been caused by national government directives and budgetary constraints but it was difficult for many parents to accept this explanation.

In November 1968, the parish councils of Bearsted and Thurnham learnt that following the review by the Secretary of State, approval had been given to seventeen County Primary School schemes for 1969-70 but Bearsted was not among them. The parish councils then requested a joint meeting in January 1969 with the County Education Officer to discuss the delay. The councils were advised that it was possible that the new school would be included in the building programme but it would be the programme for 1973-1974 at the earliest.[10]

Local opinion held that the five-year delay was due to the likelihood of enormous residential development in the Weavering area. The development of Madginford had been accompanied by the construction of two new schools. If this was an indication of the educational planning for the area, a new school would be required in Weavering instead, as the needs of Bearsted children had slipped further and further down the list of priorities.

Once again the parish councils of Bearsted and Thurnham wrote letters on a joint basis and there was further coverage in the press. This is a transcript of the report from the *Kent Messenger*, 28 February 1969:

School crisis puts parents' back up

ANGER is increasing against delays in building the new school at Roseacre, Bearsted. Now a petition, signed by 265 parents has been sent to Mr. John Wells, M.P.

On Tuesday night a joint meeting of Bearsted and Thurnham parish councils had decided to send further protests to the Secretary of State for Education and Science and to Mr. Wells.

A copy of the petition, organised by Mrs V.M. Scott, of 57, Mallings Drive, Bearsted, was read to the meeting.

Tuesday's meeting followed an earlier meeting of the two councils, when Mr. P. W. Tomlinson, divisional education officer, answering criticisms of the building delay said that the school was on the 1973-74 building programme.

They also heard a report by Mr. Martin Corps, chairman of Bearsted Parish Council, who inspected Bearsted School on its 130th anniversary.

They said that the rear boundary of the school was bounded by a railway which was embanked some six feet above the school playground about eight feet away.

The report makes several other points including: A brick air-raid shelter is used for handicraft classes; outdoor lavatories; poor fire escape facilities; a playground 'about large enough to accommodate a netball court.'

Asked by Viscount Monckton what he thought was the worst aspect of the school, Mr Jenkins replied: 'The site is completely cluttered.'

Mr J. H. Nicholson, a Thurnham parish councillor, who is also Maidstone Rural Council's engineer and surveyor, supported the parents' letter and agreed with the need for a new school.

The Permanent Under-Secretary of State at the Department of Education and Science was advised of the grave concern held by the parish councils about the delay in the provision of the new building for the school.

A few weeks later, following a meeting with the parish council and some parents, the Member of Parliament for Maidstone, John Wells, raised a question in Parliament about the lack of a new building. He presented a petition signed by 265 concerned parents. Further help was offered by Viscount Monckton who raised the issue in the House of Lords. He also wrote to the *Daily Telegraph* and his letter was published on Thursday 27 March 1969 It remains a matter of speculation as to whether all this attention finally resulted in some long overdue decisions.

On 9 October 1969, the Divisional Education Officer called to advise that the Local Education Authority expected the new school to feature in the next list of building approval. This most welcome news was confirmed at a Managers' meeting the following week.[11] It was included in the 1969-70 programme and construction was scheduled to start in April 1970.

However, all the previous hours of planning and discussion as to the facilities required in the new building came to nought. The previous designs were abandoned in favour of one already used for Joy Lane Primary School in Whitstable. Somewhat surprised by this volte-face, Vernon Finch immediately paid a visit to the school at Whitstable. He found a flat-roofed, rather modern box-like structure that was not as attractive as the previously proposed brick building. Nevertheless, despite the imposition of a new design and some concerns about this rapid turn of events, there was really no choice in the matter if a new building was to be secured. The construction was estimated as taking twelve to fourteen months to complete. The relief for the parents in the village was immense.

Other parts of the curriculum now required some updated, and different teaching methods. In 1970 Bearsted School was one of the first primary schools to address the matter of sex education for the children. There was great concern about this and a distinct element of apprehension amongst the parents. Mr Finch decided to tackle this by holding an evening at the school where there was a brief discussion about the content of the lessons. The BBC films that were due to be broadcast on the *Merry Go Round* series of school programmes were shown. By treating the matter with complete honesty and directness, the fears of the parents were allayed. These arrangements became a regular event for parents. Mr Finch was able to record in the log book that there had been no adverse criticism but on one occasion a father had fainted when watching the footage of the delivery of a baby!

The cultural life of the school was considerably enlivened by a visit from the Eastern Michigan University Madrigal Group in 1970. Vernon Finch had been invited to an earlier concert by Trevor Webb and they both realised that the children would appreciate an exceptional musical performance. After some consultations and a series of adjustments being made to a comprehensive schedule, the group gave a performance to the school.

Mr Finch recorded in the log book:

> 15 June 1970
>
> Being a warm sunny morning, the school was gathered in the playground with their classroom chairs and formed into a semi-circle. The guests then gave a planned twenty-minute programme. The response from the children was so enthusiastic that the 'concert' continued for a further fifteen minutes – only the shortage of time prevented more!
>
> In return for the guests, class 3c gave a demonstration of Maypole dancing – an experience the American visitors fully appreciated – which they performed remarkably well. Our percussion group trained by Mr T Webb…then performed for the visitors with great success.
>
> After a rapid lunch, the guests spent every remaining available minute meeting and talking with our children – apparently the only experience of its kind they had enjoyed on their tour of English Colleges and Universities. The whole visit to our School was an immense success for both visitors and our children – resulting in the guests leaving us 30 minutes later than planned!

Visits by the Madrigal Group became a fixture in many later United Kingdom tours. This photograph was taken during the first visit. The visitors and their Director, Professor Emily Lowe, are pictured below with the school percussion group:

(Photograph courtesy of the Kent Messenger group)

On 5 April 1971 there was a telephone call to the school at mid-day, for which Vernon Finch must have felt that he had waited a life-time. It was from the owner of a house adjacent to the Roseacre site to advise that the contractors had arrived. Work on the new building began at 11.40am with the erection of the Clerk of Works hut. Roseacre School was finally underway!

The final day for the children attending school at the Bearsted Green premises was 29 March 1972. However, a few days before this several photographs were taken of Upper and Lower School in front of the building.

The arrangements for the photographs were memorable for some Old Scholars: it was strange that the children in the back row had to stand on wooden benches on the pavement. The youngest and smallest children sat on chairs at the front. Both the benches and the chairs completely blocked the pavement. As it took some time to arrange the benches and other seating for the photographs, there were other, rather more informal photographs taken showing the children sitting in the front garden of the school.

In order to be in the correct position to take the Upper and Lower School photographs, the photographer had to stand in the middle of the road. This meant that the traffic stopped and any pedestrians that wanted to reach the shops or the rest of The Street had to walk in the road. Mr Finch commented that if the photographer did not hurry up and press the camera shutter there was a good chance of a traffic accident! The photographs are shown on the next two pages.

This photograph shows the Lower School: [12]

(Original photograph by Sloman & Pettit)

(Original photograph by Sloman & Pettit)

On the final afternoon of the term there was a small, but deeply poignant, ceremony held to mark the closure of the buildings. It included prayers of thanksgiving for the past benefactors of Bearsted School and the years of history that were now drawing to an end. They were read by the vicar of Bearsted, Mr Waghorne.

This photograph is from *The Gazette* newspaper, 4 April, 1972. The child turning round to look at the photographer has been identified as Thomas Soloman.

(Photograph courtesy of the Kent Messenger group)

As Mr Finch recorded in the log book:

<u>29 March 1972</u>
This afternoon the final Assembly of the school was held at 3.15pm. After a hymn and closing prayers, the school left the assembly hall and, in single file, the classes slowly made their way to the lawn at the front of the school and then gathered around the war memorial and flag pole. The school bell was then tolled at five second intervals whilst the Head Boy and Girl slowly lowered the Bearsted School flag, the children watching in silence. When this ceremony was completed, the children returned to their classrooms to collect their belongings and then went home. Many of the older children were obviously moved - one summing up the occasion with the words 'It's just as if the school has died, isn't it?'

As subsequent events were to prove, it was not the death of Bearsted School but a moment of metamorphosis.

Chapter 12
Adaptation and Growth

There were many delays and uncertainties throughout the construction of the new school building. These resulted in a complete disruption of the schedule that had been carefully devised to ensure a smooth removal from the old building at Bearsted. The planned completion date was 3 April 1972 during the Easter holidays.

The school had a new name: [1]

Roseacre County Primary School

A badge and tie had been devised to help the children and the staff assimilate the new identity of the school. Roseacre was one of the first primary schools to have a distinct badge which is shown below. It was designed by Vernon Finch to reflect upon the name 'Roseacre' and was in the shape of a shield. It featured a maroon background with two black rooks over some chevrons. The chevrons were alternately silver and blue and were intended to depict the use of the land prior to the building of the school: a ploughed field with an abundant water supply. At the bottom of the shield was a cross as a reminder of the church foundation. There was also a plain maroon badge with a silver monogram of the initial letters of the school, RCPS. The monogram badge was intended for items such as berets which were worn by some of the girls. The new tie was maroon with a thin silver diagonal line to evoke the main colours of the school. It was already being worn by some of the children before the school relocated.

(Illustration courtesy of Roseacre School)

The start of the first term, which should have been 20 April, was delayed for four days as the construction company had been declared insolvent on the very day that completion was due! The building was nominally finished but it was not fit for occupation as the interior was filthy. The grounds and three playgrounds were in a similar condition.

All the staff, supplemented by extra cleaning staff, worked feverishly to achieve a building that was in a fit condition to admit the children. In a later article[2] Vernon Finch recalled some of the more amusing incidents that occurred in the construction of the building. This included an electrician leaning his ladder against a wall to install some internal wiring, only to find himself and his ladder propelled out through the front door as the wall collapsed!

The unfinished state of the school led to a description of the relocation as 'moving old wine into a new and very rough skin'. The new premises were a single storey, of a roughly square-shaped construction, arranged around a central courtyard with a hall which had large windows on the southern aspect. The hall was to be used for assembly purposes, PE and Drama lessons, and had a climbing frame that folded flush with the wall.

This plan[3] shows the layout of the school:

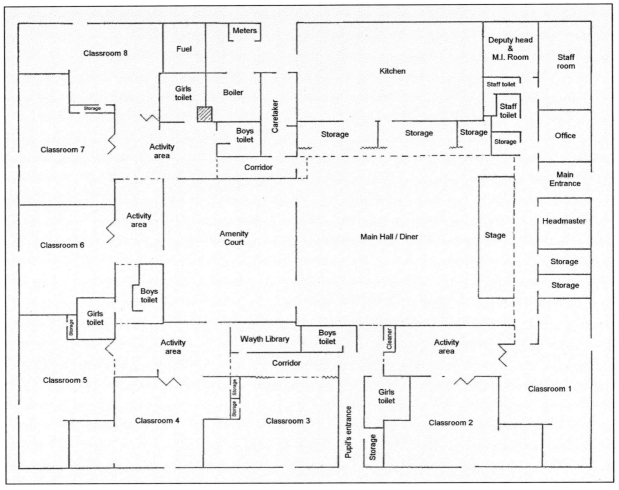

(Illustration courtesy of Roseacre School)

The main entrance was on the north-western boundary with a road built from The Landway. It was felt that this route would be safer than Roseacre Lane which was viewed as too narrow for increased traffic. Jonathan Wraight recalled many children also using an 'unofficial' footpath which led from the Roseacre Lane corner of the school field to the playground once the school was open.

The eight classrooms, school kitchen and boiler room were arranged around the eastern, southern and western sides of the square, with the fourth side comprising a set of offices and the staff room. Each classroom had an external door that led directly out into the playground area, and a set of internal large wooden screen doors. The screens folded back so that the children could use the 'activity areas' that were formed by the internal corridor. There was some doubt whether all the classrooms would have these screens as the architects plans showed parts of the building to be truly 'open-plan'. However, the practical need to achieve some sound-proofing for class lessons prevailed.

The activity areas adjacent to the classrooms were fitted with long white sinks for easy cleaning after art and science lessons, together with work-top surfaces and cupboards. The sinks had long tubular plugs that were slightly shorter than the sides of the sink in order to prevent flooding by overflowing water. However, Mr Finch was less than impressed when he had to point out to the architect that there was little chance of flooding. The taps had not been sufficiently offset to fill the sink but directed the water straight down the plug hole! They were later adjusted. All the activity areas had 'mobile cloakroom trolleys' which were on wheels for the safe storage of coats and PE kit. It was quickly realised that these were impracticable and were eventually replaced by fixed coat pegs.

The Wayth library was situated near to the third and fourth year class rooms. Vernon Finch asked for it to be accommodated in a room constructed in an 'activity area', and to feature a wall of half-glazed panels to enable visual supervision of the children within. The room was actually built with full height walls. Once again, Mr Finch intervened to correct the oversight and half-glazed panels were eventually installed.

The earlier dispute over the stage in the hall was resolved with the installation of a platform that was installed as 'temporary', but inevitably became permanent. This was supplemented with some large wooden blocks that had originally been offered as part of the negotiations over the stage. Within a year, a full provision of stage lighting and audio facilities had been installed but it was some time before the stage received curtains. Unusually, the stage furnishings were specially designed to be in proportion to the children. The maypole was carefully installed in a corner of the hall.

To accommodate the greater number of children now attending, Vernon Finch devised another school house. It was called 'Dering', after an old, established, family that had lived in Thurnham in the seventeenth century. The house colour was red. Another small wooden house shield was added to the weekly house score pegboard, which had been transferred to the new assembly hall.

The weather station and the aviary were installed by the brick-edged pond in the courtyard. They were carefully transferred by Alan Cecil with some assistance from Mr Finch as there was very little clearance through the courtyard door! The memorial sundial was also moved into the courtyard where it remains. Mr Finch was reluctant to move it as he felt that it was part of Bearsted School. However, no-one knew what future lay ahead for the old building which was now empty and there were concerns that the sundial could be temptation for vandals. In addition to the sundial, the school bell and the climbing frame also transferred to Roseacre. It was not possible to move the flagpole, so a new one was eventually installed.

Roseacre opened its doors for the very first time on 24 April 1972. Many Old Scholars recalled the very new smell of the building and the atmosphere replete with the pungent odours of paint and varnish. For Lower School children there was the new experience of lessons sitting around plastic-topped tables to work, and storing essential possessions in sets of grey plastic trays racked in cupboards. There was continuity from the old premises though as the traditionally-styled wooden dual locker desks were transferred from the old building. These were used by the Upper School as preparation for arrangements that they would encounter at secondary school.

Another example of continuity from the old premises was the Tuck Shop. It was still run by the children, supervised by a teacher, but it was now accommodated in Mrs Rayner's classroom at mid-morning play-time. Regular deliveries from the United Biscuit company were keenly anticipated and many children assisted with the delivery by stacking the boxes containing *Crispie Crisps*. A further novelty in the new building was eating dinners served on cardboard plates and bowls as the new supply of crockery had not yet arrived. If the meal included gravy or custard, the blue and white willow-pattern design soon became soggy and more than once there was a hole in a plate caused through enthusiastic use of cutlery!

Although there had been some attempts at landscaping, it was cursory. In places the grounds were little better than a rough construction site. There was a large roughly-grassed area which seemed to stretch as far as a child's eye could see, but actually extended from the playground behind the school to Roseacre Lane. It was later to be used for the new Thurnham Infants School.

The area featured a huge pile of earth which had been left behind by the builders. It was named 'The Mound' by some of the children and almost immediately declared out of bounds when a large wasp-nest was uncovered on top of it after several children had been stung The unfinished state of the grounds and field meant that the annual sports day in June, took place on the playground with no track and field events.

The freedom of playing on the village green at lunch time had now gone, but children regularly explored the brambles which grew profusely at the top of the field next to Roseacre Lane. Thomas Soloman recalled that it was very satisfying to make 'secret paths' and tunnels in the vegetation in this area. More intriguing were the bedstraw and horseradish plants that grew in the same area just by the old wooden field gate. The girls tried to stick the bedstraw plants on to each other but some boys dared each other to eat the horseradish. Several boys were horribly sick as a result!

The main exit route from the school ran by the headmaster's office. If he was available, Vernon Finch would lean out of the window to remonstrate over crooked ties and admonish the evident lack of care over shoelaces. It was all kindly meant and ensured that his 'Ambassadors for the school' presented a neat and tidy face to the world. It soon became the local custom in the autumn that residents of The Landway with fruit trees, would place surplus produce in wooden seed trays left on garden walls. This kind gesture enabled many children to collect an apple or pear to eat on their way home.

The school was officially opened and dedicated on 6 October 1972. Few people attending the event were aware that Mr Finch had been advised by the Education Office that it did not approve of an Official Opening for a primary school. Undaunted, and confident that Roseacre was going to be different, he made the arrangements anyway. The event was attended by Mr Partridge, the Assistant Divisional Education Officer, the Managers, members of both Bearsted and Thurnham Parish Councils, and parents. The Guest of Honour was Major-General the Viscount Monckton of Brenchley CB OBE MC, accompanied by Lady Monckton.

There were a few eyebrows raised in the Kent Education Committee offices by the invitation to Viscount Monckton, as he was a Roman Catholic. However, Vernon Finch reminded the Committee was now designated a County Primary School and no longer a Church of England foundation. Viscount Monckton had greatly assisted in the battle for the new building and Vernon Finch was determined that bureaucracy was not going to stand in the way of a public opportunity to say a heartfelt 'Thank You'. In the event, the vicar of Bearsted, Mr Waghorne, led a short service of dedication accompanied by the choir and orchestra.

This is the prayer of dedication:

```
              6th October, 1972

       IN DEDICATION OF ROSEACRE SCHOOL

    Blessed art thou, O Lord God, for ever
 and ever;  thine is the might, the majesty,
   the dominion, and the glory;  all we have
  and are is thine but of thine own give we
                  unto Thee.
    Accept, we pray, this school which we
   dedicate to thy service, and as thou hast
   blessed it in the past so we ask for thy
 guidance and assistance in the years to come:
  that whatsoever things true and pure, lovely
     and of good report may here abound and
  flourish;  preserve in it an unblemished name
  and use it as an instrument in thy service and
  for the furtherance of thy truth, through thy
      Son, our Lord, Jesus Christ.  AMEN.
```

(Reproduced courtesy of Roseacre School)

From the Official Opening programme:

```
                    Kent Education Committee

                ROSEACRE C.P. JUNIOR SCHOOL
                Bearsted, Maidstone, Kent.

             THE OFFICIAL OPENING OF THE SCHOOL
                             by
         Maj. Gen. The Viscount Monckton of Brenchley
                     C.B. , O.B.E., M.C.

                 Friday, 6th October, 1972

                     * * * * * * *

                   THE ADDRESS OF WELCOME
          The Assistant Divisional Education Officer
                      C.F. Partridge, Esq.

                 THE SERVICE OF DEDICATION
             Conducted by the Rev F.C. Waghorne

                 Hymn: O Worship the King.
                   Prayers and Blessing

              THE SCHOOL ORCHESTRA AND CHOIR

               PRESENTATION TO THE SCHOOL
      The Chairman of Bearsted Parish Council, Martin Corps, Esq.

                 THE OPENING DECLARATION
              Maj. Gen. The Viscount Monckton

        'NON NOBIS DOMINE'   SUNG BY THE SCHOOL
              Words by Rudyard Kipling
              Setting by Roger Quilter

              THE NATIONAL ANTHEM
```

(Reproduced courtesy of Roseacre School)

A specially commissioned oil painting of the old Bearsted School building by a local artist, Mr Archie Morris, was presented by the Chairman of Bearsted Parish Council, Mr Martin Corps, and was unveiled by Lady Monckton. Viscount Monckton sat down on some wooden staging blocks at the side of the hall that were the same level as the children, and gave a short address. He concluded with a motto:

Always take your work seriously, but never yourself!

One of the first changes was largely due to the lack of an official access to Roseacre Lane. Vernon Finch had earlier argued that although no longer a church foundation,[4] Christianity would always be one of the fundamental influences in the school. Major religious festivals had previously been marked a service at Holy Cross church. This now became a memory because a long journey through The Landway estate on foot to the church was deemed inadvisable. Instead, the vicar came to the school to lead services such as that for Ascension Day. In later years, this particular service was taken on occasion by the Bishop of Maidstone accompanied by the vicar of Bearsted. The Bishop always took care to explain his symbols of office as the children were fascinated by the mitre hat he wore, and his crozier.

Although the immediate problems with the new building were addressed once finance and labour were available, others took longer to remedy. The wholly inadequate landscaping and drainage of the grounds caused persistent problems which became evident fairly quickly into the first term. Any heavy rain usually resulted in flooding on the playing field and sometimes extended up to the building itself.

The end of the first year was celebrated over two evenings with an 'end-of-the-year' summer Prom concert; 133 children took part. On the second night, two things added to the atmosphere of the concert. The headmaster's appearance in a white jacket similar to that of the conductor, Colin Davis, had caused some comment. Also, two flags appeared in the front row to be waved in the 'Prom' tradition! The year was concluded by the presentation of a gift token from the fourth year children to Mr Finch as a completely unexpected present: he was much moved by their generosity and thoughtfulness as they left the school.

The next few years brought much growth and many changes as the school established itself into new routines to meet the demands of an evolving curriculum. It took some time to adjust to the new building as the numbers of children attending steadily increased. The core curriculum continued along a disciplined framework of learning defined by the class teacher but there were changes. As a result of developments in educational policies and thought, children of roughly the same ability worked together in Group Working, but each group studied different subjects at the same time. As children progressed through the school, the size of the working group was reduced. The curriculum was subtly modified to encompass periods of whole class teaching, and increasingly individual working as projects and themes were introduced.

All the clubs that had been previously available at the old school building continued. These included Chess, Draughts, Art & Craft, Needlework, Drama and Verse-speaking. The entries for the Monckton Art Cup and the trophy for Craft were of a consistently high standard. The work submitted for these two prizes was displayed in the hall. Mr Finch recalled it took nearly three days to mount and hang all the paintings and drawings. The needlework and other pieces of craft were also carefully displayed to the best advantage. On many occasions this work completely filled the available space!

The Maypole team continued to give regular displays at local fêtes and fairs and were invited to dance at Leeds Castle. This became a regular event. The first performance was in the courtyard of the castle. Mr Finch took along the wooden benches that were used during school lunchtimes so that the parents could sit down to watch. In later performances, the dancers were awarded the accolade of being allowed to perform on the croquet lawn. The castle managers specially requested that Mr Finch continued to bring along the wooden benches as they felt that it added to the ambience of the occasion!

This photograph shows some of the dancers:

(Photograph courtesy of Vernon Finch)

New clubs were also set up: gymnastics and swimming were popular as progressive award schemes such as those offered by the British Amateur Gymnastic Association and Amateur Swimming Association were followed. Both of the latter were overseen by Mr Cecil. A large wooden shed to accommodate the growing collection of rabbits and guinea pigs was erected by the main playground entrance. The children were encouraged to care for the animals through a system of Pet Monitors.

Some long-serving members of staff left and new appointments were made. Miss Daphne Clement retired in 1973 after twenty-six years of service to the school although she returned occasionally to give illustrated talks about her travels in the Holy Land. Mrs Pauline Sisley took over from Miss Clement as deputy head. Pauline Sisley's subsequent departure brought the return of Alan Cecil who had previously left to become deputy head at Boughton Monchelsea Primary School.

The musical reputation of the school continued to grow as Vernon Finch was able to develop a policy of giving every child the opportunity to learn to play a musical instrument. An increasing number of concerts and plays were performed. The high standard of both the performers and the productions were always appreciated by the audience. Particular care was always taken over the set design and scenery. However, these high standards led to an unexpected situation. One evening, dressed in very old clothes, Mr Finch stayed late to build part of the set for a pantomime production of Cinderella. The design for the coach had caused some problems as it was based around a small trolley that was tapered to one end to achieve a degree of perspective. At 11.45pm, the doorbell to the school was rung. Two policemen were making enquiries following a telephone call from a local resident who was concerned that all was not well at the school. The policemen were rather surprised to be advised by Mr Finch that Cinderella's coach was under construction! A quick inspection sorted matters out before midnight. Mr Finch was grateful for the concern raised by his activities and the indication that the school had now become established in the community around Landway.

The next two photographs show part of a regular orchestra practice in 1973. It was almost unique for a primary school in Kent to have this number of children playing stringed instruments. The tympani were equally uncommon.

(Photograph courtesy of the Kent Messenger group)

(Photograph courtesy of the Kent Messenger group)

The advances in musical instrument playing consolidated into a permanent arrangement with the Kent Music School as their peripetatic teachers now gave individual lessons in school. Gradually, as more children began to play instruments, orchestra practice evolved into separate 'junior' and 'senior' sessions.

In 1971 the Youth Orchestra had commenced at the old Bearsted School building. This was started by the older children who had just left the school but still wanted to play and give musical concerts together. Bernard Cley gave great help with the training of the violin section of the Youth Orchestra. Trevor Webb was the accompianist for rehearsals and concerts. After the move to Roseacre, the Youth Orchestra continued to flourish although Mr Webb had to relinquish his support and was replaced by Mr Markham Chesterfield.

Around this time, fairly regular invitations were accepted for both choir and orchestra to give concerts in different schools and churches in the area. Concerts, plays and other productions given by the children always had a very significant musical content so the participants consistently experienced performing together. On many occasions Roseacre joined up with other schools - a concert with Balgowan School, Beckenham was particularly successful, as was a concert at Rye parish church. The confidence gained by the children was invaluable and many Old Scholars have had distinguished musical careers. Andrew Snowdon, built upon the foundation of the performance experience gained from his years at the school and achieved the distinction of becoming House Master and Lay Chaplain to the choir of King's College, Cambridge.

On 29 June 1977 the Dean and Chapter of Canterbury Cathedral gave permission for the choir to present an informal choral recital in the cathedral which achieved great acclaim. From the log book:

This morning sixty seven children of our school choir gave a short choral recital in Canterbury Cathedral from 11.30am to noon. The programme demanded two-part singing and included:

Ave Verum (Mozart)
Panis Anglicus (Cesar Franck - sung in Latin)
Ex Ore Innocentium (John Ireland)
As I Outrode this Enderis Night
Riding on a Donkey (A Carol).

The programme (sung completely from memory) began and ended with a two-part presentation of Psalm 84 *How Amiable are Thy Dwellings*. The choir was accompanied by Mr Markham Chesterfield and Mr Trevor Webb using a delightful small Collins pipe organ. The choir sang from the tiered stands erected for the Canterbury Choral Society's presentation of Verdi's *Requiem* at the eastern end of the Nave. The quality of the singing surpassed my expectations and was apparently enjoyed by approximately a thousand visitors sitting in a fairly full nave! A number of visitors were kind enough to express their appreciation to me personally after the performance. The Reverend Alan Humphries, Cathedral Sacrist, remarked that the choir 'sang superbly'.

It was the start of a regular engagement which was to last over five years. Subsequently, the choir also sang in Rochester Cathedral. This photograph shows the choir standing in front of the quire screen at Canterbury Cathedral on a later occasion:

(Photograph courtesy of Vernon Finch)

In 1973 the Kent Education Committee removed the selection procedure to secondary school through examination at eleven for children. Up until this time, it was generally acknowledged that a school was performing particularly well if twenty-five percent of the children that were eligible for the examination were entered. At Roseacre, forty percent of the children were routinely entered for the examination.

Under the new system, children automatically transferred to local high schools in Maidstone. After two years of continuous review, children who were assessed by the high school to be of sufficient ability, then transferred to technical or grammar schools. The secondary high schools for Roseacre were Vinters High School for Girls in Union Street and Vinters High School for Boys located in Huntsman Lane. Later on, children also transferred to Senacre Secondary School in Sutton Road and Swadelands School in Lenham.

Housing developments continued around Bearsted and the school roll began to rise sharply. Barely two years after opening the new building, with the roll standing at two hundred and eighty nine, a mobile classroom had to be installed in the grounds. It was the first of three such classrooms that were added to the school.

In 1975 it was decided to review the system of Managers whose duties now extended to cover all the schools in the Bearsted area. As a result of the deliberations, the Managers decided that it was more appropriate to have separate bodies for each of the two schools at Madginford, as well as Thurnham Infants and Roseacre. The first meeting of the newly constituted Managers took place in January 1976.

The role of Managers was again under national review in 1981. Following parliamentary legislation, they were replaced by School Governors whose role and responsibilities significantly changed. Governors were now legally responsible for both business and education activities within the school.

A visit by Dr Rhodes Boyson, Under-Secretary of State for Education and Science on 4 February 1982 was an important moment for the school. Dr Boyson was accompanied by several members of the County Education Committee and the Chairman of the school governors. The visit gave partial recognition of the high academic and pastoral standards that were being achieved at Roseacre. However, one Old Scholar remembered the visit only as a group of men touring the building, constantly talking and all wearing very similar suits!

In July 1986, Vernon Finch announced that he had decided to retire after twenty two years in office. His decision was influenced by the fact that he had contracted cancer, for which he had received surgical treatment in 1984. Nevertheless, it was with very mixed feelings and considerable thought about the matter that he resigned from his post as Headmaster in July 1986. Mr Alan Cecil became Acting Headmaster until a new head teacher could be appointed.

Vernon Finch's term of office had overseen a quiet revolution in education in Bearsted. He had endured the successful struggle for a new building and accompanied the school as it moved through the difficult early years at the new location. He retained the values of traditional education but was quick to introduce new ideas where appropriate. However, it was his contribution to the development of music in a junior school that was truly remarkable. In particular, he will be remembered by the children that started to play instruments and learned to appreciate the cultural value of music which was carried through into their later lives.

A new chapter in the life of Roseacre School began with his successor, Mrs Dawn Perry.

Chapter 13
Into the Millennium

Mrs Dawn Perry began her duties as Headteacher in April 1987; the fourth woman to be appointed to a long tradition. Her tenure of office witnessed many changes. Almost immediately, old adversaries demanded attention: the provision of sufficient accommodation in a building that needed constant maintenance. Although the building was only fifteen years old it was already far too small for the number of children on the roll.

During summer holidays, building work started on the new Thurnham Infants School. This required the three mobile classrooms to be re-located to the Landway entrance side of the grounds. Work then began to re-surface the flat roof to the school. During the third week of August, heavy thunderstorms and rain resulted in part of the building suffering flooding. Most of the damage was quickly repaired but the start of the Autumn Term was delayed for a week whilst staff prepared the school for re-opening.

This calamity was followed a few weeks later, by the Great Storm which spent the night of 15 October blowing a turbulent path through the country. All the schools in the county were subsequently closed the next day. The damage incurred to the school was thankfully small: the loss of a television aerial and a gate to the oil tank seemed minimal compared with the havoc wreaked upon other parts of the village and county. The *Royal Oak* public house by the Green at Bearsted lost its external namesake but a replacement was planted in December and some children from Roseacre attended the ceremony.

Dawn Perry brought with her a special interest: very bright and intelligent children. Staff were encouraged to undertake special training in this aspect of teaching. Schemes of 'differentiated' work were developed: these were appropriate to the ability of the child, but still fitted into the lesson plans. Links were also formed with the National Association for Gifted Children and Oxford University in their research programmes for able children. Such work has been one of the most recent outstanding aspects of the school.

In 1987, the Minister for Education introduced the National Curriculum as part of the 1988 Education Reform Act. There was further legislation in the Act that was to affect Roseacre. The provisions reduced the powers of the Local Education Authority and encouraged school governing bodies to consider opting out to become 'Grant Maintained'. Schools that took this step would be funded by a grant directly from the government. On 5 June 1989, Roseacre was inspected in the new style of continuous assessment required by the Act. As the power of the Local Education Authority diminished, there was increasing local management of the school. On 3 April of the following year, Roseacre became responsible for finance and the first budget was produced. A copy of the budget can be found in Appendix Eight.

The government also wished to determine levels of knowledge for children at a defined age. This idea was developed over the next few years into the 'Key Stage' tests which would examine children at the ages of seven, eleven and fourteen. Once the programme of testing had been established, children commenced their career at Roseacre having been already assessed at Senior Infants level, or Year Two as it became known. There was another round of testing in the final year at Roseacre, or Year Six, prior to moving onto secondary education.

In January 1989 the new Thurnham School was opened. Both schools now shared the same approach road. At the start and finish of the day, there would now be many more children, parents and cars in the same area. To reduce the number of children using the road, a new main entrance for the pupils replaced the caretaker's store. A traffic calming scheme was implemented with a speed hump outside the main school doors.

Whilst all this change had been taking place, distant shades from the past were present when the 150th anniversary of a school in Bearsted was commemorated in 1989. The celebrations took the form of a 'Victorian Fayre' which was held with staff and children in Victorian dress. There was a display of Maypole dancing and other activities included many Victorian games and sideshows. It was very different to 1839 when another, rather smaller building had been opened to educate the children in the parish.

The move to local management and financial control accelerated the introduction of computers into the school although it was some time before the administrative potential was fully achieved. The first computers had been installed in the early years of the 1980s, overseen by the enthusiastic Mr Cecil. In 1987 a NIMBUS computer system replaced one based on BBC Micros. A few months later the class lists were typed onto a computer system and stored on a disk for the first time. By 1991, Roseacre had an e-mail address and the staff were tentatively using it. It was a small start to a revolution that was to ultimately lead to the demise of the written log book as the daily entries are now entered on to a computer.

Early in 1990 the need for further maintenance and repairs became startlingly apparent when part of a wall in Class Two fell down. An investigation revealed that at least one wall near the external door in every classroom had been built without the insertion of wall-ties and so was liable to collapse at any time! This frightening discovery resulted in urgent discussions with the Education Department over the need for repair and a possible extension. A timely decision was made as the mobile classrooms that had been installed since 1975 could not have lasted much longer, despite regular maintenance. The number of children to be accommodated was certainly not diminishing.

The new extension comprised four classrooms, a music room, toilets and a secure store room on a split level accessed by a short staircase. It was completed on 19 September 1991. Ironically, the new split level was similar to the previously rejected plans from 1967! Later on, a small stair-lift was added to cater for any pupils who might experience difficulties in climbing the stairs.

The new accommodation was named 'Thornacre' in a competition won by Charlotte Acton who was a pupil. This time there was no argument about an official opening! The ceremony was performed by the Member of Parliament for the Mid-Kent Constituency, Andrew Rowe, on 22 November. A facsimile of the opening programme is shown overleaf. A plaque in the extension commemorates the opening and an acer tree, donated by the Chairman of the Governors, was planted in the grounds.

By the time the Thornacre extension was completed, the governors at Roseacre had been considering the advantages of 'Grant Maintained' status. The consultation about the matter amongst the staff and parents was exhaustive. Finally, a ballot of parents was overseen by the Electoral Reform Society in 1991 which resulted in widespread approval but it was not until 22 February 1993 that the Secretary of State approved Roseacre's change of status. A new title was designated for the school:

Roseacre Grant Maintained School

Mr Bernard Head, employed as a Bursar some months previously, was appointed Business Manager as a firmer financial footing needed to be achieved. It was envisaged that the school could now effectively be run as a business through a series of structured development plans. Areas of the school that benefited from the extra money were improved staffing, extra resources for the children, and a continued improvement of the premises.

The new status and title of the school were incorporated into the new sweatshirts that were introduced as part of the official uniform. They were navy blue and very smart in appearance, bearing the Roseacre badge on the left hand side. They were immediately very popular.

This is a facsimile of the official opening programme:

ROSEACRE SCHOOL BEARSTED

OFFICIAL OPENING OF SCHOOL EXTENSION
BY ANDREW ROWE, M.P.
Friday, November 22nd 1991.

BEARSTED SCHOOL ~
Extracts from the School Log
And Looking Ahead.
Introduction by the Chairman of
Governors and the Headteacher

1. A musical tradition begins:
   School Recorders.
2. Victorian Schooldays and the
   Victorian Headmaster
3. "Kate Wins a Scholarship ~ 1930"
   from "The Family From One End
   Street".
4. The Second World War ~ children
   from Plumstead are evacuated to
   Bearsted
5. Moving to the present site ~ 1972
6. Roseacre in the 1990s
7. The story of the extension, 1991.
8. Preparations for Europe ~ 1992.
9. The school of the future.
10. The musical tradition continues ~
    The Senior Choir.
    We shall all join the choir in
    singing "The Lord's my shepherd".

Following the concert we shall
adjourn outside, where Andrew Rowe
will plant a tree.
Refreshments will then be served
in the new extension.

(Reproduced courtesy of Roseacre School)

Entry arrangements into secondary schooling were once again under re-consideration following the introduction of the Key Stage tests in the early years of the 1990s. In Maidstone, the 11+ examination was re-introduced to determine entry into secondary education. In January 1993, the first examinations held at Roseacre since 1971, were taken by Year Six children. This was eventually followed in 1995 by the first Department for Education Key Stage Two Standard

Assessment Tests. The children took two papers in Mathematics and Science and three papers in English. A small group of able children sat an extra paper in Mathematics. All the papers sat nationally were externally marked.

Life was not all work though, as later in 1993 the first Year Six residential trip abroad took place during the week 28 June to 2 July. A group of children visited France and the trip culminated in a visit to Euro Disney in Paris. Dawn Perry commented in the log book that it had been a wonderful, if exhausting, experience, but she had also brought back some Minnie Mouse ears! Residential trips were later expanded to include Year Five children. They have been offered the chance to spend a week at a working farm or to participate in outdoor activities such as canoeing, hiking and abseiling through a resource centre. There are non-residential activity programmes available for children who prefer to stay closer to home.

Around this time, the school began to receive enquiries about entry from parents who were thinking about settling in Kent to be closer to work demands in the Continent. When the Channel Tunnel was officially opened in 1994, theory gave way to reality. Roseacre's contribution to the new means of travel was a mural painting by Year Five children. The official unveiling at the Folkestone terminal was witnessed by a party of the artists. Two months later, the Tour de France visited England and flashed by a party of children who had travelled down to Ashford for the event.

The school had attracted considerable attention from many quarters since the move to Grant Maintained status. In recognition of the high standards achieved by the children, Dawn Perry was invited to meet the Prime Minister.

This high note was promptly tempered by the news of subsidence in the playground. The records were checked concerning a previous incidence in the playing field during Mr Finch's headship. This had been thoroughly investigated and resolved by pumping concrete into the hole. Another full investigation ensued but it was not resolved until April 1996 by which time the subsidence was estimated to extend sixteen metres below ground. It had been caused by earlier quarrying and the extraction of Fullers Earth. As the remedial work was completed, and the protective barriers were finally removed, there was a slightly eerie reminder of a previous industry in the area which had made its presence felt.

In 1995 the 50th anniversary of VE Day was commemorated. On 9 May, a 'street party' was held at the school with both children and staff in 1945 costume. The visit of Mrs Edith Coales to see her son's name on the war memorial sundial in the courtyard was a poignant moment for everyone, as was her later visit in 2002. On both occasions she talked to the children about her life through wartime and the reign of Elizabeth II. Edith recalled, with particular pleasure, how the children sat on the hall floor by her feet, listening intently, as she spoke to them about John. The 'Thank You' letters, signed by the children, that she subsequently received, remain treasured possessions.

Later in 1995 the work to refurbish the classrooms occupied by Year Three children was completed. The classrooms had been reshaped to reflect the move away from the 'Group Working' current at the time the school had been built. Unremittingly, the roll had risen and it was decided that an extension to provide two further class rooms was required. In 1996 a start had been made on the foundations but there were also other building works continuing in the school. Mrs Perry recorded in the log book:

<u>Summer Holidays 1996</u>
Extensive building work. Year 4 classrooms extended and refurbished. A new glazed corridor built across the end of the courtyard. The result is a very smart school. Since becoming Grant Maintained in April 1993, every classroom has been extended.

In addition to the two new classrooms, an additional room was added on a corner plot to house the library in the Thornacre area. As the building work was completed through 1996-97, the library stock was reviewed and replenished. The building was now in better shape than 1972! This diagram shows the new layout of the school:

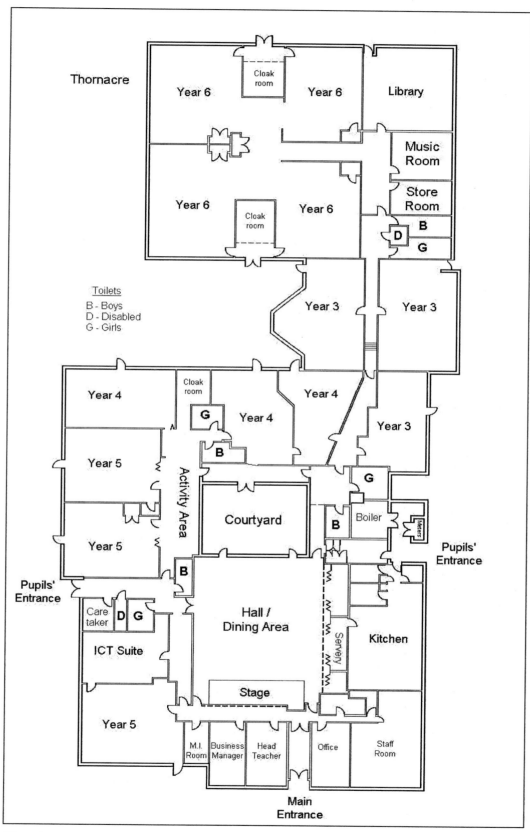

(Illustration courtesy of Roseacre School)

1997 was a year made brilliant by the Silver Jubilee of the relocation to the Roseacre site. To mark the event a photograph was taken of the entire school and a copy hung in the foyer. A new Latin motto was adopted:

Labore ludoque gaudeamus

(Let us be happy in work and play)

The Jubilee events included an Anniversary Concert and an Open Day during which visitors were served lunches and teas. Messrs. Rickwoods of Bearsted supplied two anniversary cakes so there was an historic link to the old Bearsted School building as the Rickwoods premises now occupy the site of Perrin's Stores at Chestnut Place. The celebrations concluded with an anniversary picnic lunch on the playing field for all four hundred and seven children on the roll.

Barely a week later, the new Labour government indicated that it was considering the future for all Grant Maintained schools. A review was to take place into all expenditure in education. Roseacre prepared for the first OFSTED inspection and report with this uncertainty as a backdrop. It was decided that the Grant Maintained schools would receive funding once more through the local education authority in order to achieve a greater equality of funding between all state schools. Schools that were previously Grant Maintained would now be known as 'Foundation' schools. Roseacre became a Foundation school on 1 September 1999 and is now known as:

Roseacre Junior School

In 1998 a plan was developed to build a Greek-style miniature amphitheatre with a tiered brick seating area. Parents were thoroughly involved in the fund-raising for the £20,000 project which opened in a year later. Together with an attractively-planted garden area, it is generally used to enhance lessons such as English, drama, geography and history. The photograph below shows the amphitheatre following completion of the landscaping.

(Photograph courtesy of Malcolm Kersey)

Roseacre thoroughly celebrated the Millennium! A photograph of the entire school: children, teachers and other staff was taken shortly before it was announced that the school had been awarded 'Beacon School' status. This was in recognition of the high academic and teaching standards achieved and delivered. To mark the event, the Union flag was unfurled on the flagpole and the happy atmosphere was almost palpable! Later on in the year, a twenty-five minute video about the school: *Welcome to Roseacre Junior School* was released for sale by Wizard Video Productions Limited. The video sold very well.

Ancient and modern times were considered by the children through an historical pageant which took place on the playground and used the new amphitheatre as a backdrop whilst the weather and daylight permitted. The performances coincided with some very hot weather. On the first night it seemed rather appropriate that as the death of Thomas à Becket was depicted, there was a crack of thunder and rain poured down! There was a hasty adjournment of proceedings whilst the production transferred to the assembly hall.

Some aspects of everyday life in Millennium times were highlighted by several separate projects. Information Technology is now present across the curriculum and it was felt that an appropriate project to commemorate the Millennium and benefit the children would be the establishment of an Information Communication and Technology suite. It was overseen with great enthusiasm by Mr Mark Geadah. The suite offers all children the opportunity to use computers and Internet access. Lessons now include word processing, databases, graphics and programming.

After the Millennium celebrations, the children were keen to commemorate the Golden Jubilee of Queen Elizabeth II's accession. Mrs Barbara Thomas, a member of staff, had the good fortune to receive a ticket to one of the two very special Jubilee concerts held in the grounds of Buckingham Palace. Mrs Perry made a special trip to London in order to witness some of the Jubilee festivities and took many photographs. Later they wrote down some of their impressions and memories. These were used, along with the photographs, to arrange a wall collage about the Jubilee. Many parents were just as fascinated as their children by the display and spent some time looking at it!

The performances of the maypole team at local events were rather special in the Golden Jubilee year too. During the performances at Bearsted Fayre, Otham Fête and the Bearsted Brownie and Girl Guides Summer Fayre held at *Snowfield*, many local residents talked about the long tradition of this dancing practised by the children at the school. Robert Skinner would have undoubtedly approved of the fact that the tradition, begun under John Sarjeant's headship, and developed by him, had continued to the present day. This photograph shows the Maypole team in performance at Otham Fête in June 2002:

(Photograph courtesy of Malcolm Kersey)

The school celebrations for the Jubilee included a summer concert and a pageant of children's literature. The orchestra and choirs performed at the Kent Music School premises at Astley House to immense acclaim. The pageant featured excerpts from the work of children's authors ranging from Enid Blyton through to J K Rowling with singing, dancing and poetry performed by the classes. Many parents sitting in the audience commented on the apparent confidence and enjoyment shown by the children as they performed their items. A copy of the programme, which was printed on aptly gold coloured paper, is shown below:

"FIFTY GOLDEN YEARS OF CHILDREN'S LITERATURE"

Afternoon Performance - Monday 1st July
Evening Performance - Wednesday 3rd July

YEAR 3 - presents Tales from Enid Blyton

Introduction
Song - "The Faraway Tree"
Dance - Fairy Dance
Five on a Treasure Island
Song - "Row Row"
Song - "A Policeman's Lot"
Noddy
Song - "The Faraway Tree"

Interval

YEAR 5

5R	BFG by Roald Dahl
5W	The Church Mice by Graham Oakley
	Summer Holiday by Graham Oakley
5G	Charlie & The Chocolate Factory by Roald Dahl
5W	Rats by Graham Oakley
	The New Parson by Graham Oakley
5R	Matilda by Roald Dahl

Afternoon Performance - Tuesday 2nd July
Evening Performance - Thursday 4th July

YEAR 4 & YEAR 6

Year 6CA	The Bash Street Kids from The Beano
Year 4HC	Playground Poetry
Year 6DT	Chitty Chitty Bang Bang by Ian Fleming
Year 4BT	"When I grow up!" Aspirations for the future

Interval

Year 6CL	Harry Potter and The Philosopher's Stone by JKRowling
Year 4HB	People, Poems & Pets
	Year 4 choir
Year 6GM	The Lottie Project by Jacqueline Wilson

There will also be refreshments provided, courtesy of the PTA. Tickets for the Grand Draw will be drawn after the performance on Thursday 4th July.

(Illustration courtesy of Roseacre School)

All these celebrations were something of a swan-song for Dawn Perry. It had been announced in May that she had been appointed to the Local Education Authority as a member of the Kent Primary Excellence Team of Advisors. During Mrs Perry's tenure of office, Roseacre coped with many changes that affected everyday life to an almost unprecedented degree. It is due to the highly professional, dedicated staff and governors that the school has smoothly adapted through the recent changes to status and different methods of funding.

After Mrs Perry's departure, Mrs Beth Lloyd became Acting Headteacher before appointment as Headteacher on 20 February 2003. This was announced to the children in a special assembly held in the school hall by Mr Peter Begbey, Chairman of the Governors the following day. The children spontaneously erupted into applause! Mrs Lloyd has now taken up her place as the eighteenth teacher to be appointed the charge of the school. She is the fifth Headteacher of the school but possibly the first teacher to admit purchasing a car of sufficient length to accommodate the maypole, should it require transporting!

During the winter months, the lower part of the playing field continued to suffer from poor drainage, quickly becoming water-logged. It was decided to solve this problem by installing a games pitch with all-weather playing surface. There was a substantial financial contribution from the Parents Association.

The playing surface was officially opened on 6 June 2003 during a "Summer Open Afternoon". The special guest was John Colyer who has a company supplying cars for use in feature films. He brought along a Ford Anglia which had featured in one of the *Harry Potter* films as the car driven by the Weasley family. It was very popular with the children who were rather hoping that some of the magic evident in the film would rub off! John Colyer was invited by Mrs Lloyd to cut a ribbon stretched across the pitch.

(Photograph courtesy of Babs Jossi)

This photograph shows John Colyer duly declaring the surface open for use.

A new chapter has now begun as the school progresses into the twenty-first century. Whatever changes and challenges may have to be met in the future, the staff will meet them with fortitude and courage, mindful of the traditions embodied in the school and of a distinguished history. These traditions and hope for the future are perhaps best expressed in the school motto:

Labore ludoque gaudeamus

(Let us be happy in work and play)

Epilogue
Resurgam: A New Life for the Old Building

133 years passed between since the application in July 1839 for assistance towards establishing a school in Bearsted until the school departed on 29 March 1972.

Before the official announcement of the school's relocation, the vicar of Bearsted, Mr Waghorne, was in correspondence with the Director of Education for the Diocese of Canterbury about uses for the buildings once they became vacant. He was advised that once the buildings were available for sale, as an educational trust was involved, legally, the proceeds of any sale, had to be applied to educational work within the diocese.[1] Any plans of both the parish council and the parochial church council of Holy Cross church, Bearsted were limited by this restriction.

Consideration was given to erecting some temporary mobile classrooms for Thurnham Infants School but it was dismissed as impractical for the school to operate on two separate sites. A scheme to sell off School House separately from the main buildings was also not realistic, particularly as it was still occupied.

One idea that was only partially explored was to convert part of the building into flats for old people. A much later plan to rent part of the premises as a day centre for elderly people in the parish did not proceed either. Despite the failure of these plans, everyone in the village and diocese was keen to guard against the very real possibility of the sale of the premises leading to demolition.

In 1973 the Post Office gained permission to open a temporary office in the entrance hall. Two years later, after much negotiation, the Kent Library Service opened a branch library in the main building in September 1975. This was a much needed facility in the village. Previously, villagers had relied on regular visits from a library van and were also able to borrow from a small supply of books accommodated in the Women's Institute Hall.

This photograph shows the building now in use as Bearsted Library:

(Photograph courtesy of Malcolm Kersey)

181

Current facilities that are available in the library include a photocopying service and access to the Internet. The building is also used as a contact point for Neighbourhood Watch and a police surgery opened in May 1998. Residents are encouraged to use the library as an information and publicity point. It is a popular place to display posters about forthcoming events. There is now a small gallery in the foyer which many local artists and organisations use to stage small exhibitions. The library is also occasionally used as a venue for lectures on subjects of local interest.

Playgroups, nurseries, and schools are encouraged to visit the library and the staff undertake reciprocal visits. The staff also offer an advisory service to the local schools about their book provision. A 'Story Time' is held once a week for younger children during which the staff read stories and talking about them. By pursuing this policy of access to all, Bearsted is particularly fortunate that the tradition of educational provision is continued in the building erected specifically for that purpose in 1839.

In 1992, Guy Thomas, a local resident, led a welcome proposal to List the main building, which would safeguard it against future inappropriate development. However, the Department of the Environment was advised by English Heritage that a survey had been undertaken in 1984 and on this basis, it was concluded that parts of the building did not fit the criteria for Listing.

The building now lies within the Bearsted Green conservation area. However parts of the School House premises, used for storage purposes by the library, are already markedly deteriorating. It is apparent that there is an urgent need for a programme of regular maintenance if effective conservation is to be achieved.

Although the building cannot be demolished without a grant of consent, in view of the pressure for development on all areas of vacant land in the vicinity, it may now be appropriate to reconsider the matter of further protection.

Appendix 1
Headteachers of Bearsted and Roseacre School

Mr James Simmons	Master	*surmised from opening of school in 1839 (listed on 1841 Census) - up to 1843?*
Mr John Peirce Mrs Frances Peirce	Master Mistress	*from 1843? (listed on 1851 Census) - 1856*
Mr Samuel Taylor	Master	1856 - 1870
Mr Samuel Johnson	Master	1870 - 1872
Miss Love Jones	Mistress	1872 - 1874
Miss Elizabeth Vincent	Mistress	1874 - 1879
Mr Edward Barnacle	Master	1879 - 1881
Mr William Smith	Master	1881 - 1884
Mr John Day	Master	1884 - 1897
Miss Agnes Barclay	Mistress	1897 - 1905
Mr James Cripps	Master	1905 *(six months)*
Mr Frank C Goodman	Master	1905 - 1930
Mr John Sarjeant	Headmaster	1930 - 1937
Mr Robert Skinner	Headmaster	1937 - 1964
Mr Vernon R Finch	Headmaster	1964 - 1986
Mr Alan Cecil *(pro tem through post as Deputy Headmaster)*	Acting Headmaster	1986 - 1987 *(six months)*
Mrs Dawn Perry	Headteacher	1987 - 2002
Mrs Elizabeth Lloyd	Headteacher	2002 to present day

(Acting Headteacher pro tem through post as Deputy Headteacher prior to appointment 2003)

Appendix 2
School Prize Winners

From details found in the log books:

School Prizes distributed for good conduct February 1867

First Class
Emma Patten
Elizabeth Lurcock
Frederick Knowles
Thomas Matthews

Second Class
Maria Glover
Ian ….. Tolhurst *(name partly illegible)*
Thomas Rose
William Stanford

Third Class
Kate Hewitt
Sophia Rose
William Edwards
Hubert Cheeseman

Fourth Class
M A Tolhurst
Isabel Woolet
Herbert W…….. *(name partly illegible)*
Fred… …..ason *(name partly illegible)*

Fifth Class
Lucy Hodge
William Woolet
Herbert Hickmott
William Hewitt

List of Prize Winners 1906

Attendance Medals
Minnie Shorter, Victor Pollard

Attendance Certificates
Minnie Shorter, Victor Pollard, George Cooper, William White, Emily Baker, Alice Smith, Mildred Higgins

Books
Minnie Shorter, Victor Pollard, Ada Rose, Horace Medhurst, Winifred Jeffrey, Olive Rideout, Olive Hunt, James Torry, Herbert Baker, Charles Rixon, Violet Marsh, Ellen Blackwell, Frank Walkling, David Boulden, Fred Wilkinson, George Fuller, Fred Naylor, Wilfred Wilkinson

List of Prize Winners 1908

Bars to Attendance Medals
Victor Pollard (3rd year), Kate Torry (2nd year), Frank Torry, Reginald Allcorn, George Cooper

Attendance Medals
Elsie Fuller, Frances Rose, John Baldwin

Attendance Certificates
Enoch Turley, James Thompson, Basil Hazelden, Jos. Thompson, Ambrose Goodhew, Mary Hickmott, Kate Terry, Mildred Wilkinson, Alice Smith, Flossie Apps, Robert Rose, William Thompson, Alice Elliott, Thomas Ellis, Harold Allcorn, John Shoebridge, Ralph Hazelden, Alfred Hunt

Vicar's Prizes for Scripture
John Gasson, Ivy Stringer, Kate Terry, Fred Wilkinson, Alice Elliott, Stanley Bates, Lizzie Harland

Headmaster's Prize
Minnie Shorter

Wayte's Prizes
Emily Hodges, Herbert Tree, Florence Ellis, William Kennett, Henry Marsh, Ettie Baker, Lily Rixon, Reg. Allcorn, Flossie Apps, William Thompson, Elsie Fuller, Albert Shoebridge, Kate Torry, Mildred Wilkinson, Mildred Higgins, Vivian Briseley, Alice Smith, Minnie Baker, Nellie Jeffrey, William Hodges, Victor Pollard, Ben Attwood

Annual Prizes 1909

8 April
The annual Prize distribution took place this morning, the prizes being distributed by Mrs W H Whitehead, the vicar also being present.

Bars to Attendance Medals
Frank Torry, John Baldwin, Reg Allcorn

Attendance Medals
Ben Attwood, James Elliott, Henry Marsh, Alfred Hunt, Harold Allcorn

Attendance Certificates
Alice Elliott, Lizzie Martin, May Sharp, John Marshall, Thomas Ellis, Ellen Ellis, Florence Hickmott, Viola Hunt, Kate Terry, John Sharp, Robert Rose, Joseph Thompson, Victor Pollard, Richard Baker, May Shorter

Vicar's prizes for Scripture
Charles Stringer, Daisy Attwood, Lizzie Martin, Albert Tree, John Sharp, Violet Marsh, Ivy Stringer, Nellie Jeffrey

Headmaster's prize
Nellie Sharp

W H Whitehead prize for Drawing
Ben Attwood, Arthur Sent

Wayte's Prizes
Emily Hodges, John Shoebridge, Fred Wilkinson, Reg Allcorn, Frank Torry, Florence Hickmott, Mildred Higgins, Richard Baker, William Thompson, George Hunt, Mabel Holmes, Mildred Wilkinson, John Baldwin, Minnie Shorter, Frank Walkling, Eliza Harland, Flossie Apps, George Fuller, Hettie Baker, Victor Pollard

Annual Prizes 1910

<u>3 June</u>
Yearly prize-giving distributed by Mrs Nugent, accompanied by Miss Nugent and the Rev P Nugent, who addressed the children on 'Character'.

Bars to Attendance Medals
Frank Torry, Reginald Allcorn

Attendance Certificates
Bertie Earll, John Sharp, Lizzie Harland, May Shorter, Elsie Sent, Florrie Hickmott, John Marshall, William Sharp, Alfred Tree, Herbert Tree, Nellie Earll, Annie Merrall, Douglas Sharp

Vicar's Prizes for Scripture
C Stringer, Norah Baker, Emily Hodges, William Sharp, Vernon Elliott, Kate Terry, Mildred Higgins, John Sharp

G W Swinerd Prize for Needlework
C Hunt

W H Whitehead prize for Drawing
Herbert Hill

<u>Wayte's Prizes</u>
Claude Brisley, Elsie Sent, Bertie Earll, Florence Hickmott, Victor Pollard, Frank Walkling, R Baker, Ethel Gladstone, George Hills, Ivy Holmes, Elsie Baker, Ellen Ellis, Douglas Sharp, Jesse Tree, Charles Colgate, James Elliott, Hilda Tolhurst, Ethel Baker, George Fuller, May Shorter, Ivy Stringer, Fred Wilkinson, Flossie Apps, Lizzie Harland

Annual Prizes 1911

<u>7 April</u>
The annual distribution of prizes took place this afternoon, the Vicar and the Curate being present. Miss Nugent handed them to the winners. The school was addressed on the 'Benefits of Self-Control'.

Bars to Attendance Medals
Florence Hickmott, Alfred Hunt

Attendance Medals
Ellen Ellis, Alice Elliott, Holly Holmes, Herbert Tree, May Shorter, Bertie Earll, Vernon Elliott, Ronald Hunt, Percy James

Attendance Certificates
Ella Jeffrey, Jessie Tree, Winifred Elliott, Douglas Sharp, Harriett Selves, May Sharp, Hilda Tolhurst, Gwendolene Elliott, Ivy Holmes, Norah Baker, William Bennett, John Shoebridge, John Marshall, William Sharp, Robert Henderson, Hy. Jos. Selves, Kate Terry, George Fuller, William Ellis, Jack Baker, Ellen Elliott

Vicar's Prizes for Scripture
John Sharp, Lydia Marshall, Gwendolene Elliott, Dorothy Myles, Ivy Holmes, Oswald Higgins, Jesse Tree, Douglas Sharp, Gladys Holmes, Winifred Taylor

Wyatt's Prizes
Alfred Hunt, Ronald Hunt, Joyce Radwell, Ethel Swift, Sidney James, Charles Colgate, Ronald Marshall, Holly Holmes, May Sharp, George Hills, Ella Jeffrey, Florence Hickmott, Olive Hunt, George Fuller, R Baker, Laura Henderson, James Elliott, Jesse Baker, Bertie Earll, May Shorter, Fred Wilkinson, Claude Brisley, Elsie Sent, Dorothy Attwood

Undated List of Prizewinners.

This list is undated but was found enclosed in the log book 1908-1921. It provides a good indication of the type of books that were distributed as school prizes.

Vicar's Prizes for Scripture

John Sharp	*Martin's Drilling*
Lydia Marshall	*Seven Idols*
Gwendolene Elliott	*World of Ice*
Dorothy Myles	*World of Ice*
Ivy Holmes	*Royal Pardon*
Oswald Higgins	*The Two Shipmates*
J Tree	*Picture Book*
Douglas Sharp	*Picture Book*
Gladys Holmes	*Picture Book*
W Taylor	*Picture Book*

Wyatt's Prizes

Alfred Hunt (for Attendance)	*Guy's Ordeal*
Ronald Hunt	*Stories of Jesus*
Joyce Radwell	*Birds and Nests*
Ethel Swift	*Something to Find*
Sidney James	*Something to Do*
Charles Colgate	*David and Goliath*
Roland Marshall	*Favourite Tales (?)*
Holly Holmes (Attendance)	*Dean's Little Daughter*
May Sharp	*Edith's Charity*
George Hills	*Eric*
Elda Jeffrey	*Little Pearl*
Florence Hickmott (Attendance)	*A Brave Lassie*
O.Hunt (Needlework)	*Two in a Tangle*
G Fuller (Drawing 1st)	*Mali of Lily*
R Baker (Drawing 2nd)	*Captain Polly*
L Henderson (Geography)	*Edith's Charity*
J Elliott (Geography)	*Chronicles of Durnford*
J Baker (Arithmetic)	*Marshall Vavasour*
B Earll (Punctuality)	*Cruise of Katharina*
M Shorter	*Fan's Silken String*
F Wilkinson	*Athabasca Bill*
C Briseley (Politeness)	*Charley Ashley*
E Sent (Industry)	*Nora*
Daisy Attwood	*Curly's Crystal*

Appendix 3
Curriculum 1897

This information is taken from the log book:

<u>Work done in March, April, May 1897</u>

Standards IV, V, VI, VII   taught by John Day
Standards III, II   taught by Pupil Teacher

<u>**Standards VI – VII**</u>
Reading   Grouped with 4-6 pages
Writing   Short compositions on easy and familiar subjected
Arithmetic   Standard VI Fractions - first 4 rules
                 Compound Fractions
                 Finding factors of numbers as 625

<u>**Standard VII**</u>   Interest, Time, Water, Principles of per centage,
                 The 'Mil' system

<u>**Standard V**</u>
Spelling   About six lines of 'unseen' dictation and reproduction of a short story - about 6 lines

Arithmetic   GCM, LCM Factors as in Standards VI - VII, addition & subtraction of fractions.
                 Easy practice of simple problems

<u>**Standard IV**</u>
Spelling   Exercise on the silent letters, 'unseen' exercise of 6 lines
Arithmetic   Multiplication by factors etc e g 121 = 11+ 11
                 Division (Money) factors, Long measures - yard, foot etc

<u>**Standard III**</u>
Reading   60 pages of each Reader
Spelling   A simple piece from above
Arithmetic   Addition, Subtraction (Money), Division,

<u>**Standard II**</u>
Reading   50 pages of Readers
Spelling   Words of one syllable
Arithmetic   First 4 rules, Multiplication of two figures
                 Division to 7 places

Mental exercises for all Standards dealing with the £, lbs, year, hours

<u>Infant Classes taught by Miss Eaglestone</u>

Singing   By ear only from commencement of school year 1 March 1897

<u>**Standard I**</u>
Reading   To end of Practical Reader
Writing   Names without transcription
Arithmetic   Addition with problems
                 Mental, Money to 10/-

<u>**First Class**</u>
Reading   To end of reading book
Writing   Names, capital letters, easy words
Arithmetic   Mental Value of money to 7/6d
                 Halves of numbers to 30,   2 & 3 Multiplication Tables

Babies
Reading   Small letters
Writing   Letters o, a, d, g   Figures 4, 6 & 9
Recitation   *The Glass House, Grandfather's Maid, Benjamin and His Dog, Granny's Comforter, A Little Boy's Troubles*

Songs: *'Try', My Hands, The Robin. Oh Mousey*

Kindergarten

String Mats, Fraying, Stencilling, Coloured Drawing, Bead Threading, Brick Building

Scripture: Old Testament - Stories from the Creation to the Destruction of Sodom
New Testament - Early life of the Saviour from St Matthew and St Luke

Upper Group Old Testament   Kings   taken by Canon Scarth
New Testament   St Luke   Ditto
Catechism
Prayer Book - Morning Prayer

Recitation   St Matthew XXV 31-46
St Matthew X 28-42

Lower Group Old Testament   Early Life of Samuel
New Testament   Stories from the Acts
Catechism The Creed and Explanation

Recitation   Psalms 1, 13

Class Subjects
History   George I & II   Outline   Standards IV - VII
Geography   Scotland
Recitation   *Mary Antony* - 30 lines

Standard III
Geography   England - Physical Features
Recitation   *The Sunbeam*

Standard II

20 lines of *The Spring Walk*

Drawing   All Standards....Early figures and Scales

Songs: *Waves of Sound, Good Night, Come,Come*
Singing in the Upper Room by note to 31 May, Infants by ear

Following acids in the Stock Cupboard:
HNO_3 - Nitric Acid
H_2SO_4 - Sulphuric Acid
HCl - Hydrochloric Acid

$KClO_3$ - Potassium Chloride
$CaCO_3$ - Calcium Carbonate
$CaSO_4$ - Calcium Sulphate
Hg – Mercury
P – Phosphorous
S – Sulphur
Ca – Calcium
To illustrate Object lesson NaCl (Sodium chloride):

Appendix 4
Centenary Week 11 to 17 June 1939

The log book entries for Centenary Week:

Bearsted School was erected in 1839, so the above week was set aside for celebrating the Centenary. Two committees - a ladies and a gentlemen's were formed to carry out arrangements, and they worked splendidly and with great enthusiasm. The following activities were arranged and all were duly carried through.

Sunday
Commemoration service in the Church. The Lord Bishop of Dover officiated and gave an address, other clergymen were:- the Rev G A M Griffiths (vicar), the Rev G Luckett (curate), Rev K Haslam (Chairman of Committees), Rev Scutt (Vicar of Thurnham). After the service the children presented a photo of the school to the Bishop of Dover.

Monday
An Open Day was arranged for parents and friends, including an exhibition of old school photographs and original and later title deeds, including the foundation deed of April 1840.

Tuesday 8pm
'Friends of the School' Association in the studio of 'Bell House' by kind permission of Mr and Mrs R L S Monckton.

Officers:	President	W H Whitehead Esq., Under-sheriff of Kent
	Chairman	Mr R L S Monckton
	Secretary	Mrs J Monckton

A committee was also formed.

During the evening Mr A Voisey gave an interesting talk on Young Farmers Clubs and Mrs Monckton showed a film she had taken of the school. The senior old scholars, Mr C Wilkinson and Mrs G Walkling were presented with signed photographs of the school.

Wednesday
The Second annual athletics sports were held on the Green at 5.30 between teams representing the two houses, Bertie and Fludd.
Results:- *(left blank here)*

Thursday
Cricket v. Headcorn won 107 to 37

Batting:

			Bowling:		
Humphrey	1		Vane K	3 for 19
Brown D	30		Swift D	5 for 13
Baker J	0			
Vane K	4			
Swift D	11			
Bentley S	13			
James M	35			
Weller A	1			
Walkling S	0			
White P	11			
Cannon (not out)	0			

Rounders v Headcorn lost 2 -14

Scorers *(left blank here)*

At 8pm the Old Scholars formed an Association in the School:

Officers	President	Mr C Wilkinson (Senior Old boy)
	Chairman	Headmaster
	Secretary	Miss S Wilkinson

Appendix 5
Second World War Memorial

This is the log book entry which gives details of the dedication of the memorial sundial:

27 July 1949

School closed this afternoon as an occasional holiday, for the dedication of the War Memorial as below:

Alfred + Dover (Bishop of Dover)

W H Yeandle (Vicar of Bearsted & Chairman of the Managers)

next two signatures illegible - Churchwardens and Trustees of Bearsted School

The sundial was first planned as a memorial to Flight Engineer Eddie Keay and Flight Serjeant John Coales. Eddie Keay was School Captain and Captain of Fludd prior to the war, and was followed as school captain by John Coales, who was also Captain of Bertie. Eddie Keay took up motor engineering, John Coales went into Messrs Larkin to learn accountancy. The former joined the Home Guards as soon as he was old enough, the latter the ATC. Both volunteered at about the same time for the RAF, Eddie going into Bomber Command on Lancasters and John as a Fighter Pilot.

Eddie was missing from a heavy raid and no more has ever been heard of him. John survived the war but was killed in a Tempest V fighter while on duty, after having taken part in the Victory Fly past in London.

The influence of these two boys while here was magnificent, and no two boys in any type of school could have given of their best with such loyalty for the common good and in a manner entirely divorced from thoughts of self. Their schoolfellows, and many more who knew them supported the idea of the sundial. Later it was found that three other old boys were also killed, equally well-known and well liked before I came here. Notes regarding them will be added later.

The sundial was dedicated at 2.30 p m by the Lord Bishop of Dover in a touching but simple ceremony, the front of the school being crowded with sympathisers who had known them.

After the ceremony a folk dance display was held at *Snowfield* by kind permission of Captain and Mrs Litchfield-Speer.

Appendix 6
120th Anniversary Week 1 to 8 July 1959

This is the log book entry which gives details of the 120th anniversary week celebrations:

1 July Founders Day

10am	Communion Service	Bishop of Dover
2.30pm	Presentation of Inter-house Shields and Cups including awards by	
	Sir William Rolfe Nottidge at Women's Institute Hall	
	Unveiling of Commemorative Plaque in School Hall	

2.30pm - 8.30pm Open Day

2 July Senior Old Scholars Day

Old Scholars who were in the school in 1899 or before (60 years ago) visit
Followed by a visit to Hastings and tea at Sedlescombe

3 July Sports Day

7 July Concert for Children

8 July Concert for Adults at Women's Institute Hall

<u>Managers</u>

Rev J Long
Mr J Ellis
Mr Markinck
Mr R L Monckton
Mrs R J Bartle

<u>Guests</u>

Captain J Litchfield RN (retired) OBE MP
Bishop of Dover
Sir William Rolfe Nottidge (Past Chairman Kent Education Committee,
                                    Kent County Council))
Mr G L O Williamson & Mrs Williamson
Miss Maplesden Noakes (Chairman Divisional Executive)
Mr W Moore (Deputy County Educational Officer)
Miss Morphew (Vinters Girls School)
Mr Voice (Maidstone Boys Technical School)
Mrs Stockport (Thurnham School)
Miss Barnacle (Daughter of former headmaster)
Mr Tala Sasa (Solomon Islands)
Rev Sarkies (Curate of Bearsted)

also: Mr & Mrs T A Campbell of New Zealand House set off but the car broke down!

Awards presented 1 July

Whitehead Cup	Barty House
Monckton Art Cup	Janet Parsons
Sir William Rolfe Nottidge Crafts Cup	Penelope Keast (presented at concert)
Boys Swimming	Christopher Judge
Girls Swimming	Marilyn Wise
Chess Cup	Malcolm Belt
Draughts Cup	Dennis Cleggett
Verse Speaking:	
4th year	Rosalind Cooper
3rd year	Martin Prestman
2nd year	Susan Rabbatts
Bishops of Dover Shields	
Games	Barty House
Competitions	Barty House
Athletics	Barty House
School Work	Tied
Swimming Shield	Fludd

Appendix 7
The Early History of Roseacre

There are number of interpretations to the derivation of the name 'Roseacre'. Most sources agree that at least two elements of the word are Anglo Saxon: *hrōc*, meaning 'rook' or possibly, *Hrōc*, which could indicate a personal name. The second element, *œcer*, is also Anglo Saxon and indicates 'a cultivated piece of land'.[1] It is possible that the area became informally referred to, or known as, 'the land of the rooks'. Later on, it would be used as a place name recording the locality, but it is probable that when surnames came into common usage in the Twelfth and Thirteenth centuries, the name was then adopted by people originating from this area.

The use of the word as a place name took around five hundred years to achieve a regularised form. An early indication of the word 'Roseacre' being used as a personal name was recorded on 26 July 1242, when a man called Poteman de Rokesakere gave evidence at a form of inquiry in Henry III's reign to establish how much land Robert de Hucham had held 'of the King'.[2] In early medieval times, the name was recorded in some Lay Subsidy records. Lay Subsidies were an early form of taxation and under the Hundred of Eyhorne (an administration district that included Bearsted), a payment of 11 pence was made by Hugh de Rokesacre in 1334-1335.[3]

Several centuries later, a version of the Roseacre name is found in an indenture dated 1701.[4] The document details a scheme for land ownership and management by several people including Edward and Sarah Brice of Bersted and Thomas Brice of Boxley. Although the document describes Edward and Sarah as holding tenure of:

land in Rocksaker alias Russecar Street in the parish of Bersted

evidently they were not living there as the property, comprising a messuage, garden and bankside, was occupied by William Boghurts of Aylesford. Edward and Sarah agreed to pay William £3, together with any lawful interest, in order that he would leave and they could then hold and use the land for the tenure of their lives. The land would then pass to Thomas Brice and his heirs. It is likely that Thomas was Edward's brother or another close relative. It was considered noteworthy in legal documents that Roseacre was slightly set apart from the main village of Bearsted.

A surviving mortgage indenture dated 1735 gives another version of the name and a small history of a further part of the Roseacre area. Following a default upon a mortgage dated 27 May 1728, Thomas Rich of Debtling, yeoman, and William Lake of Rainham, yeoman sold it to Robert Dawson. The area is described: [5]

that messuage or tenement (commonly called Russikers) with the outhouses, lands, gardens, orchards and appurtenances thereunto being and containing in ye whole by estimation two acres be the sum more or less situate lying and being in Bersted aforesaid in the said county of Kent.....

There is one further set of documents concerning land holdings within Bearsted and Thurnham that seem to reflect the development of the Roseacre name and area.[6] The Barber and Ballard families, although based in Goudhurst and Horsmonden, held land, tenements and messuages in Bearsted between 1745 and 1828. Many of the documents describe the area:

that one other Messuage or Tenement with the Garden and Bankside thereunto belonging with their appurtenances containing by estimation half an acre of Land more or less situate lying and being in Rocksaker also Stretton Street in the parish of Bersted. [7]

As the properties expanded and developed, the area acquired a proper definition. The name gradually regularised to common usage as 'Roseacre Street'. The Roseacre area of Bearsted was definitely set a little apart from the rest of Bearsted village and, at one time, may have functioned as an independent hamlet. This is borne out by some of the early Nineteenth century trade directories for the county which refer to 'Roseacre Street' and estimate it to be a quarter of a mile west from the main village of Bearsted.[8]   In this respect Roseacre seems to reflect the linear pattern of settlement that is typical of Kent.

In 1948 the chosen site for the new school building in Roseacre Lane was part of Roseacre Farm, owned by Mr Bradley. The main farmhouse was originally situated off The Landway, and down a track which later became called Fauchons Lane. Plantation Lane was then known as Bradley's Lane. Aviemore Gardens and Fauchons Close were later built on the site of the farmhouse.

Appendix 8
First Local Finance Budget 1991

The details of the budget inserted into the log book:

	£
EMPLOYEES	
Teachers	226,400
Supply Teachers	4,000
Caretakers	5,000
Classroom Assistants	0
Welfare Assistants	0
Midday Supervisors	7,320
Senior Supervisory Assistants	0
Clerical Assistants	9,370
Advertising Non-teaching	0
Staff Interview Expenses	75
Advertising Teaching	425
Total Employees	252,590
PREMISES	
Maintenance of Buildings	3,600
Maintenance of Grounds	4,687
Fixtures and Fittings	0
Fuel Oil	1,820
Electricity	5,000
Gas	300
Other Fuels	0
Rates	0
Rents	0
Water	440
Sewage	600
Cleaning Heating and Lighting materials	690
Total Premises	17,137
TRANSPORT	
Transport to Classes	0
Public Transport	0
Car Allowances	1,000
Total Transport	1,000
BSAE	14,720
SUPPLIES AND SERVICES	
Laundry and Protective Clothing	70
Toilet and First Aid	620
Postage	150
Telephone Rentals	500
Telephone Calls	500
Staff Subsistence	0
Total Supplies and Services	1,840
Contingency Reserve	8,427
GROSS EXPENDITURE	295,714
INCOME	0
NET EXPENDITURE	295,714

Notes to the Text

1 Why Build a School in Bearsted

1   Will of Edward Godfrey 1709
CKS Ref. PRC/17/83 Folio 35

2   p.510
The History and Topographical Survey of the County of Kent
Edward Hasted
Volume V - first published 1798
Reprinted 1972 EP Publishing Ltd

3   *Op. cit.*
Will of Edward Godfrey

4   *The Parochial Library of All Saints, Maidstone and other Kentish parochial libraries*
Nigel Yates
Archaeologia Cantiana Volume XCIX (1983)
Kent Archaeological Society

5   William Streatfield is listed as a Registrar for Births and Deaths, but not Marriages!
Pigot and Co. National Commercial Directory
Kent Surrey and Sussex 1839
Facsimile Text 1993 published by
Michael Winton, Norfolk

6   pp. 163-165
Entry for Bearsted
History, Gazetteer and Directory of the County of Kent 1847
Samuel Bagshaw
Kent Archaeological Society Library

7   p.xv
A History of Education from 1760
H C Barnard
University of London Press (6th impression with amendments 1969)

8   *Ibid.* p.5

9   *Ibid.* pp.57, 9-11

10-11   *Ibid.* pp.63, 67-69

12   *Ibid.* pp.98-99

13   p.51
Education in Rural England 1800-1914
Pamela Horn
Gill and Macmillan 1978

14   *Op. cit.* pp.98-99
H C Barnard

15   *Op. cit.* p.51
Pamela Horn

16-17   Minutes of the Proceedings of Canterbury Diocese Education Society Board
CCA Ref. U45/A1

18   First Annual Report, Canterbury Diocesan Board of Education 1840
CCA Ref. U45/B1

19   *Op. cit.*
Minutes of the Proceedings of Canterbury Diocese Education Society Board

20   *Op. cit.*
First Annual Report, Canterbury Diocesan Board of Education 1840

21   p 27
        Enterprise in Education
        Henry J Burgess
        SPCK Press 1958

22-23   *Op. cit.*
        First Annual Report 1840 Canterbury Diocesan Board of Education

24   Deed dated 6 April 1840 and enrolled in Chancery 10 February 1842
        CKS Ref. U/1872/T/1

25   p. 1
        A History of Bearsted and Thurnham
        published Bearsted and Thurnham Local History Society 1978

26   *Op. cit.* p. 510
        Edward Hasted

27   Bearsted Tithe Map 1842 and apportionment 1844
        CKS Ref. P18/27/2,3

        Alderman Lucas used the business experience gained from the negotiations over this lease later on in 1840 to consolidate some of his own assets and land holdings. He lived in Wateringbury and offered to build a school for the children of the poorer inhabitants of the village providing he was granted thirteen acres of land at Canon Heath which was part of the manor of Canon Court. After protracted negotiation, the Dean and Chapter of Rochester, as Lords of the Manor gave the Alderman the desired thirteen acres on payment of one shilling per annum Quit Rent. See:

        Wateringbury in the Past
        W A Bolt
        Wateringbury Local History Society 1986
        CKS Ref. C 15 0497694

28   Bearsted Parish Chest Records
        CKS Ref. P18/25/1

29   A Visitation was a regular inspection of the parish by a Bishop or Archdeacon which often resulted in a list of works to be undertaken. The work resulting from such an event was usually listed in the Bearsted parish records separately to the annual accounts.

30   Document detailing Terms of Union with National Society dated 14 December 1839
        CERC Bearsted School file

31   Bidingfield Wise died 11 March 1840. His death was registered 17 March 1840.
        His will was made on 26 August 1839 and proved 21 April 1840.
        His named executors were his wife, Ann and his eldest surviving son, Lewis, together with William Gascoygne.
        CKS Ref. PRC 17/110 384 Folio 0189011

32   1851 Census for Bearsted. (The spelling of the surname Peirce is from the Census)
        PRO Ref. HO107/1616

33   Emily Peirce was born 13 June 1843 at Bearsted
        She was registered by her father, John Peirce, on 30 June 1843. The registrar was William Streatfield!

34   1841 Census for Bearsted
        PRO Ref. HO 107/456/7

35   The National Society Index of Schoolmasters records a James Simmons, listed as a fully trained Master, as teaching in Margate around 1846. It is possible that the post at Margate was his next promotion.
        CERC

2 The Development of the School up to 1914

1   Conveyance and Deed for Bearsted, Thornham, Debtling and part of Boxley
National School, 6 April 1840
Enrolled in Chancery 10 February 1842
CKS Ref. U/1872/T1

2-4   *Op. cit.* p.39
Henry J Burgess

5   1839 plan for Bearsted School
CKS Ref. DE/S/18/1

6   Bearsted Tithe apportionment drawn up 1842 for the Tithe map dated 1844
CKS Ref. P18/27/2,3

7   Application for aid, 6 August 1847
CERC Bearsted School file

8   p.244
A History of Education in Great Britain
S J Curtis
University Tutorial Press 1968

9   *Ibid.* p.238

10   *Op. cit.* p.51
Pamela Horn

11   United School Plan 1848
CKS Ref. DE/S/18/2

12   Application for aid, 7 May 1855
CERC Bearsted School file

13   Thurnham School Minute Book 1870-1899
Gordon Ward Collection
Kent Archaeological Society Library

14   *Op. cit.* p.130
A History of Bearsted and Thurnham

15   Holy Cross Parish Magazine, Bearsted September 1899
CKS Ref. P18/28/11

16   Letter dated 2 October 1879
CERC Bearsted School file

17   pp.11-12
Administrative County of Kent Endowed Charities
HMSO 1907
CKS Ref. XK 370

18   Indenture 22 July 1892 re Exchange of strips adjacent to school with John Perrin, grocer
CKS Ref. U/1842/T3

19   Receipt for Bearsted National School
CKS Ref. P18/25/1

20-21   Printed balance sheet for Bearsted National School 1894-95
CKS Ref. P18/25/2

22   Architects Certificate of Inspection 1901
CKS Ref. P18/25/4

23   The school was already in receipt of a £12 fee grant for children attending the school
aged between three and fifteen years.
Letter from Board of Education 1902
CKS Ref. P18/25/3

24 Letter dated 7 January 1903
CERC Bearsted School file

25 Holy Cross Parish Magazine, Bearsted October 1902
CKS Ref. P18/28/12

26-27 pp.11-12,20
The Centenary Magazine 1839-1939
R Skinner
CKS Ref. BX 94051530

28 Entry in log book, 23 March 1908
Bearsted School log book 1893-1908
CKS Ref. C/ES/18/1/3

29-30 *Op. cit.* p.20
R Skinner

31 Report concerning architect's proposals 1909
CERC Bearsted School file

32 The main object of drill exercises seems to have been to instil a sense of discipline and prompt obedience in a large group of children rather than scientifically structured physical exercises.

33 Holy Cross Parish Magazine September 1909
CKS Ref. P18/28/12

34 Grant awarded 27 May 1910
CERC Bearsted School file

35 Entry in log book, 12 January 1910
Bearsted School log book 1908-1921
CKS Ref. C/ES/18/1/4

36-37 Entries in log book, 3 October, 24 December 1910
Bearsted School log book 1908-1921
CKS Ref. C/ES/18/1/4

38 Grant awarded 27 May 1910
CERC Bearsted School file

3 Staff, Training & Teaching at Bearsted School

1 *Op. cit.* p.36
Pamela Horn

2 1841 census for Bearsted
PRO Ref. HO 107/456/7

3 *Op. cit.* pp.56-58, 64 *passim*
Pamela Horn

4 *Ibid.* p.42

5 The entry for Bearsted in *Monckton's Directory for Maidstone and the neighbouring villages*
published Walter Monckton, 1854
Gordon Ward collection
Kent Archaeological Society Library

6 *Op. cit.* p.60
Pamela Horn

7 p.147
Upon the Quarry Hills - A History of Boughton Monchelsea
Paul Hastings
published by Boughton Monchelsea Parish Council 2000

8   *Op. cit.* p.256
       S J Curtis

9   Minutes of the CCE 1852/53
       I
       p. 68
       Pupil Teacher Broadsheet
       Quoted in
       Lowly Aims and Lofty Duties
       Ruth Jennings
       Sheffield Academic Press 1994

10   Minutes of the CCE 1847/1848
       p.clxxiii-xlxxv
       Op. cit. p51
       Ruth Jennings

11   *Ibid.* p 51

12   *Op. cit.* pp.64-66, *passim*
       Pamela Horn

13   Holy Cross Parish Magazine, Bearsted 1874-1881
       CKS Ref. P18/28/8

14   *Op. cit.* p. 59
       Pamela Horn

15   *Ibid.* pp.111-112

16   pp.16-31, *passim*
       Education and policy in England in the 20ᵗʰ century
       Peter Gordon, Richard Aldrich & Dennis Dean
       The Woburn Press 1991

17   Document enclosed in log book 1908-1921
       CKS Ref. C/ES/18/1/4

18-19 *Op.cit* . pp.16-31, *passim*
       Peter Gordon et al

20-21 pp.226-228, *passim*
       The History of Maidstone
       Peter Clark and Lyn Murfin
       Alan Sutton Publishing Limited 1995

4 The Effects of Social Problems on the School

1   *Op. cit.* pp.126-127
       Pamela Horn

2   *Kent Messenger* 18 July 1891
       Particulars of sale Freehold on Church Farm, together with Roundwell Brickyard.

3   It is likely that Rev Cullum was an occasional visitor to the school although this is not
       recorded.

4   *Op. cit.* p.52
       A History of Bearsted and Thurnham

5   Coxheath Poor Law Union Death Register 1886-1889
       CKS Ref. G/Ma/Wic/502/3

6   *Op.cit* p.161
       Peter Clark and Lyn Murfin

5 Illness and Disease in the Village and School

1   pp.193-194
Labouring Life in the Victorian Countryside
Pamela Horn
Alan Sutton Publishing, reprinted 1995

2   *Op. cit.* p.144
Paul Hastings

3   *Op. cit.* pp.193-194,
Labouring Life in the Victorian Countryside
Pamela Horn

4   *Op. cit.* p.156
Peter Clark and Lyn Murfin

5   Document enclosed in Bearsted and Thurnham school log book 1908-1921
CKS Ref. C/ES/18/1/4

6   Document enclosed in Bearsted and Thurnham school log book 1908-1921
CKS Ref. C/ES/18/1/4

7   Bearsted and Thurnham school log book 1908-1921
CKS Ref. C/ES/18/1/4

6 The Curriculum Before the First World War

1   *Op. cit.* p.33
Henry J Burgess

2   *Ibid.* p.140

3   *Ibid.* p.85

4   Holy Cross Parish Magazine, Bearsted August 1875
CKS Ref. P18/28/9

5   *Op. cit.* p.258
S J Curtis

6   *Op. cit.* pp.16-31, *passim*
Peter Gordon et al

7   p.3
The Victorian and Edwardian Schoolchild
Pamela Horn
Alan Sutton publishing 1989

8   *Op. cit.* pp.46-48
Labouring life in the Victorian Countryside
Pamela Horn

9   Holy Cross Parish Magazine, Bearsted February 1882
CKS Ref. P18/28/10

10   *Op. cit.* pp.16-31, *passim*
Peter Gordon et al

11   Document enclosed in Bearsted and Thurnham school log book 1908-1921
CKS Ref. C/ES/18/1/4

12   Holy Cross Parish Magazine, Bearsted July 1909
CKS Ref. P18/28/12

7 Celebrations, Commemorations and Holidays

1   There was also provision for the Boxing Day holiday to be transferred to the following Monday if the 26th December fell on a Sunday.

        p. 10
        Leisure Pursuits in Kent 1850-1914
        Group Research Project 1973
        Kent Library Ref. C 15 0387466

2   *Maidstone Telegraph*
        21 June 1890 edition

3   Linton/Coxheath Poor Law Union Records
        School Attendance Committee
        Minutes Volume 1 1889-1903
        CKS Ref. G/Ma/Npe/1

4   *Op. cit.* p.135
        A History of Bearsted and Thurnham
        It is not known whether the garland was paraded in return for a small donation. In some areas of the country there were special verses that accompanied the garland:

> The first of May is Garland Day
> So please remember the garland;
> We don't come here but once a year,
> So please remember the garland.

        p. 59
        A Calendar of Country Customs
        Ralph Whitlock
        Batsford 1978

5   pp. 69-73
        A Season at Rosherville Garden
        George Frampton
        Bygone Kent
        Volume 17, No 2
        Meresborough Books 1996

6   p. 10
        British Empire Exhibition, *Official Guide*

7   *Op. cit.* p.144
        A History of Bearsted and Thurnham

8   Holy Cross Parish Magazine, Bearsted 1898 -1906
        CKS Ref. P/18/28/12

9   *Flower Mission 1875 -1905*
        J J Pearson
        Journal of Kent History
        Autumn 1977, No 5

10   Linton/Coxheath Poor Law Union Records
        School Attendance Committee, Minutes Volume 1 1889-1903
        CKS Ref. G/Ma/Npe/1

11-14 Holy Cross Parish Magazine, Bearsted 1875-1879
        CKS Ref. P18/28/8-11

15   Holy Cross Parish Magazine, Bearsted 1902
        CKS Ref. P18/28/12

16   Parish Council Accounts, Silver Jubilee 1935
        CKS Ref. P18/29/8

17-18 Holy Cross Parish Magazine, Bearsted 1935-1938
        CKS Ref. P18/28/18

19 Letter from Education Department, Tonbridge Road, Maidstone
    to clerk of Parish Council, 21 April 1937
    CKS Ref. P18/30/5

8 The Development of the School and Curriculum: 1914 - 1937

1   *Op. cit.* pp. 205-206
    Peter Clark and Lyn Murfin

2   *Ibid.* p.205

3   *Ibid.* p.207
    Some allotments were provided in 1916 by the County Council.
    Maidstone Town Council formed a Food Control Committee in 1917.

4   The upper photograph is not dated, and there are no other details about it. However, it is
    likely that it includes the youngest children in attendance at the school. Several of the
    girls are holding china dolls and one girl has a teddy bear. Careful examination of the
    bear reveals it to have a long snout - like the majority of the early bears produced by
    companies such as Steiff. Steiff started production around 1903 but teddy bears only
    really became popular about 1913.

    The lower photograph was used as an illustration of the children between 1917 and 1918
    in the *Centenary Magazine*. It bears the original printing instructions on the reverse.

5   *Op. cit.* p.156
    History of Bearsted and Thurnham

6   *Op. cit.* p.226
    Peter Clark and Lyn Murfin

7   *Op. cit.* p.157
    Peter Gordon et al

8   *Op. cit.* p.228
    Peter Clark and Lyn Murfin
    By the time of the Hadow Committee's next report in 1931 the local re-organisation of
    separate junior and senior schools had already been achieved.

9-11 *Op. cit.* pp.111-116, *passim*
     Peter Gordon et al

12 p.1
    *Educational Broadcasting - a report of a special investigation in the County of Kent
    during the Year 1927*
    Carnegie United Kingdom Trustees
    Comley Park, Dunfermline 1928
    Kent Library Reference C 150252393

13 *Op. cit.* p.157
    Peter Gordon et al

14 Application for a grant, 5 March 1935
    CERC Bearsted School File

15 p. 18
    The School Meals Service: From Its Beginnings to the Present Day
    Nan Berger
    Northcote House 1990

16 In a report to the School Managers dated 9 October 1956, Robert Skinner mentions that
    £40 had been raised in the previous year in addition to the voluntary funds:

    > 'so we can now purchase or assist in purchasing a proper full-size Maypole, a set of portable
    > goalposts for the Green and paving stones to cover the paths in the nursery beds...'

    but even this report does not make clear whether the school actually owned a Maypole by
    this time!

17   *Op. cit.* pp.29-30
R Skinner

9 The Sweet and Bitter Years: 1938 – 1946 Centenary and War-Time

1   pp.7-31, *passim*
Education in the Second World War: a study in policy and administration
PHJH Gosden
Methuen & Co Ltd 1976

2   *Ibid. passim.*

3   pp.67-71
Kent at War
Bob Ogley
Froglet Publications

4   *Op. cit.* pp.72-92
PHJH Gosden

5-6   *Ibid.* pp.183-209, *passim*

7-8   p.121
East Kent Within Living Memory
East Kent Federation of Women's Institutes & Countryside Books 1993

9   From the Internet websites: www.cwgc.org.uk, www.bomber-command.info, and from correspondence held by Irene Bourne (née Keay), sister to Eddie, it has been possible to piece together this information:

Edward Thomas Joseph Keay, had been the second School Captain and a Captain of Fludd before joining the Royal Air Force Volunteer Reserve. He was a Sergeant, RAF No 1896361, before becoming a Flight Engineer, 195 Squadron, Royal Air Force Volunteer Reserve. The squadron had been formed at Duxford, Cambridgeshire, in November 1942 and was based at Wratting Common, Cambridgeshire from November 1944.

Sergeant Keay's Lancaster Bomber (HK683) took off 23 November 1944 from RAF Witchford, Wratting Common at 1256 hrs for a raid on Gelsenkirchen, Germany. On the out bound flight, the aircraft caught fire and crashed in the sea, west of the Dutch island of Walcheren. All the crew members were reported as missing.

Although Eddie had actually been posted as 'Missing' by the Royal Air Force from the return of a bombing raid on 23 November, the telegram advising the family of this was dated 24 November 1944. It was less than three weeks before his twenty-first birthday.

From the Bomber Command diary:

> 23 November 1944
> 168 Lancaster planes of No. 3 Group carried out a GH (*anti-radar)* bombing raid through cloud on the Nordstein oil plant at Gelsenkirchen (*near Essen, Germany*). The bombing appeared to be accurate. One Lancaster plane was lost, registration HK683.

10   John William Coales had been the first School Captain and a Captain of Bartie in 1938 before joining the Royal Air Force Volunteer Reserve. At the time of his visit he was a Flight Sergeant, R A F No 1806859, with 35 Squadron. He served in many places in the Second World War including the Mediterranean and South Africa. He took part in the Victory Fly Past over Buckingham Palace. He died 27 June 1946 whilst on active service, aged twenty one. He was buried in the war cemetery in Hanover, Germany.

10 Chance, Change and Two Anniversaries: After the Second World to 1959

1   Letter to Minister of Education, 18 September 1946
PRO Ref. ED161/8141

2   Bearsted School file
CCA Ref. DCb/GT3/1

3   This epitaph had first been used on the Kohima Memorial. The words are ascribed to John Maxwell Edmonds (1875-1958), an English Classicist, who had assembled a collection of popular epitaphs for the First World War, in 1916.

4   Holy Cross Parish Magazine, September 1949
CKS Ref. P18/28/21

5   See footnote 1

6   Permission for an additional temporary classroom, July 1951
PRO Ref. ED 161/8141

7   pp.36-39
Focus on Roseacre County Junior School, Bearsted
Kent Education Gazette, December 1974

8   Deed of Conveyance, 14 April 1953
PRO Ref. ED 161/8141

11 New Opportunities: 1960 - 1972

1   Will of Charles Wayth,1851
PRO Ref. PROB 11/2157

2   It is possible that the details of the administration of the bequest were in an earlier log book which has not survived.

3   "Thinking Day" was intended to commemorate and celebrate the birthdays of the founders of the Girl Guides and Scout Association, Lord Robert and Lady Olave Baden-Powell. Wolf Cub Scouts changed their name in 1967 to Cub Scouts as the Scout Association felt the name sounded rather more modern!

4   No one seemed to be aware that similar flooding had occurred in 1890 and 1906 as described in an earlier chapter. At that time there were no school buildings in the vicinity.

5   Official Notice for new school at Bearsted
CKS Ref. P18/30/18

6-7   Sketch Design of proposed school, Draft III
November 1967
Unpublished papers and correspondence held by Vernon Finch

8   Sketch design of layout of proposed school, Draft IV, November 1967
Letter to Divisional Education Officer from Vernon Finch dated 11 December 1967
Unpublished papers and correspondence held by Vernon Finch

9   Letter from Kent Education Committee dated 15 October 1968
CKS Ref. P18/30/18

10   Correspondence Bearsted and Thurnham Parish Councils dated 18 November 1968
CKS Ref. P18/30/18

11   Bearsted School file
CCA Ref. DCb/GT3/1

12   The author is in the back row, left hand side, third from left!

12 Adaptation and Growth

1   The inclusion of 'Roseacre' in the name for the school was first suggested by the Divisional Education Officer, Mr Tomlinson, in a letter to Mr Finch dated 15 November 1967.
Unpublished papers and correspondence held by Vernon Finch

2   Focus on Roseacre County Junior School, Bearsted
Kent Education Gazette
December 1974

3   Plan of Roseacre School 1972
        Unpublished papers and correspondence held by Roseacre School

4   In a letter to the vicar of Bearsted, Mr Waghorne, in 1968, the Diocesan Director of
        Religious Education had discussed the matter of the loss of church school status. He
        advised:

> 'the law on the matter was that an existing school could only be transferred to the new site and
> retain church status, if the numbers remain more or less stable. The growth of the population of
> Bearsted means that the number of children in the school compared with the original number in
> the Development Plan was first approved, has grown so much that the new buildings required
> are large enough to constitute a new school. The Department of Education and Science have
> ruled that when this situation arises, the new buildings must then become a new county
> school....'

        Bearsted School file
        CCA Ref. DCb/GT3/1

Epilogue   Resurgam: A New Life for the Old Building

1   Letter dated 24 June 1971, from the Director of Education, Canterbury Diocese to the
        vicar of Bearsted, Mr Waghorne
        CKS Ref. P18/25/7/1

Appendix 7 The Early History of Roseacre

1   p.202
        The Place Names of Kent
        J K Wallenberg
        Uppsala 1934

2   The inquisition took place in 1242 but the document recording it is dated 1258
        Esc. No 6 42 Hen III 1258
        pp. 242-247
        Inquistiones Post Mortem
        Archaeologia Cantiana Volume III (1860)
        Kent Archaeological Society

3   pp.58-170
        The Kent Lay Subsidy of 1334/35
        Edited H A Hanley and C W Chalklin
        Medieval Kentish Society
        Edited F R H de Boulay 1964
        Kent Archaeological Society

4   Indenture Rocksaker alias Russecar Street 1701
        CKS Ref. U838 T238 (Bundle T233-240)

5   Mortgage concerning Russiker 1735
        CKS Ref. U108 T1

6   Rusaker, also Stretton Street 1745-1828
        CKS Ref. U82 T58

7   Rusaker, also Stretton Street 1745
        Conveyance by Lease and Release, Mr William Barber to Mr John Barber
        CKS Ref. U82 T58

8   Entry for Bearsted
        Kelly's Trade Directory for Kent 1855

Select Bibliography

Original Records and sources:

Located at the Centre for Kentish Studies, Sessions House, Maidstone, Kent:

Bearsted Primary School Deeds	CKS Ref. U 1872 T1-3
Bearsted School Records	CKS Ref. C/ES 18
Bearsted Parish Records	CKS Ref. P18
Maps and plans	CKS Ref. DE/S/18
The Centenary Magazine 1839-1939	CKS Ref. C150821493 K/Bearsted
Thurnham School Records	CKS Ref. C/ES/369
Maps and Plans	CKS Ref. DE/S/369/1

Located at the Church of England Record Centre, 15 Galleywall Road, London SE16 3PB:

Bearsted School File, National Society records.

Located at the Canterbury Cathedral Archives, Canterbury Cathedral:

Canterbury Diocese Education Society Board	CCA Ref. U45/A1
Canterbury Diocese Board of Education	CCA Ref. U45/B1

Located at the Public Record Office, Kew, Richmond, Surrey TW9 4DU:

Bearsted School File	PRO Ref. ED/161/8141
Wills	PRO Ref. PROB/11
1841 Census	PRO Ref. HO107/456/7
1851 Census	PRO Ref. HO107/1616

Simmonds Aerofilms Limited, Gate Studios, Station Road, Borehamwood, Herts. WD6 1EJ

Aerial photograph of Bearsted, 11 May 1959   Ref. A75229

Other Sources:

A History of Bearsted and Thurnham
Bearsted and Thurnham History book committee 1978, revised 1988

Focus on Roseacre County Junior School
Vernon Finch
Kent Education Gazette   December 1974

No Return Tickets!
L. Grace Dibble
L. Grace Dibble 1989

History of Maidstone
J M Russell
1881, re-printed John Hallewell, Rochester, 1978

The History of Maidstone
Peter Clark and Lyn Murfin
Alan Sutton publishing 1995

East Kent Within Living Memory
East Kent Federation of Women's Institutes & Countryside Books 1993

West Kent Within Living Memory
West Kent Federation of Women's Institutes & Countryside Books 1995

Bygone Kent (Volume 17 No 2)
A Season at Rosherville Gardens - George Frampton
1996 Meresborough Books

Bygone Kent (Volume 21 No 12)
Bearsted Green Bakery - Rowland Powell
2000 Meresborough Books

The History and Topographical Survey of the County of Kent
Edward Hasted, 1798
Volume V
Re-printed E P Publishing Ltd 1972

Villages around old Maidstone
Irene Hales
Meresborough Books 1980

History and Gazetteer of the County of Kent
Samuel Bagshaw 1847

Return of Owners of Land 1873
W E Baxter
Sussex Express Office 1877

Wateringbury in the Past
W A Bolt 1986
Wateringbury Local History society

The Parochial Library of All Saints Maidstone and other Kentish parochial libraries
Nigel Yates
Archeologica Cantiana
Volume XCIX (1983)

English Popular Education 1780-1970
David Wardle
Cambridge University Press 1970

The Growth of British Education and its records
Colin R Chapman
Lochin Publishing Second edition 1992

Materials for the Local and Regional Study of Schooling 1700-1900
W R Stephens and R Unwin
British Records Association 1987

Educational Broadcasting
Report of a special investigation in the County of Kent during the year 1927
Carnegie United Kingdom Trustees
Comley Park
Dunfermline

Education in Rural England 1800-1914
Pamela Horn
Gill and Macmillan 1978

Labouring Life in the Victorian Countryside
Pamela Horn
Alan Sutton publishing reprinted 1995

The Victorian and Edwardian School Child
Pamela Horn
Alan Sutton publishing 1989

Britain since 1945: a political history
David Childs
Routledge 2001

Education & policy in England in the 20th century
Peter Gordon, Richard Aldrich & Dennis Dean
The Woburn Press 1991

Education and the Social Order 1940-1990
Brian Simon
Lawrence & Wishart 1991

Lofty Aims and Lowly Duties: Three Victorian Schoolmasters
Ruth Jennings
Sheffield Academic Press 1994

Microhistories: Demography, society and culture in rural England 1800-1930
Barry Reay
Cambridge University Press 1996

A Calendar of Country Customs
Ralph Whitlock
Batsford 1978

Newspapers:

Maidstone Journal 1786 - 1880

Maidstone and Kentish Journal 1853 - 1911

Maidstone Gazette 1815 - 1851

South East Gazette 1866 1869, 1940 - 1951

The Gazette 1980 - 1981

Mid Kent Gazette 1981 - 1982

Kent Messenger and Maidstone Telegraph 1859 - 1910

Kent Messenger 1911 to present day

Index